Rhik Samadder is a writer, actor and broadcaster. He has a regular column with the *Guardian* and created their cult 'Inspect a Gadget' feature. He has written for the *Observer, GQ, Men's Health* and *Prospect* magazine, as well as being a guest, presenter and host on various radio shows. Rhik studied acting at Drama Centre London and has appeared on HBO, BBC, ITV, C4 (credits including *Coronation Street, Emmerdale* and *Doctors*) as well as a lead role with the RSC.

'By turns laugh-out-loud hilarious and devastatingly sad.'
Nathan Filer

'The bravest book I've ever read.'
Christie Watson

'Utterly human and readable and hits you slyly
with relatable, complex, brilliant explorations of
a family's inability to communicate.'
Nikesh Shukla

'It's honest and funny and beautifully painful.
The writing is graceful and kind, even when it
hurts a little to remember it's a memoir.'
Joanna Cannon

'A brilliant sometimes hilarious
sometimes heartbreaking book . . .
Read it. It's brilliant.'
Aisling Bea

'This astonishing book is carrying me,
making me laugh, and felling me in equal measure
. . . it's a beautiful thing.'
Jojo Moyes

'*I Never Said I Loved You* is a work of fucking art.
It's as wrenching as it is funny.'
Stuart Heritage

'One of the most electric, enchanting,
engrossing and energising memoirs of self-harm,
self-loathing, grief, eating disorders, suicide
– and sex – that you will read.'
Sunday Times

'This is really, really, really good.'
Jenny Colgan

'It is taking me forever to read *I Never Said I Loved You*
because I have to keep pausing to let out the breaths
I'm holding, or the gasps, or the bark-laughs, or the
sucker-punch, throat-catching sobs. What a ride.'
Jack Monroe

'Astonishing . . . I am undone, in a good way.'
Polly Samson

'Both funny and touching.'
The Telegraph

'Equal parts hilarious and heartbreaking.
What an absolutely riveting read.'
Nikita Gill

'An extraordinary achievement; both painfully honest and laugh-out-loud funny – often on the same page. Utterly compelling, raw and hilarious, no one else could have written this book.'
Felicity Cloake

'Hilarious and brilliant.'
Marina Hyde

'I have always loved Rhik Samadder's writing. And now there's a whole book!'
Jessie Burton

'Heartbreaking, funny, raw, brave and – yes! – even better than the egg thing.'
Erin Kelly

'Extraordinary.'
Susannah Reid

'A feel good mental health memoir . . . both touching and funny.'
Daily Telegraph Magazine

'It's one of the best books I've ever read.'
Emmy the Great

'I was so massively moved by it.'
India Knight

RHIK SAMADDER

I NEVER SAID I LOVED YOU

HEADLINE

First published in 2019 by
HEADLINE PUBLISHING GROUP

First published in paperback in 2020 by
HEADLINE PUBLISHING GROUP

5

Cataloguing in Publication Data is available from the British Library

ISBN 978 1 4722 5070 4

Designed and typeset by EM&EN
Printed and bound in Great Britain by Clays Ltd, Elcograf S.p.A.

Headline's policy is to use papers that are natural, renewable and recyclable
products and made from wood grown in well-managed forests and other controlled
sources. The logging and manufacturing processes are expected
to conform to the environmental regulations of the country of origin.

HEADLINE PUBLISHING GROUP
An Hachette UK Company
Carmelite House
50 Victoria Embankment
London EC4Y 0DZ

www.headline.co.uk
www.hachette.co.uk

For my father
May the time be now

Contents

Introduction *xiii*

1. How to Keep Going *1*

2. How to Remember *21*

3. How to Die *51*

4. How to Be in Your Body *80*

5. How to Be in Other People's Bodies *110*

6. How to Grieve *144*

7. How to Be Alone *176*

8. How to Let Go *201*

9. How to Work *234*

10. How to Be Free *264*

Introduction

Christmas morning, 2010. I'm in bed with my mother, in a Bangkok sex hotel. It is my thirtieth birthday. How have things got this out of hand?

To wind back a little, I hadn't been looking forward to a fourth decade. My father had died three years before and I'd responded, with great resourcefulness, by having a comprehensive breakdown, ending a nurturing relationship, and moving back home. I couldn't work, or go out, and didn't want to be seen. A life shrunk to four small walls was all that seemed manageable. I was watching *The Lion King* a lot, and doing all the voices.

So when my mother announced we were going to Australia and Thailand for Christmas, I was unresponsive. Having been in the UK since 1979, she had recently become a British citizen and wanted to celebrate, by flying as far away from Britain as geographically possible. She wanted me to see the Great Barrier Reef, she said. I pictured men in shorts, throwing pigskins at my head. But I had no other plans.

The Australian leg was ... not good. I became extremely sick, something of a signature move. My mother, basically a toddler, had us pinballing between territories like they were rides at Alton Towers. In three weeks, we flew from Perth to Cairns to Melbourne to Darwin. We spent about forty minutes in Alice Springs. She was loving it; I was dragging the meat of my own carcass around. We went to Sydney for a single night, which I spent staring at a toilet bowl. In one airport, I looked so rough they nearly didn't let me on the plane; they thought there was a serious possibility I was carrying bird flu. The night before we left the country, my ex called me on a hotel lobby phone to tell me our dog had died.

Like I said: not good. Still, there was everything to play for. Christmas in Thailand sounded like an idea from a 'thirty things to do before you're thirty' peak-experience hit list, the ones that fixate on kayaking, taking ayahuasca on Machu Picchu, or inconveniencing dolphins in Cancún. However, those lists are aimed at sexy young couples who like house music, not a depressed 29-year-old and his elderly mother. Don't imagine beach huts or tinsel-strewn palm trees. Owing to a lack of online hut-booking facilities, and mobility issues, we were to spend the week sharing a Bangkok hotel room.

Many people may have a dated, stereotypically seedy mental image accompanying the words "Bangkok hotel room". Those people would be correct. Instead of chocolates, the staff had left condoms on the pillows of the bed. The bed my mother and I were sharing. The 'door' to the bathroom was a barely frosted glass slat: a saloon door to a nightmare. A week on a porn set was not how I'd pictured becoming a man. At least, not like this.

So there we were, Christmas morning in a Buddhist land, my birthday, no tinsel, surrounded by sex aids. The thing was, with nothing else to do, we sat in the room and talked. I couldn't remember the last time we had. Depression had left me uncommunicative, paralysed, angry with the world. There is so much shame attached to not being able to function, and I knew my life hadn't progressed. I was turning thirty having not realised any dreams. I felt small.

Finally talking though, it became clear none of that stuff mattered to her. I'd done nothing in my whole life to make her proud, yet, unfathomably, she was proud anyway. She'd used her savings for us to be able to go as far away as we could, to show me things, for me to be happy.

I asked her about her life, which I'd never done, having always assumed I just emerged from a fog in the 1980s. She told me she'd been born in a trench in Burma during the war. How her mother had suffered too much to bear, and died young. How my mother raised her siblings. How later, after the death of my father – her husband – she'd refused to give up on life, and instead taught herself a new skill every year: conga drumming, sculpture, digital story-telling. We talked about what it means to surrender your Indian passport for ever, and take a British one. I realised

I came from somewhere, which is to say I realised I was alive.

No one tells you the truth about adulthood, which is that you spend most of it missing people, and only a handful of moments last. Sometimes we have to force ourselves to not shut out the people we love, because they're all that keeps us here. I wasn't magically transformed that Christmas – I'm still grumpy, ungrateful and complain a lot. But I started to understand; and I started to mend.

This book is an attempt to tell the story of a depression, and how I got out of it. To understand an idea is to own it, and that day I felt the condition weaken its grip; opening up the possibility that I could slip its chokehold, perform a Russian legsweep and flip myself up to stare down its nostrils. I wanted to bark questions in its face. 'Where did you come from? Why are you so greedy? Why, if you live inside me, do you want us to die? Why does your breath smell like that?'

I will get no reply, because my adversary is a chemical imbalance in my brain. Or a psychic hangover, oozing through the fractures of childhood. Or a tiny statistic in a social epidemic. Or a genetic hand-me-down, a family heirloom like a box of old spoons. Or a tentacled kraken, unpeopling my vessel, dragging my men down to the depths.

But I'll keep talking, because I want to tell this story. Stories bring us comfort, even when they are not comforting stories, because the moral of every one is that whatever we have experienced, we are not alone. They can be a hand in the dark, a reminder that others have struggled, and prevailed. Mental health is perhaps the most serious topic we have, which is why it can be so boring to read about. But the truth is there is often a great deal of absurdity to our most harrowing experiences, which is a healing thing to remember when we feel out of joint. We need more Tales of Depression. Gather round, children, let's talk about Great Aunt Stephanie, who sent sixty consecutive tweets to Sandra Bullock because she had no one else to talk to! Have I told you about the time your father cried for three days because he saw a tree that looked like an old man? And wouldn't let us turn any lights out? He was like a difficult baby! That sort of thing.

In the past I have told myself that I was not human. That I had no family, that I was marooned from an alien species. Probably a superior species; it's just the air here wasn't good for me, which was why I walked bent double and felt tired all the time. But it's not true. I just wanted to feel special, to claim compensation for things I had suffered, at the cost of sealing myself away from others. It was incorrect, but it was also a waste of resources. The things that made me feel totally alone then are now what bind me most tightly to others.

According to Jung, 'The greatest and most important problems in life are fundamentally insoluble. They can never be solved, but only outgrown.' He knew things,

Carl. This book is about the deepest problems I have faced, and how I began to move beyond them. The going gets rough on ground like this. We'll be stopping off at self-harm, grief, eating disorders and suicidal thoughts. (Though there will also be sex, knife crime and supermodels. I've got you covered.) Perhaps unsurprisingly, I've found the episodes most painful to recall are those that hurt other people, especially those close to me. Questions ignored, responsibility not taken, love unexpressed – by trying to make things better for myself, I made things worse for them. This book was always intended to be a sort of reverse treasure map, of the ways I lost my bearings, a catalogue of starless nights. Yet another idea quickly entwined itself around that initial project. I began wondering what freedom really consists of, and not just for myself.

That is why the other purpose of this book, running through its pages like a seam of golden regret, is the urge to mend. In my struggle towards better mental health, I have acted in ways that were paranoid, cowardly and selfish. Surly and aggressive. Treacherous and cold. (I'm pitching the *Snow White* sequel to Disney as we speak. It's going to be called '*Coal Black*: When shit gets real, princess'. Don't steal my idea.) I have been, like the result of a fox's digestive process, a toxic little shit. While the whole book could be seen as a letter to those I have let down or left behind, I am quite a literal person, and have thus written a series of actual letters to close each chapter.

They are addressed to the people who still rattle around my heart in unresolved ways. I needed this, to close the same chapters in my life. There was no other way to do it. I don't have all your numbers.

1

How to Keep Going

I stare at some turds and think about existence. Sunlight glints off the water that uncoils slowly through this park, next to the street where I grew up. In the distance, young people laugh among themselves. A pigeon struts the grass defiantly, while in the water a duck stands ankle-deep, looking at a confusion of twigs, a hurricane survivor surveying the wreckage of his home. I'm not sure if ducks have ankles.

How does one survive a life? For some reason, this is the thought that has been pressing itself upon my mind since I made a decision to write about – well, my mind. Specifically, the way it goes wrong.

It's not a welcome question. All I want to do is set down how this particular problem feels, the tangible effects it has had, and what has helped. Even that's hardly straightforward – akin to walking face first into thick smoke, hoping the fire will become more clearly visible. A relationship with depression has been the longest, most intimate and yet opaque I've ever known. It's always been the two of us; a miracle we've stayed together so long. The key to any good relationship is knowing where the other is coming from, but this has always been a great mystery to me. Where does this paint-it-black, Chicken Licken shit come from? Was I born with a black frame of mind, or did I adopt it? Strange thing, to be a puzzle to yourself.

I have to get past the possibility that no one cares. Even I don't want to hear about depression, because it's depressing. The word sounds like air leaving a lilo. But perhaps this is a smokescreen for how difficult I find it to talk about feelings. I have often taken circuitous routes to avoid it, talking so obliquely that few could understand when I was asking for help. There was an astrophysicist I started hanging around with towards the end of university, known for brewing strong pots of opium tea, passing shrooms around like chocolate raisins, and dispensing wiggy lectures of a cosmological bent. I recall hitting him with this at the end of a late night.

'Do you ever think about how one day the sun will be a faint disc, dying in the sky, unable to protect us?' I had been preoccupied by the death of the sun recently, fixated on the universe drifting, losing touch with itself.

'What faint disc?' he scoffed, rousing himself on the tattered sofa. 'You do know the sun will grow before it dies? That it'll be huge and red and boil the seas and melt mountains and then the Earth will be physically dragged into its surface and disintegrated?' I didn't. 'Dude, we don't know how this ends,' he added, pouring more tea.

'The universe, if there is just one, could collapse at a point of maximal expansion, and vaporise everything in a split second. Which you have to admit is cool.'

I sensed I should be more upfront, but it felt too threatening. Later, I tried speaking to one of my teachers, a backwards step given I'd left school a decade ago. Miss Regent had always been supportive and interested, as well as impeccably cool, so agreed to meet for a catch-up, high atop the Brutalist architecture of the National Theatre, an unhelpfully dramatic setting.

'How is movement even possible? There's so much inertia,' I began, apropos of nothing, lacking the momentum to explain what I meant. I didn't possess language to contain the wilderness within. I wanted to frame what I was feeling rationally – from a distance, without risk – then be presented with an answer.

My old teacher took a beat, then started to draw on a napkin. 'The thing about inertia is it's what happens when the forces acting on an object are exactly equal,' she said, sketching a box pressed by arrows from different directions. 'It doesn't mean nothing's happening.' An intriguing idea, way over my head. She drew more squiggles, indicating that taking away one side was as powerful as adding to another. 'Is it acceleration you want, or to change direction?' The weird thing was she had taught me English.

Depressives are constantly advised to be more open, to speak up, as if the only problem is our blushing reticence. But if one does find the nerve to speak directly, there's no guarantee you'll be heard. Wandering the city weeks later with nowhere to be, I saw a friend, Giles. We'd always had an easy relationship, though not too close. I would sometimes sleep on his sofa after group nights out, and he'd pass me primer CD mixes of Detroit techno that I listened to once.* He crossed the road in greeting, asking how I was, a coded British phrase that means 'please don't tell me'. But at that time I wanted only to lie down and never get up, so decided to play an honest hand.

'I'm . . . tired of life,' I confessed. It felt good to tell someone. There was a long, uncomfortable pause.

'Does that mean you're tired of London?' he quipped, backing away from the cliff edge. A bookish riff on a Dr Johnson quote: 'When a man is tired of London, he is tired of life.' I laughed to show I got it, while feeling incredibly alone.

Now, I can see that I didn't need jokes or differential calculus or cosmology. I needed to be honest with myself about how bad I felt, and to ask a professional for guidance. I needed someone to tell me I would be okay.

Scientific accounts of the major bummers – depressive personality disorder, bipolar II, cyclothymia, whatever your poison – only tell a portion of the story, but what do they say? That depression is almost certainly hereditary. Genetics determines whether we grow flat feet, have

---

* I don't mean 'for a period of time in the past'; I mean I listened to them once.

blue eyes, or a predisposition to complex mood disorders. Depression runs through families like a Soho rickshaw driver. Funny how people talk about a genetic lottery, as if we originally had a say in the numbers.

So, who dumped these ingredients, this box of thistles and ketchup, at my doorstep? An enquiry needs suspects, and here are two in the frame, one of whom is inconveniently dead. From memory I can construct the picture of my father. Health problems, financial anxiety, an inflexible daily routine of fish dinners and *Columbo*. But also practicality, tenacity, an ability to see into the future – none of which fit my experience of depressive symptoms. Let's downgrade his status to 'person of interest'.

My mother, on the other hand – there's certainly something fruity sprouting in that neck of the woods. My mother has claimed that trees talk to her, and one birthday, she presented me with a breakfast of Parma ham, popcorn and the DVD of *127 Hours*, the self-maim mountain-porn movie starring James Franco. I remember a time she hadn't been responding to messages for a few days and I careened home in a state of panic to discover she had been keeping her phone in the bin. 'If I'm senile, I've been senile since I was twelve!' she laughed. If anyone asks me why I am the way I am, I usually point at her.

But this won't stick either. She has more friends than me. She takes herself off to trade conferences around the country for pleasure, is always air-drumming to any piece of music she hears, and frequently pieces no one can hear. She may be mad as a mug of plum chutney but she is essentially happy. So now where should I look? There's no one else to ask. I have no siblings. I don't know any other family really. I'm aware some do exist, but they are 4,990 miles away in India. You could get to the International Space Station and back ten times covering the same span. It's ten times further than the Proclaimers would consider an acceptable long-distance relationship, and they're pretty desperate.

Throughout my twenties, not knowing my relatives had never struck me as a problem. The entire idea of family was strange to me. (This mainly came from watching the bald Mitchell brothers in *EastEnders*, who were constantly sleeping with the wrong wives and making each other bankrupt. If I ever needed an alibi for murder, family seemed like a good bet. Otherwise, the whole thing looked like a pain in the arse.) In the absence of family, however, strange ideas had taken root in my head from a young age. That I wasn't from anywhere. That I had no backstory and was free to be whoever I chose. Yet that didn't appear to be working out: my first choice, given unlimited avenues, probably wouldn't have been 'unemployed actor who has a nervous breakdown at twenty-seven'.

As my mental state deteriorated, I began to take solace in the idea that I wasn't even a person. I would take ostentatious offence when described as human, which must have been tedious for everyone.

Receptionist: Are you one of the people who signed up for Bodypump Aquatics?
Me: I'm not a person.

I should have asked about my family history earlier. Before it was too late. My parents and I had never had a talkative relationship. Distance from them, and a mystery concerning their lives before me, as if such a thing even existed, was a good exchange for privacy in my own. Besides, I knew it would be another dead end: my mother's mother had died while giving birth to my mother's younger sibling. There's no good question to ask about that, little light to be shed. Some conversations will always be too late.

But as with any good mystery, my initial assumptions were wrong. I remember an eavesdropped conversation, during the year I had crashed and burned. I'd moved back in with my mother and rendered myself housebound, contact with the outside world withered to nearly nothing. I was for some reason crouched halfway up the stairs – a grown man at this point, mind you – listening to my mother talk about her childhood with a friend on the phone. That wasn't the unusual part, but my paying attention was. She was explaining that she hadn't had a mother to turn to, since her own mother had been an invalid. I'd been told she never knew her mother. An invalid? Was she a character from a Somerset Maugham novel? I pictured someone with an ear trumpet. I was appalled at how little I knew.

When the lights turn green, you have to drive. My mother and I were going to have one of our disastrous annual attempts at a conversation. I shuffled into the kitchen, opened the fridge and stared into its back wall. She was ironing a transfer of Mother Teresa onto a baseball cap that she would later wear backwards, making me wish I had never been born.

'You okay? Want some food?'

'NGH,' I grunted, while reaching for some cheese. (My grunts have discernible meanings for anyone forced to spend time with me, as with Jane Goodall's chimpanzees. 'Ngh' could convey anything from 'leave me alone' to higher-order propositions such as 'life is a shitshow'.) In my head, I was panicking about how best to broach a difficult subject, after years of silence, filling in the blanks, and getting it wrong.

'Are you okay, bebe? Are you too hot?'

'No.'

'Too cold?'

'No.'

'Are you exactly right?'

I thought for a second. 'No.'

Behind me, my mother continued to iron, squashing the dome of the hat awkwardly flat, to receive the saintly face. I continued to stare blankly into the fridge, not knowing what to say, my grunts for once not up to the job.

'Well, there's a pizza in the freezer, and yoghurts. Or venison.'

My mother has a Henry VIII-esque attachment to venison. Neither of us ate it, yet there were always smoked slices in the fridge. I had no idea where they came from. We were poor, and lived in Lewisham, a London borough judged the most violent place in the country by the UK Peace Index. It's possible the venison was human fallout from local turf wars.

'I THOUGHT YOU SAID YOUR MUM WAS DEAD!' I shouted at some old milk.

'She is. What's happening, bebe?'

'I mean, I thought she died in childbirth.'

A pause. 'No, she was alive. But . . . she was in bed a lot. She had severe problems with mental health. So.'

Sweat prickled my scalp. 'Okay,' I say, reaching for a Müller Light and leaving the room.

This was a lot to take in. I felt like Luke Skywalker being told his father wasn't dead, and had instead been taken over by the Dark Side. My grandmother was . . . Darth Vader? Except in real life the Dark Side doesn't give you formidable powers like electric hands and remote throat pinching. It makes you sad and small and unable to leave your room.

I needed to know more. If I was Luke Skywalker, I needed Yoda. An infuriating yet wise teacher, who was both young and old, and could guide me to understanding. Luckily my seventy-three-year-old Indian mother, who is four foot nine and speaks in jumbled-up English, fits the bill almost exactly. The problem was how to talk to her. I had never been much of a talker, and the condition had further crushed my ability to relate to others. Intimacy asked too much, and I was a coward, with a liver so lily it could poison cats. This meant that when I needed to ask a favour, deliver news or extract highly personal information, I would do so on conversational raids: approached blindside and blundered through with brute insensitivity.

I also needed a little time to digest the unsettling news, and so allowed four or five years to pass before asking a follow-up question. I had by this time learned to start talking again, but it was a foreign language, and the blunderbuss was still my conversational weapon of choice. The occasion presented itself on a dark Christmas afternoon, as we were crawling up Regent Street on foot, crowded by shoppers. We found ourselves at a momentary pause, our progress past Hamleys Toy Shop stymied by laughing children. Goodwill was in the air, and festive cheer.

'WHAT MENTAL-HEALTH PROBLEMS DID YOUR MUM HAVE WAS IT SCHIZOPHRENIA OR DEPRESSION OR WHAT?' I said, with the volume and feeling of a man in charge of a firing squad.

There was a long pause. 'We didn't know the word "depression".'

'What did the doctors say?'

'How am I to know? I was so young, no one talked about it to us.'

'People, then. What did people say?'

'They said she wasn't sane.'

I pressed on, with the sympathy of a policeman who has found drugs in his son's jacket.

'Where did it come from?'

My mother sighed. 'She lost . . . a lot of children,' she said. 'Two sons, one day after another. Young. Then her eldest daughter also died, twelve or so. It was a very sad thing, the shock of it. Then of course our eldest brother was in a very serious accident. Broke his spine and died. That was it for her.'

My internal organs were seizing up in discomfort, yet I was also aware of a strange sort of wonder. 'I remember her illness, before she died,' she continued. 'She definitely had depression; she was always alone in her room. She did her own cooking. If she ever came out, she was lost in her own world.'

Ahead of us Robert Wadlow, the world's tallest man, stood sadly under a Ripley's awning that read 'Believe It or Not!' It seemed a travesty that he should have to stand, even in statue form, under a sign that gave you the option of disbelieving in his existence. I thought about the unlikely odds of my mother being here, and by extension me.

I became aware of being pressed around by strangers, a stream of unknowable people aching in their own ways.

Behind us, a low monologue picked itself out of the general din. An older man guiding a younger, I assumed his son, who did not speak. 'Look people in the eye when you talk to them,' he was coaching him gently. 'There's no need to panic, speak clearly. You don't need to be scared.' The boy was black, in his twenties, wearing a hoodie and an unreadable expression that pierced me in the gut. Startling how the world reconfigures itself to your emotional state.

I realised I was in no way listening to what my mother was saying. This is another of my signature moves, mentally checking out of difficult conversations. To this day, if someone attempts to talk to me seriously about money, relationship problems or unchecked moles, I immediately start feeling drowsy. Where defensive narcolepsy isn't a safe option, I'll become hypnotised by a crumb of pastry caught in the groove of a stranger's corduroys, or the way they've laced their shoes. It's not the level of engagement people hope for, but I'm not in control of it. I recognise the signs of a shutdown now: the drooping head and wandering ears, the pull of disconnection and unconsciousness. The effort of resisting the spiral requires so much energy that it amounts to the same thing, but I do try. I understand it's rude to fall asleep when people are asking about your intimacy issues.

I'd initiated this conversation, which made it even stranger. I tried to focus. She was still young when her mother died, my mother was reiterating, and only remembered bits and pieces of her. Her childhood was disorienting, she explained, and they moved around a lot due to my grandfather's job in the Merchant Navy. I'd heard the outline of this history in a Bangkok hotel room, but clearly there was a lot more. I asked her to start from the beginning, and tell me everything she could.

'I was born in a seaport town in Burma,' she began, like a barnacled sea dog trading her story for snifters of grog. 'The war had begun, and everyone ran away, but my father had to stay. The hospital had been bombed, so I was born in a trench. He delivered me, though he had no training. There was no one else left.' This was an unexpectedly brutal, Cormac McCarthy-esque start to the story. 'Mother and her children – there were still six of us at this point, my younger sister not yet born – were sent away in a submarine. I don't know where we landed. Father was left behind.'

After staying with grandparents for a year or two, the family found their way to Bombay, the children sent to missionary school. But they were always in rented housing, never a place of their own, always ready to move. Eventually, while still young, they found themselves in a far outskirt of Calcutta, and things became darker. As her children's deaths mounted up, their mother became too ill to attend to those still living; with their father often away working, the surviving siblings had to raise themselves. 'We spent our lives in the streets,' she said. 'Though it wasn't actually a street, it was a track really. It led to a gun factory belonging to the Manton company, who owned the land. But it was a wild place. There were foxes, kingfishers, scorpions. I saw mongooses fighting cobras. There were snakes in the house too.'

A far cry from cosmopolitan, coastal Bombay, they were now living at the edge of a jungle, where they didn't speak the native language and were regarded as outsiders. 'That village mentality is very small. We looked different, sounded different. We had been raised quite Western, and weren't streetwise.' Already vulnerable, already alien, as the family's losses increased, so did their isolation. My mother suddenly looked tired, as if recollection was a physical weight. 'They knew she had a mental illness, so they treated us differently. There was a lot of bullying.'

My family's story struck me as a squalid cross between a council-estate drama and *Tarzan*. So much misery; it sounded like an unbelievably crap life. I looked at her sceptically, my forehead scrunched up like a Cornish pasty. 'When you're young, you don't understand these things,' she continued. 'Father never talked about anything; she wasn't seen by anyone. Her name was Kamala. He tried to give her the best treatment he could. But in those days, it was taboo that killed people more than the illness.'

What was Kamala like before the illness? I knew from the pause that my mother could not remember.

'She made beautiful embroideries. She was very good-looking. I have heard she played tennis and badminton, in Burma. And she loved to sing.'

Later that night I thought about the family I'd had neither the opportunity nor, to be honest, desire to meet. I felt the fragile thread of connection to my grandmother as if she were sitting with me, with her sewing. The ghost of a woman I never knew. Despite not knowing her story, I had in some small way – and this was the wondrous thing to me – retraced it. Had spent a long, long time unable to leave my room, retreating deeply into myself. I knew the feeling that the world outside was overwhelming, and there was no safety but in invisibility.

Which wasn't to say I knew how she felt. I may as well have looked at Christ and remembered a splinter. The worst imaginable losses had been visited on this woman over and over again. She had known horrors, and had died unhappily in her fifties. What did I have to complain about, a young man in twenty-first-century London? Patchy Wi-Fi?

You've probably heard of the phrase 'First World problems'. It's a jokey conversational hashtag white people attach to their luxurious problems, a sort of privilege dog whistle, called on themselves. 'The thing about Cannes Film Festival is it always rains – I know, First World problem.' 'Waitrose are out of popcorn for dogs. First World problem klaxon!' It is funny, but riddled with self-loathing. It implies that people from the developing world don't suffer from, for example, depression, because they have real problems, while people in the West shouldn't feel bad about anything, because comparatively, they have no problems. My family and experience have taught me that isn't the case. Anxiety expands to fill whatever container it's in, like a gas.

For decades, I didn't feel worthy of saying I had depression. The grandiosity of diagnosis struck me as showing off. Other people had been, and were, in far worse condition, with no help available to them. Misplaced guilt stopped me asking for help, a common by-product of low self-esteem. It strikes me as the height of self-denial now. Yes, other people have it way, way worse than you – so what? Perspective helps, but suffering is suffering. There's more than enough to go round. I had confused misery with a packet of Rolos, worried that I might take the last one.

The long road back to health began with fully acknowledging my black dog, and the havoc it had wrought. Depression had pushed me to self-harm, suicidal ideation and drama school. Where did this devastating force come from, and would I always be under its power? Unlike for my grandmother, the condition didn't feel like a response to a catastrophic event, unless it was one I had forgotten. It felt like a force that had been unknitting me inch by inch as I grew, like a tapeworm sucking up nutrients. How could I find its beginning, or know which effects to attribute to it? I baulked at the scale of the unpicking. It felt like too much.

When asked what depression feels like, I'm reminded that there are as many notions of hell as there are human minds to conceive them. What's worse about the water torture of negative thoughts is that it leads us into silence. The more it takes, the less that can be spoken, nothing clearly seen. Depression cuts out your tongue, takes your heart as its own. We grasp at metaphors – a black dog, an anchor, a tunnel with no lights, walls that draw in. Plumes of smoke that fill the lungs. You are dripping in oil; it coats your eyes, your nose, your mouth. You are suffocating. You are in a locked room on fire. It is a black hole, sucking in light, hungry for your atomic disassembly.

The one thing that's easy to convey, that's always at hand, is an overwhelming sense of pointlessness. The feeling is a dark echo of that childhood game in which every adult statement is met with a 'Why?' Everyone has to get up in the morning. *Why?* It's a good idea to spend time with friends. *But is it?* Everything will be all right. *How do you know?*

When our disenchantment with the world is absolute, the cost is greater than happiness. Wonder, gratitude and generosity all fall by the wayside, as well as the creative space of curiosity and flexibility, a sense of progression and our own resilience. When these things are gone, they feel as irretrievable as innocence. Now, when the mood comes upon me, an unwished visit from a dark spirit, I try to remember that there is a way back; to recover what has been lost. How does one survive a life? By keeping going, however possible. When I'm feeling faithless and I'm on the ropes, stubbornness can see me through. When I have energy, I'll come out punching, using anything at hand. Pills, psychoanalysis, CBT, extreme exercise, and some stranger paths too. If we have to fight for our mental health, we should fight to win.

Back in the park, I watch the pigeon peck at the patchy grass. 'I will not be disassembled,' I tell her. Her eye is red-rimmed, as if she's not been sleeping too well either. The duck has been joined by his mate and they shake themselves, as if readying to leave the house. They do have ankles, I decide. Unless those are knees, and go backwards. I'm not really sure.

I know that all it takes to unpick a happy ending is to stay with the story a little longer. None of us know the future, and on the days when a happy ending doesn't feel like it's on the cards, a good story is still worth the price of admission. It feels worth sticking around to keep things interesting.

My depression is so all-consuming that it's easy to imagine it has always been there, the enemy I've been fighting as long as I can remember, pulling me down, gravity's malevolent twin. But now I want to finish what I've started and bring this thing into the light, make it solid, something I can handle. This means pushing past what I think I know, into things I've chosen to forget. What stories should I tell, to make an account of myself? There are obvious triggering events or periods I have experienced. The racism of Britain in the 1980s when I was growing; body issues that came to the fore in puberty.

The standard self-flagellation that adolescence brings didn't abate as I grew out of my teens, and the loss of my father opened up a sinkhole under my mid-twenties. But I have to go back even earlier, because I have been fixated on my own annihilation since earliest childhood. And there's something else; something I find hard to think about. A memory that lies rotting like the body of a bird in the back room of a house. It's time to open all the doors, and bring out the dead.

Letter to Kamala

I always avoid your eyes.

There are seven pictures in the frame, and you are in three of those, and this is all that remains of you. Pictures of a family I don't know, in a time and country strange to me.

Such big eyes you have, Grandmother; all the better to see you with. Something is dragging you down. You cradle a child I know died too young. Oh God, was everything really so terrible back then? No one smiled in photographs in the past. You should see what we do in photographs now. We're all smiling all the time, and that's not true either.

I know that look. Where did you go, in your head? When they asked what it was like, what did you tell them? Did they ask? It's different here, we name things, try to treat them. People spend their whole lives trying to understand people like us.

I thought you died. In childbirth, I mean; that's what I was told, or what I heard. Maybe it was like you had died. I don't think Ma knew you either, not the way a daughter should know her mother. She turned out to be a strange person, but popular, you'd like her. Maybe you were strange too. Sorry this is all such a mess. Sorry I'm too late.

It was not kind to avoid your eyes.

I'll make myself look now.

2

How to Remember

A cab took me to the tube, the tube took me to the station, then the Caledonian Sleeper carried me overnight to Glasgow, where I had come to kill my mother. I'd come to tell her something that would destroy her, but I had run out of other options. It was her or me, and I made the only choice I could, because that's what survival means.

It all came down to the cost of telling this story. From the moment I decided to confront my past, I encountered resistance. Some of it was social – when people hear you want to talk about your mental-health issues, you can see the flicker of a worry, as they wonder whether you've just returned from a genocidal spree, or are gearing up to go. For some reason, it's also seen as vain to be writing your memoirs when you're in your thirties and no one knows who you are. But the biggest obstacle to writing about my life was an internal, arguably serious, handicap: the fact I didn't remember it.

I've always had an extraordinarily poor memory. I'm one of those people who always forget a face, have to look up their own phone number, wonders why I even came in here. But those are merely functional problems. I struggle with remembering things I've done, or experienced, places I have been. Alcohol might explain some short-term lapses, but I don't drink that much. I don't think drugs are to blame either. I'm always too anxious to take them, convinced that I'll get a bad batch and end up vegetative or dead.

Having said that, I recently met up with a friend after many years; she revealed the last time we'd been together we'd taken ecstasy and posed for pictures holding a gun, in a stranger's flat. A real gun; she had pictures. Someone else reminisced about her thirtieth birthday, which we'd spent together in the bath. It seems rude to tell someone you don't remember a thing like that.

The high point of bewilderment came when Amish Tom, my oldest friend and occasional nemesis, mentioned a fortnight we'd spent in New York.

'I've never been to New York,' I corrected him. 'Though I have seen *Ghostbusters* eight times.'

'It was a month after 9/11. We visited Ground Zero,' he insisted. 'The immigrations guy at the airport picked you out of the crowd and put his hand in your pants.'

'*What kind of holiday is that?*'

Amish supplied more details, each of which elaborated an increasingly implausible picture. We'd bumped into an old housemate from university halls in the Spanish portrait wing of the Met Gallery. Spent a night at an artist's squat party, where we watched a banned Karen Carpenter biopic performed by Barbie dolls. Attended a punk gig in a Hell's Kitchen speakeasy, which was full of dwarves. Stuff that wasn't like forgetting a phone number. I knew I'd never been to New York, certainly not the trip he was describing, which sounded akin to a David Lynch movie. We fought for months. One day, to settle it, I retrieved my passport from its shoebox, and turned the watermarked pages. There it was, in brute stamp. 'JFK, 2001. Admitted.' It sounded like a confession. How did I not remember? Had I been dropping into fugue states my entire life?

Hearing these stories was like sitting in the audience, watching myself onstage. I didn't recognise this Mr Hyde self, living it up with drugs and guns, while all I could remember was loneliness and the first six series of *Friends*. It dawned on me that I was making the subtle yet chasmic shift from having a bad memory to becoming a person with few memories; a much lonelier predicament. I knew facts about me that appeared on paper, where I had studied and lived, jobs I had held and people I'd written to. But my impressions of myself, the bedrock of identity, were chaotic and strung out of order, a spilled necklace badly reassembled. And that wasn't the only reason I was unsure of sharing my story. There was a strong sense that forgetfulness, and the corrosion of my mental health at a young age, were bound together. I was hesitant to step into the fog, because I knew there were monsters in it.

There are secrets you cannot let people read about in a

book first, secrets that can tear your world apart. That's why I had come all this way, to speak mine in a place far from home. I'd never been to Glasgow; at least I didn't think I had. It was always possible I had run for public office here, or had kids languishing in a tenement. It was a nice enough place, though I noticed that where the dentistry advertisements in London promised to perfect your smile, here they offered to replace missing teeth. Back home, there was a heatwave; here it apparently rained every day with a vowel in it. Curly-topped trees sprouted promiscuously, turning the city into a big bowl of parsley.

My mother had been here a few days, indulging her favourite hobby, which was attending teaching conferences. These were trade fairs where, as far as I could tell, the main business was being aggressively boring. A debate about the Finnish upper-secondary corpus would vie for audience with the next hall's lecture on Communicating Communicative Competence, and people argued about footnotes. They were held somewhere different each year, having euthanised the previous city's populace with their billboards. Ma loved them. She funded these excursions herself, saving up the way people do for a Vegas road trip, returning home loaded with mousemats, tote bags and dictionaries. She kept a mental scrapbook of the best ones. 'Oh yes, Brighton '11,' she would say mistily, in response to a question no one had asked.

I found her room in the budget hotel, where she was sitting in a nest of plastic bags, stale gingerbread and USB sticks. A laminated pass was pinned to her shawl. *I am APU and I am a VISITOR*, it said.

'What a week, we've had a whale of a time,' she sang. Her English improved whenever she'd been at a conference, except she would talk in stock phrases that sounded as if they'd been penned by advertising copywriters. 'You look tired. Would you like a cool, refreshing dip?'

'No. Let's go for a walk,' I said.

We strolled around the outside wall of a private garden, and I wondered how to say what I'd come here to say. The words seemed impossibly distant as I stared at the grassy, closed interior, and we failed at conversation in our familiar ways. I looked at her now, hobbling more than I remembered, not confident in her walking. She had falls she didn't tell me about, I knew. Well past retirement age, she was still working. I could not support her financially, probably would never be able to. Moreover, if everything fell apart for me again, she would have to provide for both of us once more, feed us and keep the heating on. We didn't talk about these things.

After we'd circled the square eight times, I began to gently lose my mind. What's more, we had a whole day to fill, which we'd no doubt spend sitting in the hotel eating sweets with websites printed on them. My mother decided we should have an adventure instead. She rummaged through one of her horrific totes, pulling out a brochure for Highland tours by coach.

'Why not take in breathtaking lochs and dramatic

landscapes!' she declaimed. 'The best of Scotland is on our doorstep!'

'Talk normally,' I snapped, but didn't say no.

Owing to her distrust of the internet, we spent two hours tracking down a tour kiosk that no longer existed, except on a paper map. In the end, I booked the tickets on my phone, and told her the dry-cleaning business that stood on the same site had sold them to me.

'What a world!' she marvelled, as we found the coach stop, and climbed aboard. The coach taxied past a fish and chip shop serving a Justin Bieber haggis, as well as a statue of Wellington with a traffic cone on his head, and a pornography shop that offered video-to-DVD conversion. 'What a world,' she said again. I told her, with annoyance, that the tour hadn't started yet. We pushed out of Glasgow, easing through new mist, then picking up speed in the land to the north. We skirted lakes mantled with spruce, boulder-strewn pastures, idyllic cabins. I'd chosen a seat on the opposite side of the aisle, on my own. There was a lack of sentimentality to the lavender view, one I appreciated. Behind me, two girls from Stockholm oohed and aahed at the bruised clouds and patchy moss and every new feature we encountered.

'Doesn't this look exactly like Sweden?' I said, twisting around.

'I suppose it does,' replied the blonder of the two after a moment's reflection, slumping in her seat.

I realised I should do it here, in the settled calm of the

coach, driving through this in-between place where we would never set foot again. I willed myself to cross seats and start talking about what had happened when I was young. Tell her about the thing I had done, that I could not forgive myself for. But the driver had started to relate Scottish trivia as we drove between plunging crags. 'We'll be passing quite near Paul McCartney's house,' he said, playing 'Mull of Kintyre' through the speaker system. 'Though he did sack the caretaker a while back, and the grass has been sold for silage.'

The miles spooled out like ribbon, as my silence deepened. The driver's commentary started to unravel, like a man who had talked alone too long. He delivered a forty-five-minute account of the Glencoe Massacre, in which the Campbell clan had accepted food and shelter from the MacDonalds, before arising in the night to slaughter their hosts, leaving only seventeen men alive. 'Try and imagine what it was like, not just for the murdered, but those who escaped, only to freeze to death on the midwinter hills to your left.' Furls of fog hunkered on the hills, obliterating the shape and detail of the ground. A Japanese girl at the rear of the coach whimpered, after a slight translation delay via her parents. I stared out of the window, willing myself to be less of a coward. 'May God have mercy on their sou— Ooh, a red deer, to the right!'

Guilt stared me down from every pass. I didn't know the right thing to do. I didn't want this conversation, and couldn't avoid it. I was about to selfishly destroy one of my mother's closest friendships. But I also didn't know how to live with a secret. My head was swimming, so I closed my eyes. Every time I opened them, the landscape became more of an abstraction; an indivisibility of sky and water, forming a full spectrum of the blues.

'Here's an island where local chieftains were taken to be buried,' announced the driver sorrowfully. 'They brought them here so wolves wouldn't dig up the bodies and eat the remains of the dead.' I thought the moment had come when we pulled up to the banks of Loch Lomond. A wave of freshness hit us as we climbed out. The air here was rarefied, the gentle lap of water making it serene, confessional. Yes, I could do it here. We were given thirty minutes to roam, more than fifteen of which my mother spent in the car-park toilet, particularly annoying as they were toilets you had to pay thirty pence to use. When she emerged, the coach party were returning to the vehicle, with the happy chattiness of the post-awestruck. Cursing her pathetic bladder, I thundered back on board without a word.

By the time the driver announced our final stop, the coastal town of Oban, I was frustrated and full of self-loathing. The Swedes and Japanese were very excited to see Oban, for reasons I couldn't fathom. The words "fishing town" have an old-world magic, it's true, but in a modern, industrialised context, what you're talking about is a ferry port. One whose most prominent architectural landmarks, according to our guide, were never completed due to financial misplanning and death. I watched a seagull pecking at the guts of what had once been a pigeon, I think. There being nothing else to do on the harbour front, my mother and I sipped tea from polystyrene cups next to a bucket of smashed crabs. The day had resolved itself in grey, and I felt hopeless. If I didn't do this now, there was no reason to suppose I would ever have the courage. And so, staring into my cup, spinning liquid sucking me down, I took a breath and broached the impossible.

'When I was young, remember when you used to work in Liverpool? I stayed home with Daddy but missed you, so sometimes you took me with you, and we stayed in the home of your friend D******. But sometimes . . . when you were out, the son, the eldest boy—' My language started to break down, burning off in the heat of its meaning. 'He made me do things.'

I have this theory that the best twist in films is always incest, because no one ever sees it coming. *Oldboy, Star Wars, Chinatown*, all classics of the genre. Am I the only person who was always hoping Ross and Monica would get together on *Friends*? I can't be. It's narrative dynamite, I'm telling you. A very close second to incest, however, is childhood sexual abuse.

It was a rule of thumb that came in handy during my years at drama school, when we frequently had to write our own scripts. Believing the stuff of drama was an evil twin, or a gun hidden in a walking stick, we'd scribble melodramatic scenes, and play them out with classroom chairs for props. Mexican stand-offs in meat-packing plants, good-hearted prostitutes who are sole witness to a murder, bad guys who get plastic surgery to look like the good guy. When you were really out of ideas though, you bunged in a sexual-abuse twist. Always in the third act, and always unearned.

example

Control tower: There's only one patch of land you can safely make a landing, given your fuel situation.
Pilot (looks out of window): I can't land there.
Control tower: Why not?
Pilot: That land belongs to the orphanage I grew up in. Things happened there. Things I will never recover from! (*steers plane into sea*)

scene.

I never wrote a sexual-abuse twist, because I know it's never a twist, or a neatly plotted revelation. It's always there, has always been there, eclipsing everything else. It's also a thief, stealing memories adjacent to it in time and space, undermining the capacity to hang onto events decades later. This is the point at which my brain started to go wrong. The place from which the blankness spread. Though I don't remember everything, I remember enough. I know I was young, because my body was small. I can't bring to mind many details of the home where it happened, but recall everything about the room. I don't remember his face exactly, but I know his name.

This was when my mother was working in the north, teaching English. I spent weeks on end in London with my father, who had to learn to look after a six-year-old single-handed, a sacrifice I repaid by begging to go and stay with my mother every moment I was awake. I couldn't bear that she was so far away from me, living with another family, that of the friend she was staying with. Wherever she was, that's where I wanted to be. I made such a problem of myself, refusing to eat, growing ostentatiously more miserable, that my parents gave in. Arrangements were made so I could spend some time with her. She was too busy to look after me all the time, but there were other people in the house. My mother's friend, highly strung and ill at ease. There were her three teenage children in the house, and I particularly remember the elder of the two boys, the quality of his attention. He liked to get me alone. Sullen in the presence of others, as soon as they left, it was as if he'd been suddenly switched on. He'd turn his attention to me, with a conspiratorial excitement that was new to me, and exciting. It was thrilling to be seen, by someone who wanted to show me things, only me, because I was special. Everything in his behaviour, from the revelation of the disguised self, to the locking of the door, told me this was privileged experience. I had the sense he could show me a new world, and that access depended on being able to keep a secret.

The things he wanted to show me were things that preoccupy most teenage boys: football shirts, cartridge-fed video-game consoles, strange magazines and ultimately his penis.* The latter he only produced when the house was empty. He took me to his room and told me to take my clothes off. Unusual, yes, and out of place, but I hadn't been taught to think of doing so as improper. It was what happened before baths or bed, a humdrum preparation best not prolonged, in case you caught a cold. I barely had a sense of myself as a body. And so I didn't understand, and I didn't object. He took his off too, but not all of them, and I was puzzled by the imbalance. Perhaps that's when I sensed something wasn't right, or maybe when a suspicion was confirmed. Either way, too late. They say you never forget your first time. Or the time after that. Or the time after that.

A momentary lapse, while no less damaging, might be easier to understand. But this was not that. It was a pattern. I can't remember how many times I went back to that room. After the first few, I tried, in an untutored way, not to be present; to just not be there, despite my little back feeling the wrongness of his weight, the slick of his sweat as he rubbed his adult genitals on mine to get excited. My mind started to fracture, the experience becoming cut-up film stock fluttering in the light, disconnected images and vivid sense. I hated the smell of his

---

* Everton, Atari, disgusting.

testicles, the way he spat on me. For lubrication, his pleasure, or my degradation? It doesn't matter. What matters is that the foul sourness would cling to my skin, scent particles lodged in my nose at night. Detectable by no one else, overpowering to me. That's still how it is.

I was marked. I was used. I was an upgrade from a sock. There was a drop of blood in the churn. Initiation ceremonies occur across all cultures, marking the threshold at which a boy becomes a man. This was my steam lodge: an airless room in the north of England with Gary Lineker and David Hasselhoff looking uselessly on, in poster form. But there's no such thing as a six-year-old man – only a child with decades of trouble ahead. Years later, reading *The Body Keeps the Score* would powerfully underwrite what I went through, then and subsequently. After trauma, our brains change, interacting with our nervous system in new patterns. Depressive responses are all but inevitable. Feelings of threat remain near the surface, with the stress hormone cortisol released on a hair trigger. Following a situation of extreme helplessness, we can lose our fight-or-flight instinct: adjusting to the reality that episodes of violation are inevitable, we give up trying to avoid them. Often, we seek them out instead. Repeating dangerous experiences of the past, in an unconscious attempt to fix them.

There are implications too for memory. Ability to recall can become fractured, victims becoming amnesiac. This resonated deeply with my experience, explained the way I forgot important people or events, mixed up blocks of years, and overlooked others. A neurological reaction to trauma explained why I was a stranger to myself.

Child abuse is a spreading stain; a gradually disfiguring ugliness. For survivors, it feels existentially threatening to acknowledge, yet impossible to think around. Impossible to be at home in your body, without at once admitting the body's total vulnerability. Most people don't know this about me, that I went through this. It is the dread I dare not speak. When I force myself to, I'm astonished at how near the surface the emotions are, horrified by my feelings of guilt, and appalled by my silence even now – why? Because it reflects my silence then?

Silence is a collusive function of the way we think about child abuse. It is the worst crime, unconscionable. Molesters are punished heavily, extrajudicially. They have to be incarcerated separately, because they stand a higher than average chance of being stabbed in the neck at breakfast. A touching vision, this, all the adult rapists and wife-murderers unable to sit by while a monster walks among them. But we punish victims with silence too. The stigma of the unspeakable cuts both ways, and is the breeding ground of shame.

The special status of child abuse obscures how exceptionally unexotic it is too. It's common, banal, and more devastating for being so. Statistics vary, but most indicate that one in five girls have been abused, and one in twelve boys. It's a meaningless figure. Here's another – one in three of these don't tell anyone. Except, by definition, later they do. What about those who never tell anyone? Children will stay silent about abuse even after they have been diagnosed with venereal disease. The real figure is unknowably high, shockingly ubiquitous. I'm staggered by how many friends and acquaintances describe similar experiences, though usually women. Either I've been exceptionally unlucky, or men are disproportionately afraid to talk about their experience. What about boarding schools, boy scouts, bad seminaries? I cannot wonder at their silence without being drawn back to my own. Why didn't I speak out?

First, saddest, the child's horror of getting in trouble. The half-knowledge that something isn't right leads to the assumption of complicity and guilt. Abuse corrupts a developing self, and as I grew into a teenager, all I had were questions I had no one to ask, and sexual self-recrimination. I tortured myself with thoughts that there was something about me that had led to this violence. Did I deserve it? Was I asking for it? Was I actually penetrated and, if not, did I have anything to complain about? Most disturbing of all, could I have enjoyed it? Finally, as an adult, I was reluctant to disturb family dynamics. It would have been a huge upheaval, and upset my parents, who had enough problems of their own. Besides, one has generally learned some ways to partially handle trauma by then. Why look for the landmines fifty years after the war?

This is how abusers get away with it – exploit ignorance or weakness, make others feel the guilt *they* should be feeling, and keep their secrets for them. They have a triple lock on our silence.

Now I know that no one is ever asking for abuse. The responsibility for sexual assault rests with those who commit sexual assault. I know that curiosity is not the same as pleasure, or consent. A child cannot consent to what they do not understand.

Back home, I did not understand who I was anymore. Something changed. I stopped speaking, developed new fixations. Retreated further into myself. I would walk through the back garden that my father lovingly tended, turning over plant pots, parting curtains of green. I'd crouch down and watch the snails coming awake. Observe their trepidation, the way their entire being could retract inside itself if their environment was disturbed. The way they would push delicately outward once more, with the telescopic jelly of their bodies, looking cutely out through pinpoints on stalks, and I wonder how they knew that a safe passage of time had passed since they were disturbed, how they gauged this, what five minutes felt like to a snail. Reaching back to retrieve the scissors from my pocket, I would quickly cut off their eyes.

It wasn't a momentary lapse. I did it again and again. What makes me sick now is the knowledge that I did not believe they felt no pain. I did it because I imagined they did. I could feel the scream and disorder of that pain, its blackness. The gutting signal jam that someone could reach inside your soul and switch you off.

For the rest of my youth I bore violation like a beacon, like a broken window. There are people who will find you interesting for the reason others find you boring, because you are quiet and cannot meet their eye. Men in parks, and parked cars, by cemeteries and schools. A curse to be seen only by those who wish you harm. When quietness was ousted by adolescent rebellion, I remained hesitant around them. I never stopped when they talked to me. I never took up their offers to buy me booze at the off-licence. If a stranger were to walk in time with me, I would step into the road, stopping traffic. I kept myself alone the rest of my teen years, and thought that I had made it. But they are patient, these men. And if you carry no safety within you, then you are never really safe.

It was my first holiday without parents, taken in the company of my new university friends. A night ferry to a French coast, then a drive into the countryside. Everything about crossing the water at night fascinated me. The fact the short journey took many more hours by darkness, as if the crossing undertaken were to some deeper place. The way they turned the lights out, so the bulk of the ferry slipped through the water like a U-boat. In the lounges, passengers snored in plastic chairs, row after row of propped-up bodies. *They're all dead*, I thought, not without pleasure, as I strolled from one lounge to another, away from my sleeping friends, savouring the feeling of being the only one alive.

That's when I became aware of a shadow in the darkness, a silhouette sliding through the sprung doors behind me. I was being followed. I couldn't see any cabin crew, only immobile bodies. Trying not to alarm myself, I found my way to the middle of a row of seats and feigned sleep. The figure set himself on the aisle seat. I pulled my hat over my eyes, to shut out a darkness I could sense growing darker. After a few minutes, the shadow moved a few seats closer. I felt pinned. Should I shout? Nothing had yet happened – if people woke up, if the lights snapped on, nothing would be out of place. It clammed my mouth. Panic rose with the figure, as he took his place in the seat next to mine. Yes, I knew this. I knew the sick lurch, accompanied by paralysis as his hands cursorily stroked my leg, then forced his way inside my clothes, manhandling my genitals, putting his mouth on me. I made no attempt to cry out, move away or communicate. The shutters were down. I was someone these things happened to.

When it was over, he took his hands off me and I fled the room, finding my way above deck. I climbed up to an area of the boat forbidden to the public. I huddled in the lee of enormous metal walls, listening to the heartbeat of the engines, as the moon scattered diamonds in our wake.

After an hour, which had felt like a night, the lights stuttered on and the tannoy came to life, playing 'Wake Me Up Before You Go Go'. I found my group, and said nothing as we disembarked. My friends were soon full of chatter and jokes, despite the hour. Driving through the French countryside, the open road and new freedoms stretched out before us. In the back seat, I pulled my hat down over my eyes, then my mouth. It wasn't even a hat with a brim. I sat mute for the six-hour journey, with a knitted beanie rolled over my face, like a crap Spiderman whose secret power was being repeatedly molested.

I don't blame the ferryman for what happened, though it is odd to be looking for sex in the plastic-seated, public area of a merchant vessel. I had inadvertently advertised myself as a boat cottager, a thing I didn't know existed. Perhaps he genuinely thought I was leading him on, and I had submitted to his advance. Despite my frozen passivity, I had even ejaculated – not the kind of blissful release that leaves you glowing, more the sort that haunts you when you close your eyes, but still. Another notch on the – well, beds hadn't been much involved to this point.

When your body replaces fight or flight with the impulse to freeze, it doesn't mean people leave you alone. My constricted throat and stiff muscles were no advantage to me, but one cannot reason with an abused body. I didn't know how it was possible that, being so terrified, I had ejaculated. Did my body judge such a response would bring the encounter to an end? Hadn't that, in fact, been true? When I remember that cramped, unwilling excretion, there was no illicit thrill. It strikes me as something akin to a shelter dog pissing in a hall.

Back with the crabs, I was working up the courage to break my mother's heart. The fear of provoking anger or disgust gripped me, the muscles in my neck tense with stress. I couldn't go on any longer, and was tired of carrying this alone. I felt a sense of momentum carrying me over my stammered words, the vertigo of the tipping roller coaster. 'Your friend's son. Made me do things.'

I was met with silence. Truly awful, and too long. I'd pushed her away for good. I used to be her Miracle Child. Was she now ashamed to have brought a dirty thing into the world? Impossible to dampen the panic quicksilvering up the sides of me – until I noticed that the silence felt soft, not hard. As if she were leaving space for me to talk more. I had left the thought open, as if more were to come. Yet I was not speaking. She couldn't read my mind; if I wanted her to understand what had happened I would have to speak again, explicitly. I started to sweat. Throat constricting, knees and elbows tight, legs tense. Pounding in my head. It had cost so much to come this far, to lift this dizzying weight, but once more cowardice won out. The conjured mirage started to burn off in the sun. I shut down.

An untested weight hung in the air between us. She looked as if she might ask something, but I avoided her eyes. 'I didn't know. That he was oppressing you, I'm so sorry,' she said eventually. 'There was so much wrong in that family.' I'd prepared myself to be the one saying sorry. I never imagined being apologised to. I was all at sea. We both were. She spoke distantly, her own difficult memories returning. She told me about the father of the house, an alcoholic who thought of his wife and children as property. 'He bashed her around.' In addition to verbal and physical abuse, he inflicted emotional humiliations on his family. Threw his sons' school certificates in the bin, because he hadn't wanted them educated, to grow into men who could challenge him. It was a house of darkness. 'He found it difficult to accept his son becoming a teenager.' The thought threw up a constellation of possibilities.

My mother had gone to that house partly to save her friend. My father had intervened too, to make their father change his ways, or leave. He left. I don't know the extent of what that man did, but he changed a few brains too. I was not the only one brutalised in that house, all of this happening before I entered the scene. Now I was a grown man, still struggling, as was my assailant, who I would learn had cancer of the stomach. Life had its hooks in all of us. I don't know what I'd expected coming into this conversation, how speaking my secret would feel. I guess I dreamed of closure, something televisual. Here was a glimpse of generational abuse, and the baton of pain.

My mother reached to clasp my hands. A wave of nausea swept over me, drawing in the foulness of crab claws and broken backs. My body could not accept tenderness; it wanted someone to blame. I watched myself turning away, walking away. Hands dug into pockets, fisting the material taut like a sail. That abused family in the north looked up to my parents after the husband left, saw them as their deliverers. But no one had delivered me. Gulls shrieked like Furies as sea air rolled in, brining us. Behind, my mother was speaking but the wind swept the words over the water. Familiar frustration, leaving a conversation furious. I passed a young gull perching on a post, button eye dark and guileless, its warm feathers speckled brown. When did their wings turn white, and eyes grow pale?

I imagined myself inside the whistling wind. Behind me, walking heavily on a bad foot, my mother was trying to catch up. 'Son, speak to me. Or write if that is easier. It will . . . there can be a redemption, for you.' I paused, battling with myself at the crossroads. Oppressing, redemption. She'd been reading too many dictionaries, getting high on her own supply.

'Talk normally,' I said, reaching for the handrails of the coach.

Back in our seats, we sat drained and silent. At least, I did. Scraping for a gesture to offer closure, or compelled by some logic all her own, my mother dug around to retrieve something from her bag, crossed the aisle and folded my fingers around it. Thirty pence, in change. 'In case you need to go toilet.' As historical reparations go, this hardly cut the mustard. And definitely wasn't televisual.

Still, in the months after that conversation, something strange started happening. Things coming back; images bellying up from the murk. My childhood, in parts. Flashes of people and places. A room of other children, me shouting at a woman to read a story. The babysitter's son, who taught me to sit right up close to the television. The feel of a particular pair of trousers. I don't know the mechanism by which these scenes return to me, or whose rules they are following. Perhaps memory is like feeling, impossible to selectively repress. It doesn't matter – to have them return is a kind of grace. I suspect just the willingness to broach a secret can open new space inside the self. This is why we look for landmines fifty years after the war: to clear the ground, and walk on it again.

The returning fragments don't stop at childhood. It's everything all at once, odd ecstasies, moments out of time and too intense. They pierce me, at inconvenient moments of the day or night, carrying me away like a time machine. Now it's me on a transatlantic flight, listening to *Rumours* by Fleetwood Mac and finally feeling safe floating above an ocean in nowhere time, while around me everyone is sleeping. Now it's the English country lane where Lily, my first love, saw something, stopped the car and got out to look – two enormous Shire horses standing, implausibly, solid as myth. I remember how they galloped towards us, eager hooves drumming thunder into the earth. I can see Eliza, the other great love of my life, and I lying in our hammock that night of the Perseid meteor shower, looking up at that electric rain falling and wondering where we were going. I remember too when my friends finally found the remote French house we'd been driving towards. We lay down on the crossroads in the middle of a new country, in the middle of the night, Milky Way spread out above us. I realised how common shooting stars are in true darkness; one only has to lie still, and look up.

Not that I'm in control; my new powers are as unbiddable as a cat. There are still chapters missing, jumbles of sensations lacking narrative, a disorienting feeling that time keeps looping back on itself. But a complete story about ourselves can only be artificial anyway, disregarding what doesn't fit, twisting the remains to shape. 'Man's life is an attempt to recover those few images in whose presence his heart first opened,' wrote Albert Camus in the preface to his own account of his childhood, *L'envers et l'endroit*, and which I read on the back of a CD, but it still counts.* How much of the past do we need? Those times when I was touched by beauty or pain; memories I still can't make sense of. It's enough to be able to break the surface, dive down for submerged items, without having to bring back the entire wreck. For me, these capsules of sensation are precious for their mystery. I'm okay with the unbiddable cat, is what I'm saying.

'He *did* put his hands in my pants,' I announced next time I saw Amish Tom. A chapter was coming back: the ludicrously into-his-job customs official at JFK, on our trip to New York. Amish took a few seconds to register this conclusion to a conversation we'd had several weeks

---

* *Scott 4* by Scott Walker. Excellent.

ago. 'And on the plane over the . . . the steward . . . gave you his own vegetarian meal. And I said it was because he fancied you.'

'You made every interaction incredibly awkward for eight hours.'

'I remember!'

Amish was less excited by my returning memories. This one was like many that came later, corroborating his side of arguments so old, any possibility of meaningful victory had expired. He'd had to let these things go, and now was missing the bigger picture, the miracle happening in his house, in my head.

We were there for our weekly movie night, pointlessly observed given our divergent taste. I didn't even know why we were friends. He was heavily political, and his idea of acceptable conversation was baffling. He'd make observations like 'a dog in the UK has a bigger carbon footprint than a Sudanese man' and I couldn't help but laugh at the image. These film nights were no easier. He'd always be pushing for Švankmajer or Parajanov, bearded auteurs and lugubrious parables about men who got horses drunk, so they could send them down mineshafts to provide sex work. 'I'm already depressed,' I'd complain bitterly. 'Why would I want to watch that?' For my part, anything was all right as long as it featured a parkour chase across a rooftop. Maybe these arguments were the main attraction for us, I realised. It was a comfort, this familiar, safe bickering. Maybe that's what family is for.

'How about this?' Amish said, trying to focus the evening. 'It's about two Icelandic brothers who don't speak, and one of them has an infected sheep.'

'Save it for Hugo Chávez,' I interjected, not in the mood for his nonsense. Or in the mood to not be in the mood, according to my theory. In any case, we settled on a film about feuding Victorian magicians, on God knows what compromised grounds.

The film featured Christian Bale and a lot of beard acting and was, I think, enjoyable. But I can't be certain. Somewhere around Christian Bale's fifth beard, I was struck by another long-buried memory. This one arrived complete – not fragmented and feeling its way first, but full sequence and unavoidably present. Suddenly, I was no longer sitting in south London with Amish Tom watching David Bowie electrocute a cat; I'm in the north of England sitting with Him, my abuser, and we are the only two people in the house so I know what's coming. He is talking, and I am retreating inside myself. A thought forms as I sit there, a plan of sorts. Normally when people run away, I'm thinking, their bodies betray them. They hold their breath, glance where they will run, stiffen their legs. They radiate fear. What if I act normally, force my body to look at ease, try to control my breath? Then from nowhere – PYAOOW! – spring up and out of the room, down the corridor, to the room my mother and I sleep in, which has a bolt on the inside? The element of surprise on my side, I could make it, lock the door and be safe. Maybe only for a day, but maybe for a week, depending on when the others would be out again. I have to try.

I soften into my sitting bones, force myself not to glance at the door. I wonder if my uncommunicativeness is drawing attention to itself as minutes crawl by, willing silence to silence itself. His words are buzzing in my head, sometimes with a lift and pause, the music of a question, before he resumes. I find this frightening, how unburdened by my muteness he is, the way he continues to talk as though we're holding a conversation. As if I am already not here. But I sit on my fear, and wait for the moment of escape to arrive. A secret moment, one that does not feel appointed, is not a moment at all, a nondescript scrap of non-time indistinguishable from those around it. Now! I spring up, and burst for the door. My twig legs numb beneath me, unprepared for action. As if only parts of my body know the plan. Unbalanced, I yank open the door, lurch through and am almost falling sideways down a wallpaper tunnel towards safety. I hear crashing behind me but I make the threshold, turning the instant I am in, fingers reaching up for the bolt.

BANG! The weight of a large body hurling itself onto the other side of the door. My hand is torn from the crenellation of the bolt, before it can be drawn, cutting my fingers as my body is thrown backwards. And he is in, standing over me on the floor. Of course he is – taller, stronger, powerful. I start to cry. Obvious now, that pure predatory instinct must have brought him to his feet a split second after I ran. There had been no stalled moment, no window of opportunity. I don't remember if he was angry or if he spoke at all, the buzzing in my brain tuning out. He came in, bolted the door and, mercifully, that's where memory once again leaves me.

I replay the scene at night still, when things are bad. Even in the few seconds it took, the meaning was clear, felt clear to me even then: I was not safe, and could not make myself safe. This is a threshold beyond which innocence cannot cross. Is it fair to lay the blame for everything that followed at his door? Hard to say. But I know I will always be a child reaching for a bolt.

Letter to my abuser

Well, fuck you, first and foremost, that goes without saying.

Would you like to know about my body now? When I talk about you, I feel light-headed, and my fingers go numb, like I'm leaving my body. I sweat heavily, my chest clenches like a fist. I can't write about you for more than ten minutes without developing a headache, so that's how long I've given myself.

I had a realisation – you're the black hole in me, the place I can't hang any lights, because it all gets swallowed. I hated you for so long. I used to think I could live just eating the hate I felt for you, but it's exhausting. I'm so tired of the way I worry about being in trouble all the time. Tired of walking like an old man, walling myself into unreachable places. Shame has been the sap of me.

I always felt I'd go blind if I looked at what we did. But that's what I've been doing, travelling back in time to where you drowned us. To feel it fully, cleanly, and then be done with it. Not being able to contain what happened in that room, it split me apart. The Big Bang, the point of no before, as if you created time. Has any of this ever cost you? Do you think about me? Because in some ways that's the most confusing thing, that we can be two people who don't know each other. Although I know your name, I think of you as Him. The whole pronoun. Both too small and too large a word, and it's all yours.

I've been going back over all this because I want to be whole again. But in the process, I learned some things about you, and they didn't make me feel better. That's been hard to make peace with, the fact that not all of this story is about me. The brutality that brought you to that place.

So I've been trying to think about something else. About what you deserve, and whether I can give it. I don't know if the capacity survives. People say it would be good for me, that forgiving leads to closure. And they're right; it would be one way to leave you behind, which is reason enough. But I'm also wondering what forgiveness is, and I think it's more. It's giving someone part of yourself, to fill their gap. You took a lot, but I'm giving you this last piece.

Because if there is a light in me, then there is one in you too, and I have to believe that about myself. So I forgive you.

Time's up.

3

How to Die

At ten, I read that it was possible to bring a bumblebee back from the dead. All one had to do was catch a specimen, freeze it, thaw it out later and witness the miracle of bee reanimation. It was a mesmerising possibility, bringing to mind the story of Lazarus, resurrected by Jesus after four days. I'd always thought of myself as an overlooked Messianic figure, having been born at the stroke of midnight between Christmas Eve and Christmas Day. To mark such an auspicious moment, my parents made up a name for me, Amurtarhik, the meaning of which was 'holiest godhead, not manifest in the world' and which I usually shortened, because people had trouble with the spelling. Apparently, you could even tie a string around the bee's leg while it was out cold, then fly it around like a kite. Jesus didn't do that with Lazarus as far as Scripture tells, but he was still a pioneer.

Of course, this had to be tried. I took to the task with zeal, stalking the park with a drinking glass and a side-plate, until I found a candidate crawling right there on the path, seemingly quite drunk. I encouraged it to totter into the makeshift gaol, and ran home to advance medical science. I'd been reading about cryonics, the preservation of living tissue in sub-zero conditions, and put all my young faith in it. The idea was that brain function could be paused, outliving cellular degeneration of the body, if the process was timed right. Once technology had filled in the blanks, the thawed subject-brain could continue to live a normal life, having woken up attached to the metal legs of a robot, four hundred years in the future.

My confused victim circled the tight perimeter of the glass, a drunken Laika on board side-plate Sputnik. I consigned the vessel to the lowest freezer drawer, next to the breaded fish fillets, and forgot about him. Five hours later, desirous of chicken nuggets, I remembered I'd earmarked this afternoon to exercise the powers of a god, and tipped him out on the floor. He didn't look grateful. He looked awful. Bedraggled stripy fur, like a jumper from a washing drum, his wings like wrung washcloths. The black visors of his eyes were blank. I looped a thread around his articulated leg, and waited. He didn't move a millimetre. I waited ten minutes more, still nothing. I went upstairs to find my mother's hairdryer, which I trained on him. He'd had density when I asked him into the glass, vibrating with a happy song, but now the warm gust blew him under the fridge. He still had the thread on his leg though, and, pulling him out, I imagined a 'Gone Fishin'' fridge magnet, which pictured me dragging a wet bee across linoleum, picking up lint and cereal cinders. He now looked even worse.

The sorrow, growing inside me. I picked the insect up gently, and took him out to the patio, where we sat in a glance of sunlight. I unlooped the thread, which caught on the combs of his legs, cleaned his fur as best I could. Held him in my hands. We sat there for an hour, warmed by the sun, with me hoping against hope. We sat there until clouds gathered themselves, and the sky darkened. The 14,000 facets of his eyes saw nothing, and I knew he wasn't coming back. None of us are.

Fun fact: did you know that if you eat a raisin underwater, you'll die? It's true. Another one: if you walk backwards during Ramadan, you'll die. It's even been proven that if you work a satisfying job, support your family and exercise for a minimum of thirty minutes a day, you will still die. Doesn't matter which path you take, we're all going the same way. They used to say death and taxes were the only unavoidables, and very rich people have proved one of those false. But there's no loophole to the hangman's noose. Which you'd have to say is a design flaw.

I spend a lot of time thinking about death. And baking; I like to bake, but I think about death while doing it. It's my own I fixate on. Will I hear the gun as the bullet leaves it? As the tiger's teeth cut through me, will there be time to smell her musk? Then I remember my life is so boring, these scenarios are closer to wishes than worries, and my paranoia descends on the everyday instead. I cross the road expecting a car to scream through the lights. Key in lock, I pause for a stranger to bring down the bat upon the back of my head. I picture the ignominious carcinoma I'm probably already living with, foot or buttock. Oh God, let it be quick. Let someone else put my affairs in order. I can't stand the paperwork.

It's always been like this. My first memory – probably around four – asking my mother if I had to die, pleading with her. I was lost in the new thought that was also a sensation, a plunging downward. An awareness of death has always been with me, and as I grew, it developed into preoccupation. I thought about it every day. I was looking for an escape from the horror boiling in my brain, and so read all the morbid literature I could lay hands on. From Pulitzer-winning *The Denial of Death* by Ernest Becker, to Irvin D. Yalom's doorstopper on *Existential Psychotherapy*, to the short stories of Hermann Hesse, I shook out books to unlock the doors of death, to take me there and back again. I reread them, muttering special lines, willing their message to enter my blood. I was relentless in my quest to find a writer who could fully explain the experience, and bring me comfort. This was, I see now, like trying to give myself a head massage with hammers.

The average lifespan is a thousand months, less in fact, and I have spent at least four of them trying to persuade the website LinkedIn to stop emailing me. Knowledge of finitude, of brevity, hounds me. I never learned to suppress their brute fact. When introduced to someone, I stare through their features, trying to discern the skull beneath the face. Imagining the black pools of the sockets, the stitch-like fissures criss-crossing their cranium. 'What are you thinking?' a girl might ask as we stare into each other's eyes. I've never liked that question. It doesn't matter how joyous events are. Whether I'm on a water slide, holding a puppy, or writing a love letter, at some point I'll think, *how many more goes do I get at this?* This is the biggest problem we face. Not death itself, but how to make peace with it.

It's the ultimate question, a spiritual dilemma. How to tackle it? Before turning to the great authors for help, I took a more conventional route to higher learning. I'd always expected to go to university, being too useless for the world of work. Yet there was no obvious area of study for me, because I didn't have tremendous grades either. I liked books – another way of saying I didn't have *loads and loads* of friends – so English was an obvious choice. But when it came time to fill out the UCAS form, I found myself bucking against the order of things. Why make life decisions based on rationality? Instead, I chose philosophy: a subject I had never shown any skill in, nor actually studied. It was an act of free will, which the course professors would soon tell me did not exist.

Looking back, the choice makes more sense than I knew. Depression is a disease of philosophy – the philosophical aspect being its profound confrontation with pointlessness. The 'why bother' that can stop one working, or socialising, or eating. Because it's true that there are no answers given to us as to why we should do anything. Earn money, maintain relationships, stay alive – why? An instinct for self-preservation? The drive for species reproduction? Because our parents told us to? These were big questions, uppermost in my mind when I arrived at University College London.

I'd chosen the place not because it was a respected seat of learning, but because I was scared to move far from home. I was only a bus ride away, but even this distance terrified me. Stepping onto the lowest rung of adulthood gave me vertigo. The necessity of cooking food every time I needed to eat, or washing clothes so as not to be clad in rags, was overwhelming. How did anyone find time to do anything else? Was this what adulthood was about, boiling spaghetti and drying socks on an endless loop? Why did functioning take up so much time? To hell with it. Let odours flow. Let noodles be abundant. Pride and personal hygiene could slide – I was here to seek the answer to the ultimate why: an understanding of death, and a reason to live. Soon I was surviving on mashed potato and turning my shirts inside out.

The only philosophy I knew was Sartre's notion that hell was other people, and the halls of residence I moved into were ready proof of that. I'd never lived with anyone to whom I wasn't related, and it was not what I'd hoped for. *Heat* magazines on the table, traffic cones in the TV room, empty vodka bottles piled around the kitchen, like snow pushed to the side of a verge. Instead of truth-seekers discussing the collective unconscious, the place was full of medical students slapping each other's arses.

'These people are morons,' I confided to Chris, as we sat up late, drawing up a list comparing famous philosophers to vegetables. He was the only other boy on my course who lived in my halls. He was from Devon, had spiky hair with frosted tips, jam-jar glasses, and a positive attitude. Still, he'd at least heard of Sartre's theory that nothingness was an experienced reality at the heart of consciousness, so I decided we'd be best friends. Not that I was there to make buddies. I needed the secrets of life and death, and had sought out philosopher kings to beseech their wisdom.

'Buffalo buffalo buffalo buffalo buffalo buffalo buffalo buffalo,' said the goateed philosopher of language in one of our first lectures. He was slumped at the desk, palm pressing into his face, as if he'd been bored once, then been frozen in the moment. He was trying to illustrate lexical ambiguity, but it was too ambiguous for me. He persisted. 'Are the bison polysemous or homonymous? It may seem clear, but the operational distinction is totally specious.' It did not seem clear. I didn't understand a word he was saying, and the longer he spoke, the less I followed. Other students were nodding, and writing things down. What were they writing? I was sitting near the front, a mistake I'd never repeat, and the lecturer could see the confusion on my face. He screwed his fist deeper into his forehead. 'All right, let's go back to basics,' he sighed. 'James while John had had had had had had had had had had had a better effect on the teacher.'

When choosing philosophy, I'd more or less pictured a Greek gymnasium. Old men and naked youths discussing moral instruction, and riddling each other. It was nothing like that. One of the very first lectures was about inductive reasoning. *There is no sound reason to believe the sun will rise each morning,* we were told, *simply because it did the day before.* That was it for me. The very last thing I needed to hear. Metaphysics, epistemology and phenomenology took as long to pronounce as they did to grasp the first thing about. Logic classes were bafflingly mathematical, and the professors were profoundly odd. One of them, a rumpled American, referred to himself in the third person because he didn't believe in individuated consciousness. He also couldn't work his phone. Another never knew when his tutorials started, or who his students were, and would simply shanghai anyone standing outside his office at random, to give them the latest on Cartesianism. Another kept me waiting outside a basement office for fifteen minutes before our first session, later telling me it was a technique he'd modified from Hitler. I liked him best.

There was a module called 'applied philosophy', which concerned real-world situations that philosophy could solve. It sounded promising. I turned up early, to glean deathbed advice. And yet the problems under discussion always contemplated scenarios such as whether it was right to give money to charity, or rescue a baby from a burning building. Where death featured, it always seemed to involve a runaway train, and the utilitarian choice between passively letting a crowd of people get run over, or flipping a switch to actively murder one.

'It feels like a lot of things have gone wrong here. I'm not taking the blame for any of this,' I whispered to Chris at the back of the class. He was assigning nicknames to the most interesting girls in the class.

'I think the lesson is: don't work on the railways,' he said.

As the first year passed, I had a major epiphany: I was not smart. This was confusing, because I was Asian, had worn glasses from a young age, and gone to the trouble of cultivating a pretentious personality. Yet it was true. I couldn't make sense of the questions others were asking in lectures, let alone the answers. Other students had a dispassionate brilliance, instantly comprehending entire arguments, probing them for points of entry like sperm at an egg. The philosophy that spoke to me was read on the side, in French existential novels that tussled with estrangement and authenticity, and whose heroes were invariably depressed. The UCL course was canonical, with limited time for voguish stuff about staring at a baguette and wondering if it existed. It dawned on me that I was at university for the wrong reasons. Rather than academic rigour, I was looking for therapy, or perhaps a priest.

On the plus side, the department also had the fewest number of contact hours of any at the university. We were taught eight hours a week, the rest of the time left to our own devices. My devices: an increasing fixation with death, an obsession that was itself running off the rails. One week, an idea gripped me. I thought about the university mortuary, where dead bodies were stored for dissection. I probably couldn't break in, but what if I got a job there? They must need porters to get the bodies in and out. That way I could surround myself with corpses, look to them for the secrets of death. But how? The answer was horrible: I realised I'd have to befriend the idiot medics, use them to hit the payload.

I'd tried to keep up with their drinking in the kitchens, but always ended up under the table, enjoying the coolness of tile against cheek. I couldn't keep up with their banter, because I didn't have enough sexual experience. At least, not of the right kind. But I knew they liked, for obscure reasons, to collect traffic cones. Mementos of big nights, they accumulated in the corridors like banded stalagmites. One got used to stepping over them, while balancing a plate of bolognese. To have the medics see me as an ally, I'd have to produce a cone to rule the others. I went out every night that week, under cover of total darkness, walking around the streets in a hoodie, until I found what I was looking for. An eight-foot free-standing circular traffic sign on legs, a shining blue coin of the gods. It was enormous. I could comfortably stand underneath it.

With Chris's help, I manoeuvred it into the house, setting it up obelisk-like in the communal front room, an offering. I went to bed, expecting the morning to bring me fame, and the keys to a morgue.

'Who could do something like that?' one of the medics was saying to another, as they looked up at the obelisk. I swelled a little. 'It's insane.'

'At your pleasure, gentlemen,' I said, immediately hating myself. They were staring at me now, as if I'd said the word "buffalo" eight times in a row.

'Do you know what this is?' interrogated the taller of the two, who had a quiff of blond hair. He didn't look grateful, I realised, or proud of me. 'This is a traffic diversion sign. That's serious. You could have been responsible for tens of accidents, or even loss of life.' An underwhelming but horribly accurate phrase, 'tens of accidents'. For the first time, I saw him not as a rugby-playing ignoramus who claimed to have invented Strip Buckaroo, but as a student physician. Someone with a future. 'You're a weird guy,' he said, suddenly bored. I figured this wasn't the moment to ask if he could get me access to cadavers.

By my second year I'd stopped reading the course texts, and looked to morbid male artists for my education: Egon Schiele, Francis Bacon, Francisco de Goya, Franz Kafka, Jeff Buckley, Darren Aronofsky. I memorised disease statistics, the processes of bodily decomposition, the way famous people had died.

'Naturally optimistic cancer patients have a better

prognosis,' I informed Chris one evening. We were sitting on the floor, rearranging his music collection from alphabetical to mood-inspired. He was holding a They Might Be Giants CD between two piles, trying to decide if they were whimsical or arch. 'A diagnosis would destroy me. Which means I'll probably die early, quaking in fear.' Chris didn't look up. He tolerated my litanies, but never joined in.

'What are you saying, something about quacking?'

I was aware how *teenage* I sounded. For years, I'd reasoned that everyone looks back on adolescent angst with laughter. One just needed to make it through those terrifying years. Now I had, and I hadn't. My fatalism had intensified. I was heavily insomniac, which I medicated via the manageable oblivions of drinking, sleeping all day and going to clubs at night. Luckily, this allowed Chris and me some crossover interests.

'It won't work. The sheer range of a band like Silver Sun defies categorisation,' he decided, abandoning his scatter of jewel cases, throwing back a vodka and adjusting his skinny tie. This was the sign that he'd had enough of death chat and was ready to head towards the lights.

London was an ebulliently optimistic place to be in the early aughts, before the Iraq War, before social media and camera phones. The club scene was going through a golden period, to which we were oblivious. An earnest boy on our course, Amish Tom, told us the best places to go. We'd often end up at electro-pop mecca Trash, which became legendary, and which Chris and I went to because it was a walkable distance from our halls. Artists played live and celebrities frequented it: Jared Leto, Scott Walker, Jarvis Cocker, the latter of whom talked to me at great length about the emergence of a new social underclass, while behind us the Yeah Yeah Yeahs were getting the party started. Through it all I felt alienated, behind glass.

'Look at these people!' I shouted, as a neon-lit crowd of proto-hipsters danced to LCD Soundsystem. 'They're in it.'

'Yeah,' Chris acknowledged. 'But we're in it too. Why are we talking about it?'

'Two thirds of suicide jumpers have dislocated shoulders,' I said. 'They change their mind, and reach back. But the force rips their arm away.'

'Let's dance.'

A few years after the bumblebee, there was the dragonfly. A walk back from school, on the last day of term, a half day, over before it began. Golden hours stretched ahead, a whole summer behind that. The leaves nudged each other, the ground was warm, and there she was, perfect on the path. She could have been Pegasus. I squatted down, wondering at the iridescent cobalt of her body, her filigree wings. Most hypnotic were her outsize eyes, each a helicopter pilot's helmet. They glowed like pearls too, lit by some force independent of the body's death. Something that had outlasted it. I snatched her up. Raced home with treasure cupped in my palms. The thought of possessing such beauty for ever was giddying.

But when I got back and laid her on the table next to my bed, I was confused by what I saw. Those lenticular, miraculous eyes were changing colour, the shimmering drama of teal and brick losing ground to a spreading, lifeless grey. Her body too was dull. I watched helplessly as the light was extinguished, embarrassed by the experience I had tried to grasp, and lost. What was the light in the dragonfly, what had I seen? Remnants of chemicals playing out in the body? Before it disappeared, the light in her had shrunk to a final, radiant pixel. The sight reminded me of the tiny black-and-white TV set that I would watch on the floor of my room, how turning the ridged knob left, past the click, would implode the picture to a brilliant, enduring spot in the centre of the dead screen, like a dying star. I'd read that the static between TV stations was, in part, the afterglow of the Big Bang; after that, I spent a lot of time staring into the hiss and chaos, trying to make sense of it.

University was not going to save my soul, I knew that. But I had a new angle on my obsession, sparked by the Scientology leaflets that would come through the door, hoping to vacuum up the young and curious. Religion was the obvious place to look for ways to cheat death. Probably not the Scientologists, whom I couldn't afford. A life beyond was religion's entire premise, probably the reason it had been invented in the first place. And so, before my final year, instead of studying, I decided to become a man of God.

Where to start? My parents hadn't pressured me to practise any beliefs as a child, though theirs was Hinduism, at least on the surface. As a child I had loved its Technicolor cartoon aspect, the monkey and elephant heroes, many-headed foes, chariot races. I loved those endless stories, of blue boy-gods who held the cosmos in their mouths and outwitted demons. But there was also another side, forbidding to a child. I would stare uncomprehendingly at our upstairs landing, covered in calendars of Indian sages, plait-bearded and sitting lotus. Contemplating infinity on faded thin paper that told you how many days there were in February. I remember posters of the venerated, four-armed Kali: black-skinned and red-eyed, wearing a skirt of severed limbs. The beloved goddess stuck out her tongue and held up a severed head dripping with blood. The most fantastic, terrifying vision. She was a destroyer, from whom even Lord Death had fled, terrified. Things were not black and white with the gods of this place, and darkness had its due. But I was scared to know more.

'You will live for ever (in the kingdom of heaven)!' read the flyer I accepted from a beatific woman on Tottenham Court Road. Clearly those brackets were important small print, but this sounded promising. Christianity was a familiar way in, and not just because I thought of myself as Jesus. Growing up in south London, with its high African population, there'd been churches everywhere. Trestle tables and sandwich boards in the street that read 'Have you heard?' and 'Good news!' Even I had to admit they were courting disappointment with juicy hooks like that. Eternal life is well and good, but if your opening gambit is 'Have you heard?', bystanders will expect a dog that can write its own name.

I should have gone into an actual church, tried a service, a joyous Pentecostal one. But I didn't want to hear myself sing, and was gripped by social anxiety about not knowing when to sit down and stand up. Still, Christianity is a broad church, and there were more introverted options. There was a Quaker meeting house near Euston station, minutes from UCL's quad. I liked the sound of the Quakers, with their philosophical rigour and porridge oats, and meetings in which no one talked unless the spirit moved them. I went, but couldn't relax because I was worried someone I knew would see me coming out. It's embarrassing to actively try to save your soul. I also met someone who had been raised in the faith, which she described as 'not all that'. Always the same people being moved, she said, usually men. Same old story. Besides, I wanted to meet God, not hang out with religious people. I began to suspect the answer lay in books.

I read the Bible cover to cover, like a mystery thriller, which in a way it is. It tells us Whodunit in the first ten words, but it was the mechanics of how Hedunit that interested me. I persevered through the endless begatting of Chronicles and the unreadable OCD of Numbers. The New Testament was moving, but I still hoped some concrete equation for cheating death might be revealed on the last page. An idea with a firmer foundation than mere faith. It basically ended with John trying to get everyone to live inside a city, 'For without are dogs, and sorcerers, and whoremongers,' which frankly sounded far more up my street.

I never got to give Judaism a proper go. I'd read the Pentateuch as a two-for-one, being the first five books of the Old Testament, but that felt like an introductory offer. I suspected the really important stuff was in a room at the back. Where it would remain. Of the Abrahamics, the Jews were the least interested in converts. There were no trestle tables outside the tube station, saying 'Look at this!' or 'I can't believe it!' I moved onto the Quran, and found exquisite verses there. Whoever does an atom's weight of good will see it. Whoever saves a human life shall be regarded as having saved all mankind. I started getting flashbacks to the train tracks and the faulty signal equipment. So verily, with the hardship, there is relief. I didn't know whether I could believe, but I believed in the grace of the writing. The physically felt balance of the words felt like it could be leaned upon. This was beauty, announcing its intention to save. But beauty was beside the point, I thought. What about the big question? The one that had brought me here. Every soul shall taste death, said Sura 3. I read further, about how the angel of death would arrive to the dying to extract the soul from their chest. What if you weren't a full believer? What if you were, for example, definitely a sinner? The angels of wrath would also be there, and the pangs of death were extremely painful. You would subsequently be thrown into the lowest point of the earth, questioned by ugly angels, then punished with scorpions and sent to hell.

None of that was especially comforting, and besides, it was after the fact. I wanted to know if there was a way I could not die at all. And then events overtook me. They overtook us all. I was woken on a September afternoon by Amish Tom, whose house I'd stayed at after a night of dancing. He told me I should come and see. His house-mates, as well as some people we'd picked up during the night, were sitting silently transfixed. On the television, we watched smoke pouring out of one of two towers, heard garbled screams that distorted microphones. We grappled with the unreality of it. We watched a second aeroplane follow the first. Saw tiny figures, like insects, tumbling from the sky, before everything fell. I knew I was looking at death. I couldn't look away.

In the weeks after the attack, my religious fervour waned. Amish had suggested we take a trip out to America, see what was happening for ourselves, and an unshaven Asian, twenty years old, was going to have troubles enough at homeland security without a Quranic codex tucked in his cabin baggage. It felt like the world had caught me up, and death was on everybody's mind. The news kept reminding us of the claustrophobic particulars of it, the terror and helplessness. There was a strain of dread in the air, and it started to take me back to the intense death fears of adolescence. The time I'd beaten on my mother's bedroom door, naked in the dead of night, summoning her from sleep to protect me from death. Exactly as I'd done at age four, but this time conscious of my pubic hair, that it was wrong to be seen like this. In a panic attack, there is no dignity. They would start to come again, now that everyone was breathing anxiety and paranoia. Anxiety is liquid fear, and panic attacks are the end point of anxiety: a total dissolution of self, an organism reduced to an overloaded limbic system. They could blindside me from nowhere, and I would find myself moaning, sweating, unable to give voice to the pressure rising inside. A soundless scream. This was dying: land-drowning as I spiralled into blackness, accompanied only by animal fear.

A week before our final exams, I fell asleep on a patch of grass outside the university library while trying to revise. We'd been out till late the night before, at a crappy little indie disco on Oxford Street, which was a language school by day. Courtney Love had been DJ'ing, at one point leaving the booth, careening onto the floor and into me, where we'd danced together a short time before the crowd mobbed her, all wanting a piece of her. A body doesn't have that many pieces to give, I thought, as the crowd carried me away from her. Kant's Copernican turn could go to hell, I thought, reliving the thrilling clamminess of her skin; now that was something worth remembering. When I woke, I was alone and hungover on the grass. I stumbled home, accidentally leaving three years' worth of notes behind. I never saw them again. At least it was a funny story, like my final grades. On the very last day, the philosophy department had a party. It was nice to connect with the other solipsists; but with warm white wine twining through my brain, I saw young people making mealy-mouthed promises to stay in touch. I heard myself speaking out loud, addressing the room. 'All goodbyes are final. Death is coming.' They must have agreed with me, because the party ended shortly after.

Was there a way back from all this fatalism, which stood between me and participation in life? I remember one final walk back from school, with another summer before me. The breeze was light and sweet, and I was taking a different path, to the house of David. He was a boy in my class, and his father was a vicar, who'd made it clear his house was open to me. With no one at my house, I would often go after school and spend time there, sometimes stay for dinner. I was daydreaming, taking my time, when I saw it. The huge black back, lustrous and tulip winged. The hinges of a powerful body, edged in yellow. I got down and stared at that anvil of a head, crowned with broad, mahogany antlers. A stunning, out-of-place beast, motionless on the path. Fearfully, I touched him. Nothing. I stroked his broad back. How long had he been dead? His limbs were stiff as I placed him in my pocket, and walked on.

I was let into the vicarage by the vicar's sing-song wife, who spoke over her shoulder as she returned to the kitchen. I wasn't listening – my mind on the dense totem next to my hip. What had he died of? Had his body just run down? Stag beetles live long lives, the vast majority of which are spent in isolation, deep underground. It felt unfair that he had been invisible all that time, and here, at the end, he hadn't made it. Standing in the corridor, the door still open, I slipped my hand inside the vent of my pocket, wanting to touch that strange smoothness again. Two points of pressure on the pad of my middle finger. The points intensified. They were coming into clarity, slow and hard. I yelped in shock, retrieving my hand. Hanging off it, suspended by its mandibles, which were vicing together, was a very undead scarab. I turned and shot my arm out, wanting to fling away the hand itself. The beetle sailed through the air, disappearing into a shrub. The vicar's wife reappeared, concerned by the noise. What was going on? 'A resurrection,' I said.

Under the surface of this fascination with death, I knew, was the desire to not be here. A yearning for escape that almost matched my terror. That *almost* was the only reason I was still alive. I think about one particular night in my teen years, the blood on my wrists, the humiliation of it. But I don't think that was the closest I came. I stared most fully into death's eye in the pitch of night, in a French village far from home. (I wasn't a WWI soldier;

I was on holiday.) My new friend Chris's girlfriend's family owned a place in the French countryside. We could go, with some of Kate's friends – a night ferry, followed by a drive, and we'd be there.

As we've seen, the ferry journey over hadn't been a simple one for me, and I arrived with more baggage than I left with, but the place was truly peaceful as paradise, surrounded by fields. For hours that afternoon, the garden had stood silent but for the coos of wood pigeons and the metronomic lull of ping-pong. And yet I felt uneasy. That same night, I left the others to a card game, roll-up cigarettes and boxes of wine. The air was like a bruise, almost crackling. The ozone and unease were an obscure call. I made excuses to leave the room, pulled on a hoodie, and closed the front door quietly behind me, to walk. To the left there was a large barn we had taken one look in and called Chicken Auschwitz, and peeking through the slats I could see a dense, worming carpet of yellow, thousands of chicks making throaty vocalisations, and giving off a smell as if evil had soiled itself. Apart from that, it was a nice barn. The road to the right was very steep downhill, so I had to creep like a cartoon burglar, feet picking a way forwards. It had been eerily still at dusk, but now that night had fallen the wind had picked up, and was building, rattling the firs around me. The hood kept being blown back over my shoulders, until I stopped replacing it. New rain pricked my face, which after a time started to feel raw, but I kept going. It meant no one else would be out. I had a fierce need to be alone, and old feelings I couldn't bear to touch.

At the bottom, I came across a lake. Actually, an enormous reservoir, cut through by a road, running over the spine of its dam. On either side, water stretched as far as the eye could see. Halfway along, a service gangway led out over the deep. I knew immediately, with the logic of a dream, that this was where I was going.

I stepped over the crash barriers, up to the locked gate of the walkway. Putting my hands on the sign forbidding entry, I vaulted up, then down, landing with a clang on the wrong side of the law. A shock how flimsy the platform felt, unmaintained, though the sound I made was swept away by the wind in the darkness. The rain was heavy now, falling on and through the thin silver lattice floor, held up on long metal stilts. Between my feet, water chopped over submerged machinery, monstrous pumps and sluices you could never see, even on a good day. Short metal fencing made a gauntlet of the way forwards, almost as narrow as my body. Clutching the rail forced my elbows out, over their boundaries. Still, they were thicker than the floor, the rails of the fencing, so I used them like crutches, swinging carefully along, letting them take some weight from the floor; but not so much that pressure from my arms might split them apart at any eroded seams. I didn't know what I was doing, but something pulled me on, further into the darkness. That's when I heard a head-filling grumble, which rolled on awfully, until suddenly it whip-split the sky. Shocking, the snap of it, as if heaven could be so brittle. A storm, like none I had ever seen. I stood under a hemispheric canopy of roiling clouds and primal fear. A flashbulb, and I saw my legs, my little body over roaring water, in terrifying wind. It was coming. It was extraordinary how I could see it coming, like a god rounding a corner, a crucible of fire at the top of the lake.

I found my way to the end of the narrow gangway, the bridge to nowhere way out over the water, facing the storm. A storm which seemed to have changed direction, and was now barrelling towards me. Rain lashed at me, but I couldn't turn away. A distance that would have taken me half a day to walk was torn up in seconds, the sky sucked up and blown out, in a darkness illuminated by jagged electrical arcs. They came frequently, unleashed and wild. Terrifying, transfixing. They burned my retinas. It was hard to look at, to stand in this power. That's when I saw the danger.

Unimaginable currents were leaping from the sky, searching for somewhere to land. I could see the bolts striking. One vicious strike, edged in red, splintered a tree at the edge of the lake into embers, which briefly glowed and then were gone. Terrifying, and beautiful. Other than the distant trees, I was the most elevated thing around. If 300 million volts somehow missed my body, surely they would find the long, metal walkway I was standing on, and enter me that way. If it struck wide of that, it would electrify the surface of the water, conduct itself up the legs of the platform, directly into me anyway. The odds were against my surviving this. This would be how I died. Not many got an exit like it.

The storm was now over me, throwing down crackling white lassos, repeatedly, without pause. And then it hit me. All this power was looking for my heart. The little electrical generator that had kept me alive this long, against my expectations. I would merge with the source. I was going home. And wasn't it what I wanted? That's what all this had been about. I was attracting death to me on some level, filling myself up, rushing towards it. Nobody knew I had come here. I'd be vaporised like that tree. There'd be no body, no letter, no trace. It was symbolic, mystical, a way to finally get LinkedIn to leave me alone.[*] It was worth it.

But the brewing cauldron ate up that huge sky, and I looked up and felt afraid. It was pure violence, not home. It was as if I had got too close to an eye, looking into it to see not some kindly window of the soul, but something else, furiously unknowable.

Panic filled me. I turned around, moaning, realising it was too late. I started to run back along the spit, grate reverberating under my feet. A slip on slick metal, a fall. My leg twisted as I landed awkwardly; pain sheared

---

[*] Sure, at this point they didn't yet have my email address. But prevention is better than cure.

through my hip and knee. The rain yowled, wanting to keep me there, the wind pinning me as I stared through gaps at the dark, boiling water below. Strobing arcs fell either side of the lake around me, and I waited for the killing stroke, wondering if I would see the flash from above, or feel the volts snaking up the catwalk, burning me to it.

Keep going, an instinct of self-preservation told me. I pulled my leg through the bars, trying not to feel the pain. Limping, I crawled along for what felt like hours, as the belly of the beast passed overhead. At the sign, I swung the wrong leg over, unthinking, and the wrench was agonising as I fell on to the other side, back with the living.

Hours later, in the dead of the night, my mind raced with what had happened. I was exhausted, my body in pain. The bed felt unreal beneath me. It did not feel luxurious. Earlier, Kate had told me to fetch sheets from a storage cupboard, and put them on a double bed in one of the guest rooms. But I was not myself that day, and couldn't hear her properly. I'd misunderstood her instructions and so when I returned I made my bed in the storage cupboard room itself, brushing aside cobwebs to lie down with the spiders. Thoughts crowded me, in the dust and smell of dry wood. That line, that had always felt so fragile, between living and dying: it *was* fragile. All choices would one day come to dust, and I would lie like this, under sheet on slab, blood pooling in a frozen body.

I asked myself if I really wanted to die. At times before,

the answer had been yes. The option felt preferable to long, claustrophobic years of panic attacks and depression, after which I would die anyway. From a utilitarian point of view, wasn't it less pain overall? I'd known people grow angry when I spoke like this. It's true that every day is a gift – but when that hasn't been your experience, people try to shame you. It's not a good place to start helping someone. When every day is a struggle, every hour contested, the urge to drop the unbearable weight is seductive. I understood that. I understand it.

If you ever come near that point, I urge you to get help, from people qualified to listen. And I urge you to listen too, because a message from the deep is trying to reach you. If you got to this feeling because you're sensitive, be more sensitive still. If life has been hard, listen harder for the grace notes. At the lowest points I've known, I thought I knew everything, could see further into what others were scared to look at. I knew nothing. Not adult love, nor the satisfaction of being useful, and while I had known suffering, I didn't yet know the understanding real loss brings. There was so much more ahead; there is always more to know. Stay open, because life only gets richer as it unfolds. We know the end of the story, but not how we get there, or who we'll be when we do.

Death was not done with me. And there was no way I could prepare for the phone call that came later, shaking me awake back home in London. You'll get one too if you haven't already. Sooner or later, we all get a call.

A letter to my university room-mate

Hi Jason

It was Mel C from the Spice Girls that put me off, I think. That was the only CD you owned. Sitting there on your shelf, reminding me of those adverts that say: If you only buy one album this year, make it this. And I'd think, who buys one album a year? And who would make it Melanie C?

Anyway, it's been twenty years, so I thought I'd write, in the hopes that this reaches you. It's a long time, and I don't know if you ever think of that time. You had a front row seat to me at my most confused, I think. I wonder how it looked from your side.

Sorry I collected every bottle I ever drank, and then started to collect other people's empties too. Sorry I stacked them up like a dry-stone wall inside our room. I'm sorry I dragged my bed frame out into the hallway, so I could sleep on a mattress on the floor, surrounded by a crib made of bottles, like the king of the sewer people. I think I was trying to feel safe, but it made the place look bad.

You used to sleep facing the wall. We never talked. It's a strange thing to live so intimately with someone and not know them. Didn't we just plough our furrows into ruts, until neither of us saw the other? It felt like you'd gone into a coma every night. Awake, you were working and tired, under so much pressure. You had your own burden; the only

78

people in the world who push their kids harder than Indian parents are Chinese parents. Actually, mine have always been supportive. Forget that. But you had it rough, from the glimpse into your situation I got. I never tried to help, and was bored by your subject: biology, or chemical engineering? Nucleotides and clumps of letters. That was unimaginative. I just heard they can make bioplastic from sea-lettuce, which I do not understand but think is incredible. It's a shame too, because I've become interested in epigenetics, specifically the way trauma might be able to travel in gene expressions, and think you might have been able to explain it to me. And I could have given you more music, or talked about books, or what was going on with me. Maybe that would have been good for both of us.

Ah, well. Next life. Whatever you're doing, I hope you learned to sleep less deeply.

I listened to that Mel C album today, by the way. It's actually not bad.*

---

* Just listened to it again, and don't know what I was thinking. It's terrible.

4

How to Be in Your Body

If you're in the market for some bad advice, get yourself a touch of clinical low mood: out it comes, sure as worms follow rain. *Stop feeling sorry for yourself. Stop thinking about it. Snap out of it.* Snap Out Of It is the mother mould of bad advice in this area, and can ferment into many pungent cheeses. One of the most annoying is *happiness is a choice, you know,* always accompanied by this inscrutable little nodding-guru thing with the eyebrows, as if the person has just told you Frankenstein is the doctor not the monster, and is waiting for your mind to be blown. *Have you tried* not *being depressed?* someone once asked me in a shoe shop, and I was stunned by the idiot-profundity of it. Furthest off the mark though, the piece of advice that makes my eyes roll so far back in my head I can see last Wednesday, is: *the thing with depression is, it's all in your head.* In a narrow, neurotransmitter-deficiency sense, that's true. It is all in your head, the same way that happiness is all in your head, and car sickness, and the idea of Japan. Depression is way more real than Japan, which I for one have never been to. Besides, it's not just the head where symptoms come home to roost.

When the downward spiral comes, the heaviness of my skull feels as intolerable as the thoughts within. Those thoughts have a physicality too: hopelessness feels like a smothering sheet, self-loathing a knife through the brain. The bones around my eyes ache with fatigue. You wouldn't want to be my toilet, because my guts are an absolute catastrophe. I experience disturbances in vision, imagined flashes across the sky. I can start to become disoriented, a physically felt confusion that means I get lost in streets I know well. I might even start to smell like a pie. All responsibility is unbearable in the throes of a downward spiral, including the tending of the flesh, which is why self-care is so easy to dispense with: the showering, brushing of teeth, taking of medication. The body takes the fall.

It makes sense that a problem which can pass from head to body can be addressed the other way around. *You should exercise. Have you tried exercise? How about that exercise, eh?* Wearying, at your most tired, to deal with advice. Advice is like being handed a large amount of foreign currency. What do you do with it? The number of times people have asked about my health problems then told me maybe I should try swimming, weights, lacrosse, a jog? A light jog? As if mental well-being were a bus I could still catch, if I left now.

Most of the time, I'd rather be depressed than exercise. I am, visibly, extravagantly lazy. Not once in my life has a bro been moved to enquire if I lift. It's clear from the Gregory Peck spectacles that I'm not an exercise person. Exercise my soul, sure: I work out answers to the oldest human problems. Deadlift the question of the cosmos. I squat God. An interest in fitness has always struck me as a defining and limiting trait, like wearing a bucket hat. It's a red flag; a warning the conversation has a low ceiling.

When I was younger, it was obvious that being smart and physically active were mutually excluding. If you voluntarily spent time in a gym, running nowhere for thousands of hours, or rotating iron plates through ninety degrees with the power of your beefy guns, you almost certainly had the depth of a cereal mascot. Anyone who had a six-pack didn't have anything else. If I'd continued thinking that way, I'd have withered away on an ottoman by now, spaghetti for legs, head entirely conical. I'm lucky for the sea change of my mid-twenties, which more or less forced me into my body.

In the last six weeks of university, something in the air alerted me to the open palm of Destiny, ready to slap me down. It was time to grow up. John, a friend on my course and a heavy-metal fan I thought I knew, appeared after finals with his hair cut short and styled, bearing news he'd sorted out a law conversion course, with an interest in property. Prior to this, his interests had been anti-establishment goatees and pale ale. I saw a fault line had appeared, with us on either side, and the ground would now carry us in different directions. Not that I was alone. A plait-bearded Swedish rocker, still on my side of the line, wept into his leathers at the change in his friend. When he spoke, he spoke in rhyming couplets, something I have never forgotten.

'You used to be a rock dude, with attitude,' he lamented with Nordic dolour, 'but now I see you, all suited and booted.'

Real life was beckoning; like all heroes, I refused the call. I didn't know what I wanted, but it wasn't anything sensible. I did have to reassess my ambitions though, which had included becoming a melancholy poet, or a beam of pure light. Neither option was practical and one of them required me to write: a lot of effort and never worth it. Surely, I thought, there must be some field of human endeavour in which unemployment was the norm. Whose players accrue glamour in opposite proportion to their social use. Of course there was. I did what anyone with low self-esteem and an ambivalent relationship to visibility does. I decided to become a professional actor.

My parents took the news with dignity. My father averted his eyes from *Columbo*, something I had never seen him do, and gripped the arms of his chair, until his brown knuckles showed white. My mother was far more vocal. 'Oooooooooh!' she actually squealed. 'Maybe I will go to drama college too?'

'It's drama school, not drama college, and I will die

before I let that happen.' They weren't the only people I had to bluntly inform of my acting plans. Lily and I had only known each other a few weeks, were barely a couple yet, but she was older and intuitive, and I knew I could trust her. 'My life is worthless. I want to be transformed, or destroyed,' I confessed. It's not clear which aspect of this suicide-bomber's-note of a personality appealed to her, but she let me move into her home, to make my commute easier.

Naturally, I was too scared to leave London, but fortunately the capital contains the most prestigious acting schools in the world. At RADA, home to the highborn, my desperate rendition of 'Consider Yourself' from *Oliver!* saw me escorted out of a tradesmen's entrance. Walking into LAMDA was like stumbling backstage at a catwalk show: the most beautiful woman I had seen in my life was showing people where the toilets were. I sensed I would never fit in at those places, especially since they had turned me down. Desperate and wondering how to assemble a pipe dream, I didn't know where to turn.

In the meanwhile, to raise the money I needed I took a job at a call centre, which paid surprisingly well considering these were fundraising calls on behalf of charities. On my first day, I was thrilled – and distantly worried – to discover it was full of actors. Being awkward and shy, it was fascinating to observe this species up close. Bitching wittily among themselves as their calls connected, they could instantly switch modes, reading the audience on the other end of the line, and becoming who they needed them to be. They'd play the solicitous nephew, banter like jocks, or grow grave as priests. They made people fall in love with them. They could seduce complete strangers into planning a future together, while cooing that two pounds a month kept an orphaned seal in physiotherapy for a week. They were trickster heroes who had stolen the gift of connection from the gods, and I wanted a piece. In our breaks, I told them I wanted to be transformed or destroyed, and asked where they would apply if they were me. *Ask us a hard question*, came the reply.

In the business, Drama Centre had earned the nickname Trauma Centre, the first casualty of trauma being rhyme. While many acting schools claimed to 'break you down to build you back up again', Drama Centre really only subscribed to half the model. Edgy, uncompromising, vaguely underground, the school and its draconian method were legendary. It was said that students were made to strip naked on their first day, like recruits at a Soviet spy academy. It proudly took in students generally deemed inappropriate: oddballs and masochists, gaolbirds and addicts, people who attracted trouble.

I wasn't convinced at first. Drama Centre wasn't an acronym, and sounded frankly similar to 'drama college'. Yet within seconds of stepping inside the building, my course was clear as sunlight. It was literally a church – a former Methodist one, with honey stone and Corinthian columns, a majestic hall, stained glass gauzing the air. There was an evangelical zeal to the students, voluntarily here on the weekend, and totally exhausted. The streets around were rough, paved with meth-heads, but within these walls young people were dedicating themselves to art, donating their bodies, doing something extraordinary. 'It's the last conservatoire training,' one of them whispered, which made me think of French windows.

At my audition, I gave them a halting speech from *The Seagull*, in which I briefly forgot my lines and experienced a few moments of out-of-body failure. I caterwauled my way through 'Rivers of Babylon', an absence of pitch somehow working in my favour.

'You have studied Brecht,' an amused Romanian approved. 'It is the ugly voice, struggling to reach the note that touches our humanity. This was exquisitely human.' It was the last good feedback I'd hear in three years, but it was enough: I was in, and could consider myself at home.

When Lily discovered where I was going, a shadow crossed her face. She had been a student at Drama Centre too, years before. She claimed not to recall the exact circumstances under which she left, but the memory made her grow slightly translucent. In her day, some teachers were notorious for giving students psychologically brutal feedback, the kind that lodged itself in your organs, before kicking them off the course. The school had a reputation for producing actors of unparalleled emotional intensity, but the proportion who graduated was similar to cadets training to be Navy SEALs, with less mental-health support.

Things had changed, but Lily was still concerned for my well-being. Knowing the school's monomaniacal spell, she also knew nothing would stop me going. She watched as I threw myself into the conservatoire hours. We worked nine till nine again, until the arc of the sun was a memory, returning home mute and hungry, to prepare work for the following day, which would be summarily dismissed as inauthentic and facile. It was basically a fundamentalist acting madrasa, and exactly what I was looking for.

Looking around at the other students in my year, it was clear the school attracted people who couldn't get along with boundaries, or were looking for an escape from civilian life. A few with prison behind or ahead of them, another who left and joined the army. An eighteen-year-old Scottish girl called Vicki could have been airlifted in from a BBC *Horizon* documentary on teen pregnancy. There was a Byronic cockney who had to be physically propped up during lessons because the heroin was making him sleepy. The school had always drawn these outsiders, and stories of its legendary alumni were lovingly circulated. Before he became Russell Brand, Russell Brand had been a nameless malcontent with a mouse living in his hair, who kept threatening to throw himself off the balcony. Tom Hardy suffered an almost romantic attachment to fighting, and broke protocol by signing with an agent in his first year, after walking around with his top off. The worst was Colin Firth, who insisted the crucial element of any good warm-up was a blood sacrifice.*

Everyone's favourite story was that Anthony Hopkins, who had studied acting under founding principle Christopher Fettes, had based Hannibal Lecter on him. Though Fettes was gone, his style lived on in the form of a younger teacher, who had been hand-picked to make people cry. James Kemp had the withholding charisma of a cult leader. He shaved his head, hair being a distraction: the weak character actor's first wrong turn. Olivier built his characters from the shoes up, but none of us were him, as we were reminded on a daily basis. 'Working up a sweat is not the same thing as having an inner life,' Kemp would note, when he sensed a chip of self-congratulation had worked its way into a student. 'Perhaps other teachers have misled you into thinking you're something special. I don't believe you. I don't believe anything about you.'

If you hadn't dropped out of school as a teen to follow the Maly Theatre Company of St Petersberg around, you were already a disappointment. The fact any of us were alive at all in the year of our Lord 2003 was unforgivable. The only movie he could wholeheartedly recommend was Bergman's *Fanny och Alexander*: not the three-hour cut-down version for the pabulum-swallowing masses, but the director's cut, which lasted three days, with a brief

* Not true. He was roundly acknowledged to be a very nice man.

intermission for whipping. 'Your idea of acting is based on a copy of a copy; it's bad. Remove the idea, or remove yourself from this class,' was his opinion of any work that hadn't emerged from eighty hours of improvisation and a spell in a gulag. At other times, his feedback was brutally rhetorical. 'Why are you walking like that? Do you need the toilet?'

If you did actually need the toilet, you were permitted to go, but not to rejoin the class. After all, actors should have full control of their instrument. ('Is your body tuned to the subtlest expression, or is it a garden hose?') If you arrived even five seconds after the scheduled start of class, you would be refused. If you were late for the first lesson of the day, you were sent home. *RADA is a holiday camp, Drama Centre is a boot camp!* we would trill as we nursed our stomach cramps, or left via the door we had just entered.

Conditions weren't uniform in their severity. The voice department was floridly eccentric, one of the teachers claiming to have learned the secret of astral projection from a shapeshifter, while I'm convinced the other was unable to pronounce the word "pronunciation". The school's new principal, meanwhile, was the bluffest Romanian I had ever met. He'd finish meetings abruptly with a Brecht quote to chew on, while making you feel you were delaying him from a restaurant table. 'It's not magic, what we do, comrades – it's work!' he would announce, halfway out the door.

What the school prized above all was movement. Actors are athletes, we were told, and should train as nothing less. This is your gym. Breakfast like a king, lunch like a queen, supper as a peasant. The movement teacher, Liana, was a twinkly Swedish sadist – what is it with Swedes? She was rumoured to be ninety-two years old, with the body of a twenty-nine-year-old, God knows whose. She would stand at the front of class in a leotard, exhorting us into stomach-shredding folds, tendon-thinning stretches, and barrel jumps for hours, until our bodies cried out, at a cellular level, to be put down. 'Sit hup on your sittings bones . . . Don't give een!' All the while a bear-like percussionist called Patrick pounded on a conga in the corner, a tribal soundtrack to unending pain.

The women were required to grow stronger, the men more flexible. Painful hours at the palm-rubbing pleasure of Liana alternated with hours of ballet, in which we learned to control the line of our torsos, unfolding into arabesques, soundlessly landing perfect *pas des chats*. Ballet, yoga, massage. Feldenkrais method, Alexander technique. Martial arts, clowning, contact improvisation. Rhythm, kilter, gravity. Revolted by the received idea that actors were namby-pamby pleasure seekers, the school invited us to become Spartan warriors of the boards. Soon our stomachs were hard, our mental resistance soft.

Our teachers wanted us to access every muscle in our bodies, until we were in total control. I mean this literally – I remember one lesson remarking off-handedly that I couldn't move my little toe. The muscle had atrophied, after years of being squashed up against its neighbour in the toe box of canvas trainers. Liana dropped to a squat over my legs, extending away from me on the floor. 'Move this toe,' she said. She was observing the digit like a vulture sizing up a sand mouse.

'Move the little toesie,' she repeated, fixing a pale blue eye upon me. The rest of the class relaxed whatever pose they'd been put in, standing on their heads with legs at nine and three, or wrapped up in themselves like a ball of rubber bands. I strained, and the toe moved – along with three others. Useless. 'Little toe is a big key. Without it, no balance.' I wondered how she would get on with my mother as I attempted to isolate the single signal I wanted. I tried again. A quiver. The little toe moved again, nosing up and sideways like a mole pushing towards the light. Such a small thing; but an awakening is always a small thing, and everything.

The desire to act, the bug actors pick up from their earliest years, is a proxy for so much that lies beneath the surface. To be seen. To be fluid and unbound. To play dress-up, give licence to hidden selves, and speak immortal words as if new-minted from our brains. To lie in, mostly. It was only once I started the training that I knew why I was there. To become real. The experience of university and a childhood of books had left me one-sided, ever-more trapped in my brain. I'd already come to the conviction that the truth was in none of those books, at least not the better part. Growing sinew and wing was a new idea. I needed to make sense of life using my body, the body that had always been a problem to me. I was here to be redeemed.

When we found our limits, of stamina and flexibility and expressiveness, we were encouraged to expand them. *You have to be able to act with your back.* There was emphasis on grace and range; we were taught to balance a stage, moving to fill its gaps while keeping our attention on each other. We studied how status was expressed physically. We watched animals in the zoo and politicians in parliament, and compared our notes.

We were taught to be psychologically merciless too. I began to see that most art dealt in essentials, but great art dealt in details. The first question of a character on day one of rehearsal, and the final thought before stepping on stage, was the same. What did they want? In every scene, characters pursue something simple. These little actions, strung together, add up to a larger, possibly unconscious directive. Their life's desire. What did they want above all else? To pursue these threads, to enable the sympathetic magic to begin, an act of identification was necessary, and so we were instructed to always speak in the first person.

What did I want?

The most essential identification, and often hardest to clarify, was with a character's internal obstacle. The invisible struggles are the ones that resonate with us all. Why does Hamlet hesitate? Why do Vladimir and Estragon not give up and go home? Is it senseless for John Proctor to not make a false confession, and thereby escape the noose? Although the characters were fictional, their situations extreme, their search for meaning was mine too. To fully embody these soul dilemmas, these bone laments and raw spots, would mean confronting my own. To 'go there', as one teacher put it. She would chirrup the words during scene study, as a student teetered at the edge of tears, holding themselves back. 'Go there, darling, go there.' A hostess with a seating plan, the main course being emotional breakthrough tartare.

But meaning doesn't come for free. Deep lessons only arise from feelings, and they were what I'd long been most mistrustful of. I never cried vocally. I blinked back tears and swallowed emotion, knowing if I opened the gates, I would be swamped. I didn't want more pain. This was probably my most British characteristic. Emotion felt embarrassing, made one physically weaker and clouded judgement. It was not seemly. Emotionality was a woman's curse, and precisely the reason you didn't want one in charge of your Zeppelin. But drama school was a topsy-turvy world, and the ability to access emotion was the highest value in this ecosystem. Outside, people kept their voices down and bottled up their feelings. We were doing the opposite.

'Recall a point in time at which you were helpless,' James Kemp said one day, because small talk is for the weak. Lessons started with him entering in silence, a student already on the spot, practising. After they had performed their scenario, Kemp would give notes, always highly detailed and exacting, occasionally gutting. But this day was different. We knew the right scene to choose, he told us, because it was probably the one we least wanted to. We would re-enact this scene, alone, playing ourselves and fighting for what we wanted at the time. The air grew chill. We knew what this was, had been warned by the years above. Mobile exercises.

From Myers–Briggs to Enneagrams, horoscopes to the houses of Harry Potter, all of us have at some point landed on a personality classification system we like, and fallen to preaching. We long for the comfort of categorisation, to be told who we are and absolved. 'There are five types of people,' we'll announce at dinner parties, having confused the sum of humanity with the Spice Girls. Drama Centre had a classification system too. Character analysis was a method-acting tool. One that blended Jungian psychology with Laban dance notation, which gives you an idea of the kind of school this was. In the system, mobility was a state of pure emotion. Real actors, we were told, possessed the strength to be totally vulnerable, going to their most guarded places, and triggering themselves. Admittedly, the majority of our professional lives would be spent balancing hors d'oeuvres, or wearing T-shirts that read *Ask me about the new Huawei P10*, but that's not why we were here. The currency of our trade was catharsis. This is what an audience pays for.

Watching people in mobile exercises was about as comfortable as watching them have an enema. Sometimes it took twenty minutes of visualising a childhood home, or a hospital room, repeating a particularly resonant line. Kemp often challenged, 'Don't let yourself off the hook.' That would do it – you'd see your peer convulse in waves, crumpling first in the torso then the face, leaving themselves weightless. It flooded the room, triggering others. It was a vital breakthrough for the actor, but it was instructive for the rest of us too. There was dignity in pain, I saw, connected to what was essentially human. It didn't matter if the scene was about coming out or breaking up, losing a pet or a grandparent. Seeing something matter to someone else, even if its conclusion was foregone, especially then, was bracing to witness and share. At the end of mobile classes we would stagger out, mute, changed. The significance of the path I had chosen was dawning. I was struck by an unremarked aspect of the job of being an actor: the calling to turn one's body into sacrifice. Feeling on behalf of others – allowing others to feel – had messianic overtones. But it would mean stripping away skin I had spent years growing to protect myself. Was this another form of hurting myself? Then I heard my name. I was called.

Brain frantic, full of nowhere to go. Walking to the front of class, wishing I could just take my clothes off instead. Maybe I still could; it would be a hell of a smokescreen. I sensed the terrible sympathy of eyes, the soft annihilation of kindness. James Kemp was staring at me, unreadable. I stood, feeling the awkward weight of the moment. I did't know if I could. I knew the scene I had to go to. Another scene from the depths of childhood, mostly shut away, but with one clear image. A sofa made up as a bed, with my mother lying in it, frail and wordless. Me standing there, helpless. 'Why . . . don't you eat?' My voice was a croak, the words sticking like flesh on ice. 'You make yourself sick.'

As adults, we can learn the truth about what was really going on, health problems we were shielded from as children. But by then it's too late to unmake our perceptions. Words like "diverticulitis" and "anaemia" mean nothing to a boy. He simply sees a mother invalided, in danger. It was always her I worried about. My father had medical issues I was shielded from too, but he was a practical person. He belonged to a group of pensioners who furiously tramped their pacemakers around the park every day, like Tamagotchis stitched inside their chests. He ate a healthy diet, vegetable heavy and rich with fish, sometimes giving me the eyes as a treat. A big gesture, because that's where the fatty acids were. The hallway proudly bore a picture of him at the gym, working a cross trainer in a panama hat, the most Indiana Jones thing that has ever happened in Lewisham.

If my father exemplified bodily responsibility, my mother expressed the opposite. Always looking after my father and others, there was an Apu-shaped hole in the agenda. Sparrow-thin, she consumed only Rice Krispies and sweets, and boiled rice on public holidays. Toothpaste gave her a migraine. She was allergic to Western medicine, from anaesthetic to ibuprofen. She was like the film negative of Muhammad Ali. *I'm so lean, medicine makes me sick!* Frequently falling ill, sunken-eyed and moaning, self-medicating with tonic water. Doctors could do little for her.

I don't know why this unresolved scene still felt so powerful to me, so deep a wound. A signpost, I suppose, to making my own body a problem. For years I waged war on myself. The confusion regarding my childhood body eventually ripened to hostility. I can't say for sure why it started, as protest or self-loathing or the desire to take her suffering upon myself, but the need to control what I put in my body began to grip in my teenage years. Fussy eating turned into self-starving, and the conscious desire to be extremely thin.

It made no sense even to me. I was much smaller than boys in my class, and hated it. It was as if having no way to become taller, to have broader shoulders or a fuller chest, I spitefully embraced the opposite. I had the sense, one I cannot explain fully, that there was a real me inside, which I wanted to uncover. I would take dinners up to my room, sweep them into a Sainsbury's bag and sneak out to the bridge in the park, emptying the bag into the river every other night. The preternaturally well-fed duck population of the Ravensbourne river owe me everything.

Initially I'd stick my fingers down my neck next to the changing room in the park, but couldn't bear the gag and burn of that for long. I preferred to eat nothing. I chewed food and spat it out, berating myself if saliva activated my swallow reflex, carrying a small amount of food down my throat. I traced the progression of hunger with satisfaction, a hard knot in the belly giving way to cramps for days but eventually dissipating altogether, leaving no hunger at all. That was always a high: the feeling of having won. Any food eaten after that would spoil things, triggering violent stomach cramps and starting the process over.

It was giddying to stand up. Sometimes I blacked out. Hunger would seep through my body from above as I lay in bed at night. I hallucinated that I could see it, a diaphanous sheet of yellow floating downward, passing through my flesh but clinging to my bones, wrapping itself around my skeleton. I had coupled my self-esteem with something I could control, and felt pride for the first time. But it was never enough. Sitting up in the morning, I despaired at the spread of my thighs. Pinched the fat around my waist with so much fascinated disgust, it came close to marvelling. I punched myself in the stomach. Dreamed of doing surgeries on myself. I did this on and off for years.

'What do you want?' A voice floated through my thoughts, and I remembered where I was. I'd been standing in front of the class without saying anything for basically an ice age. I couldn't do it. I hadn't made peace with those feelings, and couldn't bear to feel them now. If

I opened the split stitch of my mouth, cotton wool would spill forth. James Kemp was still staring at me. I waited to receive my verbal flaying, to hear that I gave abject failure a bad name, or that he was going to batter me with a first folio.

'The bigger the store of feeling, the bigger the block,' he said, almost gently. 'But you can't act with the brakes on.'

I was devastated, but I didn't cry about it. I'd taught my body from a young age to shut down raw emotion, and it was too late to override those defences. I had to get whatever else I could from the training. Luckily there were other teachings that carried weight. We were taught what was misleadingly called 'actor's arrogance', which was actually the psychologically healthy self-confidence of walking onstage and taking up the space you needed to. 'Fake it till you make it' was black-market advice, passed from older students to younger ones struggling with imposter syndrome. Most of all, before the curtain rose on a performance, the advice from the most experienced directors was always the same: throw it all away. Throw away the exercises and techniques we'd drilled, the parchments of Meisner, Grotowski, Malmgren, Vakhtangov, all the table work, all the rehearsal. Have faith that they are within you. Listen, be present, and you will come alive. This was years before mindfulness was all the rage. It did make me wonder why we'd spent eight weeks analysing the myth of Philoctetes. When it came down to it, now was all you needed.

But towards the end of my second year at the school, I still hadn't unlocked what was most important. It was now clear to me that emotion was something I wanted, needed to work with. My failure to feel in class weighed on me. I knew I had deep reserves of feeling nearby, but they were closed to me like an underground lake. I was hostage to my fear of feeling. If ever I was touched by something – a film or piece of music – I would be ambushed, incapacitated, choking back gulping sobs that were too big a response to whatever I'd seen or heard. A surge of power, shorting the circuitry. Exhausted by long hours and the demands of the work, I pretended I had let it go. I started cracking jokes more in class, distracting others. It was safer to not take things too seriously.

The big, soul-searching acting exercises hadn't worked for me, and I was in a small minority. Beyond hope. My dream wasn't going to materialise, unless I had an unanticipated breakthrough, maybe during double unicycling, or mask class. We did actually do one mask class, it being apparently an ancient art, though not one that spoke to me. I'd always thought it worse than mime. I entered that lesson in a spirit of downright sarcasm, and besides, none of us had seen the teacher before – she looked mumsy, not to be taken seriously. It was an opportunity to take a breather for forty-five minutes, before Liana waterboarded us with lactic acid. Scottish Vicki curled up underneath a chair, like a housecat. When the new teacher asked for volunteers, no one raised their hand.

'I've been watching you. You always work in the corner.'

I realised, with annoyance, that she was speaking to me, a strange smile on her face.

'Why not come and meet your mask?'

She indicated a suitcase on a table, open and full of them, linen and nylon, antic visages frozen in rictus grins. I'd sooner have put my face in a goalkeeper's glove. I got up slowly and walked across the large studio floor. Up close, the masks were even creepier. Some had furrowed brows, some were apologetic and shrugging, others overwhelmed. Even the fixed smilers were touched with mania, their extreme mirth ready to tip the other way. It was weird, this pile of contorted faces. The sort of thing you see before dying in a way that makes the news.

'Pick the one that speaks aloud, and hold it facing you,' the increasingly un-mumsy teacher ordered me. I moved to pick a mask at random, hesitated, my hand moving upward to another. For the benefit of the class, I jutted my chin, as if propositioning it across a bar. Pursed my lips, then fractionally inclined the mask away, as if it were rejecting my advances. Really killing it. People laughed.

'Meet with your mask,' dark-mum said again, so only I could hear. I glanced at the gaping mouth, the eye holes that seemed lost. I kept looking. Felt myself comprehended. Someone or something pulling at me through those gaps. I felt cold. 'Put it on, and hold back the tide.'

I put on the mask, held up my hands as if I were at gunpoint. Going through the motions. But almost immediately, something was wrong. I began slowly to push back against a weight of water that wasn't there, wearing a face not my own. It was easy to imagine the water roaring around me, elemental, furious. I spread my arms and surged forwards, was bowled backwards, drove forwards once again. Freed of self-consciousness, I felt a power rising in me. Lost and found my feet, stiffened my back and leant forwards where the resistance was greatest.

In the dark I went to the strangest place. A vision that was death, and my body before it. I knew this place. I'd been here before, when I was seventeen, drawing sandpaper across my skin. This was a form of self-harm I had invented for myself, and felt compelled towards. Messier and more painful than a clean cut; a movement from control to disorder. I would cut and fold a small square of crisp sandpaper into a V-sided blade. Then I would graze an initial line across my arm. A carpenter making a first pass through unfamiliar wood, sensing its grain. Then I would begin to saw, pulling the glass teeth through the flesh for ten minutes or more, until it had rasped through nerve, into deeper flesh.

Self-harming was not about wanting to die. It was a way to externalise my feelings, so they made sense; not deathly, but a need for coherence. Yet one particular day there was a different thought in my head. A line across the wrist. To finish everything. How long had this been building, or did it arrive in a flash? I can't remember, and am still unsure why, one day, one's worst thoughts may tip over like this. How coping strategies fail. This is my worst fear: that at my lowest point, I will be impervious to advice or sense. All I remember is looking at myself and seeing very clearly that it would be intolerable to live a whole life through as this person, every day waking up as him, with this brain, seeing through the same eyes, with no way out. No way except this. The decision made me feel strong, in place of the usual weakness.

I made the first pass. My skin was a nap of velvet rubbed the wrong way, kicking up tendrils like new shoots. I went again. I went again. An awareness of what I was doing rose up in me, and I pushed it back, trying to focus on the rough pain. Again. Again. Why had I been afraid? I tried to keep the flayed surface of the wound white – this was how it looked after each pass, as if blanched in shock. If I paused, beads of blood would seep through the subcutaneous layers, so I swept the coarse paper blade briskly. As I did, visions came to me. But they were real. A girl who didn't love me, but wrote me letters anyway. I could see those coloured envelopes, smell their bubblegum ink. My best friend, another social misfit two years older. At six foot seven, a whole foot taller than me, we made a ridiculous pair. We would eventually fall out and lose contact, but at that moment I saw the cassette mixes he made for me, lovingly curated introductions to Jimi and Joni and Gang of Four and Wire. Detailed on the liner in neat handwriting. I saw my mother too. I saw her face. Imagined how she would feel when she found me. How she would knock on the door and be puzzled by the silence, but not come in, because my privacy was important and she respected it.

I was struck by the absence of sound in the room. Butchering myself in silence, despite a screaming brain, because we cry out from the shock, not the pain. I increased intensity, not lifting the paper between one-way strokes, but rasping it forwards and back. It cut deeper yet wore the paper out faster. Sawing through the flesh was deeply painful, yet it felt as if it were happening to someone else, that I was a spectator. It was getting hard to see through the bloody custard of the wound now, though I could feel rubbery structures dancing in there. My wrist was a mess. My fingers were slick, and I could no longer feel the teeth of the glass in the flesh. I looked at my wrist, ragged and swimming in blood, and the paper could not be gripped any longer, sopping and pulling apart in my hand. I let my arm rest limp on my thigh, and started to cry. A strange bark escaped me, almost a laugh. It was as if I could see myself, a half-person bent over by lamplight, trying to buff himself to a lethal smoothness.

Why had I not used a metal blade? I stole craft knives from my father's toolkit all the time, slicing into my forearms so the flesh gaped and pulled on itself. No one had ever been sandpapered to death, outside of a *Road Runner* cartoon. I'd failed at this too. There was humiliation in the days that followed that attempt, or whatever it was. I tried to hide my improvised dressing, cotton-wool shreds messy in the wound, but people saw. At school, there were whispers and sniggers. One boy, a singer in a punk band, saw the bandage and asked why I hadn't slit up the artery rather than across. Some days, everyone's a critic.

Back at Trauma Centre, time had evaporated, like spray off waves, and I was only a faceless feeling in the dark. I'd been humiliated by that pathetic attempt at an attempt, and its abject botchedness. There was another way to see it, I now saw. My failure that night, like turning back on the reservoir walkway, proved that not all of me wanted the end. Sheer biological instinct, or stubbornness, or something else. Under all that coal-black pressure, there was something hard, glinting in the dark. I wanted to live.

The next sensation was the shiny slap of wood, as the wave broke over me, dumping me on the studio floor. The rim of the mask beaded with water. Inside, my face was running with tears. I looked around at the class, grateful for the disguise. I had little idea what I'd been doing, but I'd been doing it for ten minutes. To my surprise, they didn't look bored. And they weren't laughing. Even Vicki was awake. I saw the teacher around the school a few times after that, but we never spoke again. We didn't need to.

It took confronting all my feelings before I could begin to be comfortable in my skin, to walk with all my weight, and feel my worth. I don't think that's strange. My body has absorbed a lot. Events too painful for me to consciously acknowledge, and misdirected anger. I owe that training a great deal, as I started to take pride in what my body could do, rather than what I could do to it. There is more to wonder at in the human body than the ways it can be caged. That's what I understood here, in this terrorist cell of acting, learning that a body could move with power as well as sensitivity, and an infinite number of gestures between. Striding out as a King, hot-stepping as a Fool.

Not that this vessel will ever be anything but a mystery to me. Sometimes, even now, I have the oddest feeling of my body as a second self, that knows more about me than I do. I'll look down and notice, with surprise, my thumb closed tight inside my fingers, craving the security of the fist. A jaw ache can tell me how I really feel about someone, and I swear one of my early stress indicators is the bony lumps at the back of my skull growing more pronounced. If she ever noticed any acting out of sorts, Eliza would immediately feel for these ridges. 'Your horns are up,' she'd diagnose.

I've learned to trust and be thankful for the body, to have my back's back. Mostly, anyway. Eating disorders are diseases of perception, and their a-logic can stay with you, even after recovery. Part of me still likes how I looked when I was too thin, the definition of clavicles and ribs, when I could barely lift my arms. Part of me is still ashamed I didn't get thinner. If I feel low now, I look at how I've been eating, and ask myself if my lack of appetite is what it appears to be, or if I want to look a certain way, feel that pride again, because I lack it somewhere else.

Annoyingly, the exercise bores are right about movement and coming home to oneself. If you're feeling low, do whatever you can that earths you in your muscles, teaches you to breathe. Your other self has messages of strength and possibility. Turn it loose, let it wild. Bodies are built on the principle of recovery, that there is a way back to health. My body was constantly healing itself, far before my mind caught up. Bearing me through the world, asking nothing but the strength to serve. I had been looking for something that could defy entropy, yet it never occurred to me that we are it. Every morning we open our eyes to these recovering bodies, to a coherent self, we persist. Not for ever, but for the moment. And that's really all you need.

Letter to one of my acting teachers

*There was such a mythology to that place. I wanted to prove
myself there, to please my teachers. Funny that of all the
memories I made there, one I treasure above all is walking
out of your rehearsal.*

*You taught me once a week, but in reality it felt like much
less than that. I heard you tried to give your phone number
to a girl at her audition. I don't know if that's true, but
I know you wasted a lot of everyone's time flirting with female
students in my year, none of whom were interested. I know we
were there to push beyond bourgeois prudery; I was beginning
to understand that actors are licentious creatures. I know the
female body is the engine of the earth blah. But it's still weird
how all the pieces you directed were quite so tit-centric.*

*This one rehearsal, which you were running with priapic
inefficiency, I asked to go home. I was exhausted. You clearly
weren't going to reach my scene, especially as you were more
interested in the work of asking my female friends to sit in
your lap. I barely existed for you. You said no, and I thought,
fuck this.*

*Everyone needs a 'fuck this' moment now and then. To
find their personal boundaries, and learn to stand up for them.
I don't regret walking out; I regret not doing it in front of your
face. I went to a concert of Brecht songs that evening. Watched
the Tigerlilies perform a version of 'Remembering Marie A',*

an ode about a man in the arms of a woman, who cannot take his eyes off a vanishing cloud in the sky. Do you know, it was one of the most heart-stopping things I have ever heard, which I have not been able to forget, nor find a recording of, and therefore existed only in that moment.

Later that week in school, after the meeting I received for my conduct, one of the disciplinary panel approached me and said, 'If it's any consolation, we know he's a . . .' And then he called you a bad name, the worst word in the language, apart from the n-word, which wouldn't have made sense. It was quite consoling.

In a funny way, you're one of the most important teachers I've known. Maybe you did teach me something after all. You taught me there is no organisation, no school of learning, no church better than the people chosen to run it. Taught me to see through a myth I wanted to believe in, and that is a valuable thing. I also learned that I always have choice, and that repercussions are bearable if we stand by our choices. So, I suppose, thank you for that. Although you should stop being a cunt.

5

How to Be in Other People's Bodies

Sex. Even the word is exciting. Gauche and to the point, it doesn't just finish with a sizzle but starts with one too, cyclical sibilance for the eternal hiss of temptation. Sex sex sex. For the wretched and secular, there is no greater way to feel alive than the pleasure of the flesh. Impossible to have enough, once the scent is in your nostrils. Many of our most redemptive experiences, as well as the most shameful, involve the intimate contact of bodies, so most of the time we can neither stop thinking about it, nor stop pretending we aren't. Chasing purely erotic thrills is a uniquely human thing to do, if you count bonobos and dolphins as human, which I do.

Yet so much of sex isn't about sex. We know how the final act goes, of course: you take a willing volunteer back to yours, put on a William Shatner audiobook, make some horizontal jazz. But that's only the denouement of the play. Sex is so much more than that. Each courtship has its own time signature, and particular thrills. Fascinating, the dials of attraction and what turns them up or down.

What a tiny rip in the continuum, two people noticing each other! The subtle ratchets of flirtation like bubbles in champagne. The way a quarter-second of eye contact can hold a grain of eternity. Secret smiles, kisses from the sides of the lips. That exquisite dance with a beloved, slow encroachment to the distance at which details reveal themselves: slender hairs on the nape of the neck, freckles falling from a shelf of clavicle, speckles of shine in the crook of an elbow. The way voices can change over an evening, reverse their polarity, as lovers coil towards each other, fingering the red button of mutual self-destruction. What's not to love? Good question.

First Base

The bodies of others not constituting an existential threat to me has been a roundabout journey, made in progressive stages, like the stops in baseball. First base, in this analogy I have just invented, started with celibate adolescence, and a judgemental one at that. Sex was embarrassing, I thought. A compulsion to bad choices and wasted time. This was the mid-nineties, and the first bloom of trash-talk television. Jerry Springer provided a daily diet of scraggly Midwesterner Americans whose lives had been deformed by their besetting sins. Adultery, relations with relations, cruising for furries. There was something half-formed about these types, who gave in to temptation without thought, wore their urges so transparently. Something terrifying to this force that sucked them down, placed its hand on the steering wheel and yanked hard right.

Sex, advertising and television made clear, was the domain and prerogative of men, and something about men made me sick. It was depressing to observe groups of them on the hunt, cloaked in a nimbus of incipient violence and Lynx Africa. As a naïve young teen I intuited that the men I saw on their nights out wanted either a punch-up in the street or something mysterious between the sheets, and the proximity of the two was troubling. These men! Deep-sea creatures, eyes and mouths, heads no more than rudders to aim their bodies at a shoal of women. If a female, separated from the pack, passed them in the street, I would watch the men watching her, like savannah lions. Cold appraisal, predatory calm. Semi-involuntary movements of the mouth, like snakes tasting the air. Horrific. This wasn't a feminist perspective, mind you. I was at an all-boys' school, and didn't know what girls were. I only knew I didn't want that animalism to move within me.

This rejection of sex was basically a review of a restaurant at which I couldn't get a table. As little as I wanted anything to do with sex, it wanted less to do with me. The vulnerability of women was not the only message ratified across the culture during my childhood. There was one for me too. *Fuck off. Go home. You don't belong here.* For this reason, I will never be down with any eighties nostalgia revival. Depeche Mode are good, but for me the sound of the decade is a stranger throwing a brick at me on the walk home from school. Or a man in a white van, driving down the road we lived on, calling me a paki. Leaning out of the window so he could be heard above Bonnie Tyler. The Smiths were fantastic, but if never seeing another wall, train seat or pencil case defaced with the National Front logo means never hearing 'Frankly, Mr Shankly' again, I'll take it.

While violence and name-calling were an obvious threat, it was atmospheric condescension that ate me up like acid rain.* Part of this was the received opinion that brown people were not sexy. They did not belong on magazine covers, could not be film stars, were not to be looked at in the same way as whites. This unquestioned racism was so mainstream as to be part of the water system. White people making jokes about curry, laughing at made-up Indian names and how long they are, their compulsion to try the accent, and inability to do so without taking a left turn into Llanelli. I've always felt an affinity with the Welsh dating back to this time. They're part of the honorary clientele at my dream pub, which otherwise exclusively caters to blacks and dogs and Irish. Hard to imagine a better night out.

I hated myself. I cannot describe to you how much I hated myself. The depth of longing to fit in. Alone in my

---

* Whatever happened to acid rain? They should bring that back.

room I would stare at the hemisphere along the side of my hand, running up the length of each finger. A shoreline of brown met by the lighter, pinker skin of my palm. Odd that it should form so clear a shoreline between what I wanted and what I was. Reminded me of the flank of a great white shark, as if that wasn't the definition of irony. At some point, compelled by desperation, I resorted to using sandpaper to flay the layers of my face, hoping to reveal fair skin below. Just a scrap of Cauc beneath the Asian. I felt cursed, could not bring myself to raise my glance and look at the grotesqueness of my features, slant of the eyes, idiot plumpness of lips. In the evening, I would steal the pliers from my father's toolbox, place them over the tip of my detested nose, and crush the jaws together as hard as I could. Claustrophobia is not felt more extremely than this, the inability to bear being in oneself, entombed in your own flesh.

In a more self-empowered time, it is shameful for me to admit how much I hated my colour. Difference, body, community, self, these are domains we've learned a little more of how to claim. We have role models, jokes we are in charge of. I can only bring myself to say it for anyone who felt or feels similarly lonely. The ways we are taught to see ourselves has everything to do with the ways we want. I was embarrassed by my own desire. Although in America it remains utterly normal to see the words "no Asians" on dating profiles, we are a fraction less excluded from the conversation here. I pray we don't go backwards, because the blast radius of casual racism is large. The physical damage I did wasn't pretty. Even today, I suffer nosebleeds in the shower as a result of my efforts with the pliers, disconcerting guests with blood streaks on the towels. (Come again soon!) But the image I internalised of myself – shit-coloured, unwanted, unlovable, untouchable; that wound takes even longer to heal.

Second Base

As the joke goes, celibacy was a choice; it just wasn't my first choice. The next stage in this personal history of sex was an actual engagement with it. Being shut out of the desire system had done nothing to quell the stirring of it within me. Like bruised moss, it clung on, attached to stony surfaces. In the last of my school years, embarrassing in its predictability, I developed an attraction to goths.

Of course I did. Their wine-dark lips and marmoreal pallor were the embodiment of Thanatos, the unconscious longing for death. They were the only ones appropriately dressed for the funeral we'd been born into. For sure, I didn't understand their choices. It was unclear how a heightened awareness of mortality nudged one into lace corsets and fishnet tights, but those things spoke to me too, so I didn't interrupt. I couldn't understand why they would Other themselves, when they could pass, be part of the mainstream. But I admired their commitment to the process, the wearing of jumpers in the height of summer, facial piercings that compromised them for retail work.

But how to gain welcome with the tribe? Like an anthropologist, I needed to be smart if I wanted access. I tried to get into the music, a lot of which sounded like food poisoning being distributed via tornado. I didn't know where to buy goth clothing and didn't have any money, so had to get creative. My parents had saved up to buy me a winter coat, the lining of which I now ripped into strips, that fluttered from the hem behind me as I walked. That was the idea, anyway. In fact, they trailed limply on the floor like a sad tail, picking up gutter juice and dust. To achieve the ragged-cape effect, I had to run very fast as if launching a kite, legs slightly bowed to funnel wind between my thighs. This was not dignified. I grew my hair long and experimented with make-up, but my mother's foundation actually made me look healthier, which was no good. I bought paler stuff from Boots, but it gave my brown skin a lime-nauseous tint. In a last-ditch effort, I applied white face paint in the mirror, cheap stuff from the pound shop intended for kiddies' parties. Staring back at me was the reflection of a Mundari cattle herder covered in dung ash. It dried to a cracked finish, adjacent to the suave, vampiric effect I was after. I looked like I was actually four hundred years old, and recently exhumed.

The appeal of goth girls was their distance, in any case.

I knew I would never get close to one. Especially not running past them at full extension outside Camden Market, made up as a sexually confused clown with rickets. They would never notice me: they longed for a head-banging boy who wrote on his arms in Biro, possessed of a part-time bad attitude. They were idealised and unreal. In time-honoured tradition, I was Terrified of Talking to Women. It was only after I'd arrived at university that I dipped a toe in the water, and even then, still worried about getting wet.

Whatever the opposite of moves is, I had it. I was in a pickle when, after a few weeks, the Cornish hippy who lived in our halls of residence – the one who was flaxen-haired, smoked weed every day and had a slow, broad smile like a lazy river – invited me up to her room to chat. It was like being selected to play for England: an inexplicable nightmare that could only end in physical humiliation. Yet she was beautiful, so I had to go. Cardigan buttoned or open? Should I take a gift? Flowers? I didn't have any. In the end, I took a toffee hammer with me, because it was all I had and I needed a USP.

Zany twat, I cursed myself as the door opened to a vision. She flaxenly put my gift to one side and invited me to make myself comfortable. There was no furniture, other than the bed on which she was sitting. I clambered to the floor, brushing crumbs out of the way.

'Do you want some spinach?' It was an odd question, but I could hardly call her out, having arrived moments earlier with a shrunken hammer. I looked at her, wondering why I wasn't saying anything. Things were already going worse than I'd anticipated, and I'd been inside for under a minute. 'I'm saying we could share a bowl,' she laughed. I wondered if she was mad. She took a moment to appraise me, concluding 'You're funny.' Generous, as my only contribution had been to tell her I wasn't hungry.

I knew I should say something, progress the conversation. Should I do a chat-up line? Like from *FHM*? This was a magazine beloved of men hateful to me, yet also studied with tragic avidity by me. The mid-teen's pre-internet alternative to top-shelf entertainment, *FHM* showcased TV presenters in their bras alongside mating banter and sex tips. The latter I memorised, assuming the information would later become crucial, like Laika the space-dog boning up on atmospheric re-entry aboard Sputnik 2. Yet I sat there empty, dumb as a bucket. My mental Rolodex drew a blank. *Something something river in Alabama, you're the only Ten I See. The fabric of my shirt looks better on your floor, because it is boyfriend material.* I couldn't remember exactly, but sensed the selling was all in the telling. *Girl, do you know CPR because you are the cause of atrial fibrillation.*

As I weighed these unconvincing options, without warning, she bent over the edge of the bed and fingered my buttonhole. 'You're gonna lose that,' she said. This was unprecedented. With the unexpected contact of her hand, a leaping in my blood. I could feel the pulsing of a chrysalis. A vision of life on our Cornish alpaca farm. I would do business with fences and chickens, while she tended her jazz ferns, and in the evenings we would robustly spouse. To have something new in the world!

She rolled over and scrabbled around for a metal tin, retrieving a needle and thread, as if she hadn't already proved herself demonstrably perfect. Was she really working the sharp little wand between the tiny holes, nimble fingers gently bumping my chest? Such an inefficient way to sew, with me still in the cardigan, mute and transported. I tried to muffle the beating of my heart, as she fixed the button and liquefied my organs. It wasn't exactly Marvin Gaye, but still a hell of a lesson. I need sexual darning. It's something that's good for me.

Post-button, there was nowhere left for us to go. I had only said a handful of words, and the effort of carrying the conversation seemed to be tiring her. 'When I move my head quickly, it squeaks like there are clouds inside,' she said sadly. Those magazines hadn't prepared me in any way for this; offered no traction on the facets of a real person, in their opacity and touching weirdness. Of course, she was baked as a potato. I was equally flummoxed by her hair, and the woodland-spirit softness of her voice. Eventually things became too awkward, an unreachable itch pushing me to my feet. I had to leave the room, go and tell Chris. On my way out, a foot in the hallway and quivering, I wondered if there was room for another first. 'I know someone who likes you,' I quavered from behind the door. When she asked who, I fled, making sure we never spoke again.

Beauty is, by mathematician and poet alike, our highest truth. It pays to be beautiful. Good bone structure is a skeleton key, unlocking the doors of experience. Reproductive capital, higher wages, wider social circles, reputation. It also makes a mockery of our moral ideal: to judge things by their worth, and not their surface. I'd spent my judgemental years worrying that we shouldn't be attracted to attractive people. It was the injustice of it all that was overwhelming: watching people whose faces were their calling cards, who attracted interest and opportunity, parlaying modest talents into disproportionate success. These people didn't have to prove themselves to be accepted, they were prized and welcome. We bestow on the beautiful a nimbus of moral trustworthiness too. We're always ready to redeem the heroic-looking. Look at young Stalin, raffishly tousled, thick of barnet and hipster of cravat. Is there anything more valuable in this world than the benefit of the doubt?

I didn't want to be coerced by beauty. To respond like everyone else, the idiot apes in their check shirts and wet-look hair. What I couldn't admit was that this unhappiness was only, entirely, with myself. I needed to believe I was *complex*. That I had *a lot going on*. Constantly ruminating affairs of state, the applications of theology. If anyone were to see me asleep in my chair, I thought to myself, they would tiptoe past because it was obvious *I was doing heavy lifting.* But the truth is, I was never thinking about those things. At any given point, I was feeling bad about the way I looked.

Self-obsession is unproductive, ungenerous, above all boring.* I could have understood coding, got a SCUBA certificate, learned some bird or plant names, rather than spending years lamenting my own face. (I could have learned philosophy.) I still know no plants, can't tell my arse from an aspidistra. What a colossal amount of ourselves we pour into the mirror, looking for lines or spots, pulling the skin taut and imagining cheekbones. Holding our face at a particular angle and tension we have reserved for this nonsense, or just taking in the whole with a furious blankness, immovable and resigned. Are better minds immune to this?

It's even more pointless because we never really see ourselves. The mirror is a flat surface carrying the illusion of depth, horizontally flipped. The photons bouncing back are a moment behind the present. It is a younger you, swimming in the silver. But even understanding that, there is still no objective, fact-like us to see there. We instead see a daily diary of nurture or neglect, trauma or love. We see how we feel about ourselves. What's more, other people see it too.

Inconceivably, a few weeks after I nearly passed out because a girl touched my button, I actually had sex.

---

*. Although thank you for buying the book.

University is an extraordinary place. It was Halloween, the sexiest night of the year, and there'd been a party in our halls. One of the girls had led me up to her room for a drink, and there really were zero chairs in those rooms. When she had finished her drink, she threw the cup across the room, a gesture of such daunting lustiness my burgeoning erection left the country. I don't remember much, but know I hardly covered myself in glory. There was some mid-act coaching, 'Move your whole body,' giving rise to the distressing assumption I had been planking on her. But it was a relief I hadn't died, and useful to speculate I might have a type: brash women. A bit o' brash, and brusque. Bossy was good too.

Not to brag, but I'd lost my virginity to a girl who shortly afterwards realised she was a lesbian, and wanted nothing more to do with men for the rest of her natural life. I'd hoped we would never speak again, but she remained a good friend of friends, and I know her brothers, so we do. It's mortifying, but there's also something tender about not having lost that connection to her, and that initiation half our lifetimes ago. I'm glad it was her.

Far from being out of the woods, I was only just entering them. The past has its hooks in us, is always along for the ride. Most experiences that followed in those years, as I attempted to define a sexual self, were troubled. I was unprepared for these indefensible, enveloping encounters with other bodies. I blundered into bed with people blackout drunk, not wanting to face what was going on, afraid of what I wanted. When someone un-dressed me, I felt like a child, the memory of abuse hitting me like a bat, delayed but not lessened by the fog around it. Undressing others was fraught with the para-noid sensation that I was turning into Him. The rising of lust made me feel dizzy, like I no longer knew who I was, had woken into a body that was falling. If someone stayed over in my bed, or I slept in theirs, this conviction would worm through my brain, leading to nightmares and crying out. Desire was a parasite, one I dreamed of cutting out of myself, in a purifying act of backstairs surgery. I couldn't bring myself to penetrate anyone, couldn't see past the violence of the act. Not that it was an option; my horse bridled at the jump, heedless of the whip. When I even-tually went back on antidepressants, the traditional side effects – an explicable impotence and diminished libido – felt like a huge relief. Let's say these weren't the Justin Timberlake years.

Third Base

'Parappa the rapper,' I said solemnly, gazing into Lily's eyes and clutching a rich tea biscuit.

'Misty makes the play-offs, Pickle Finger,' she affirmed, in receipt of the secret note. I had the better half of the gazing, as she was extraordinary to behold. The spitting image of Elizabeth I as played by Cate Blanchett, anvil-trussed copper curls lending her the silhouette of a hammerhead shark. Severe cheekbones lifted the corners of her smile with forceps, as if it were evidence. We met at the call centre – a place beneath us both, as it was beneath all human souls – and from the first moment, knew each other instantly. During breaks we would look for each other the way castaways look for shore. Around us, actors complained about the casting of West End transfers. By contrast her speech was full of lyrical strangeness, and the pleasures of pure sound. I'd try to keep up.

'Sometimes I look at my hand and think, *what the hell is that?*'

She went by Lily, but I called her by her given name, Lilith, because I dug that Babylonian demonology sound. She was older, a busy artist who had lived many lives. I was a twenty-two-year-old nothing who hadn't even lived my own, so it was sensible to keep things platonic. Then she invited me over to walk Kaspar, her one-eyed hound, and by the end of the day I was wearing a pink nightdress and there was flour all over the floorboards and I stayed for six years.

It was like stepping through the back of a cupboard. Her house was an expression of her as pronounced as if she had given birth to it. Walls not so much distressed as traumatised. The effect was a satanic woodcut of blackened hearts and bare stairs, a howl of gothic masonry and animal remains. Dinner was eaten off grey metal plates every night, flirting with lead poisoning. The table was shared with a vast buffalo skull, horns the span of a paddling pool, while hanging from the ceiling were human-hair dolls, loosely woven into her body shape, like voodoo Oscars for scariest dinner. She installed me in the Moon Room, a shockingly white box containing nothing but a bed and a sash window. At least, until the morning when I awoke to a twig-cage she'd hung above my head in the night. Suspended from branches inside muslin walls were five cocoons, which would eventually hatch Indian luna moths, soft, herbal green and enormous, that laid little round eggs on the walls and windows.

Trying to formulate what we love, we find ourselves talking nonsense. It is a slippery, dancing thing. Lily was as graceful as a classical sculpture, but had an equal capacity for demented outbursts, and these are what sung straight into my heart.

'Would you like a treatment?' she would sometimes enquire during a quiet evening, solicitous as a house doctor. This was a warning shot, meaning I had seconds to put a great distance between us. 'It is a *treat*, meant JUST FOR YOU!' she would holler, pinching or hammering the tops of my thighs with her fists, which was incredibly painful. I would scream, like a child going higher on the swing. For once, I was not the strangest person in the room. I relished these twisted little lovers' tussles, the opportunity to play the straight man.

'If you had to choose a superpower, what would it be?' I asked her once, over a fancy dinner.

'YOUR superhero name is Coco Pops, and your power is turning the milk CHOCOLATE-Y BROWN!' she shrieked, which didn't even answer the question.

'You cannot be blind to the racial insens—' I started, but she was already throwing Brussels sprouts into my mashed potato, because she liked the splat. It was a nice restaurant, too. It had an atrium.

Physically, we were a comic mismatch. We looked like a folk story about a newt courting a heron, yet were in some fundamental way alike. She knew as little of conventional family life as I did – a mother who died young, a father she had never met. And I'd never met anyone with the same capacity for diving into the dark. She could weep for hours, bang her head on the walls, but always put the torment into her work. She created crepuscular objects of luminous beauty. Painfully fragile ceramics, covered in feathers and chopped-up text. She would emerge calm from her studio after a dark spell of creation, as if something had been appeased. I wondered what it was like for hands to grasp thought, and how that handling wrought a transformation. What it was like to have work that compelled.

It would be easier to separate sex and relationship, talk about them separately, but that would betray the truth. It was the safety of relationship that demonstrated to me ease and trust, with no goal outside the moment itself. Sex was not assembly instructions for flat-pack furniture, but a revelation that could burst open a universe of sensation. I'm embarrassed to recall that I cried during our first times together, when she proved that I could function.

'I think I can only be with someone if I love them,' I told her. Our coupling was the unique expression of our unique togetherness; our relationship felt miraculous and redemptive, as if I'd stumbled upon a person equally curious about climbing inside a barrel and riding it over the edge of a waterfall. Which is as viable a definition of good sex as any other. I felt that life was finally beginning.

Having chosen each other, we fell pell-mell into misadventure. One morning she drove us to a field in Flitwick to present an extraordinary sight. An army of ex-service vehicles for sale, filling the field like an incongruous battalion of insects blown up by weird science. I knew she wanted a new car, but hadn't imagined this. There were full-size buses, going cheap. We could drive – hell, we could live – in our own double decker, the way I supposed Cliff Richard did, and ride around town making people's day. Or even better, drive away in one of the hearses.

'We could paint it white, like Ecto-1 from *Ghostbusters*,' I whimpered. Lily was swayed by my description of Janine Melnitz's glasses, but upon learning the Mercedes-Death took twenty minutes to get to sixty, was swayed back. Besides, it would have been the hardest vehicle to park since a double decker bus.

'We have to be practical,' she mulled, wearing a Westwood bolero. She was looking at a classic hackney carriage, a vehicle that looked like a huge, goth ball-bearing. An hour later we were driving it home, a one-eyed dog-viscount riding in the ample rear, me perched on the navigator's flap in the cab, a seat no one knows exists. Begging to turn the light on. The black London cab became our magic carpet. Unlocking the bus lanes, it got us out of London three times as fast, with a turning circle of zero. Everywhere we went, tourists tried to flag us down, but we weren't stopping for anybody.*

We drove all over the country, as often as we could. She was a rock star to me. She'd tailgate into the back of a fishery, stride through the rubber flaps and emerge clutching two crabs and a lobster, having tucked a tenner in someone's wellington. Loaded up with a groundsheet and cookware and the *Gormenghast* trilogy, we had everything we needed. Sometimes we forgot the tent, but invariably, it would be a mild night. We'd sleep on a satin quilt in some Cornish dell, underneath the stars.

'Thank you for showing me people like us can survive,' I said.

I called her Mistress, or sometimes Sister, because we were twinned and "girlfriend" didn't seem to fit. I think

---

* We drove there in a normcore Peugot and God knows what happened to that. She probably left it in a ditch, or rolled it across the county line, and called it somebody else's problem.

she would have preferred "partner", but to my ears that was a double-breasted, pinstripe sort of a word. "Mistress" was outlaw and sexy, the kind of word that would sound right when read out on the news, after we were gunned down by a posse in New Mexico. Though now I think about it, "partner" would have worked for that too.

In the eighties she'd been one of Jean-Paul Gaultier's favourite models, with all that implies. It was always thrilling to unearth scraps of her past. Magazine articles about her, a portrait of her looking angular and otherworldly under a wide-brimmed hat, her credit at the end of a film. While I'd been avoiding local boys after school, she was clubbing with Boy George. When I was throwing a tennis ball up the stairs, she was walking leopards down the Champs-Élysées, or climbing through the roofs of Soho members' clubs, or removing all her clothes on aeroplanes. I was giddy for her stories, a tadpole swimming in a champagne bowl, and fantasised about us living them together. One afternoon, walking behind Oxford Street, a striking woman called out her name and came striding towards us. Her legs scythed the air, so scraps of it seemed to flutter in her wake. I don't remember what Lily and Naomi Campbell chatted about, I only remember the guy she was with, a man of my height and similar glasses, and the almost courtly acknowledgement that passed between us. We probably lit votive candles at the same time every night.

But she didn't like talking about it all that much, had grown weary of the drugs and damaged personalities.

Bored of spinning out a highlights reel. Never be afraid to let go of the past, she told me. The best of life is always right now. I honestly believe her main hobby was throwing things away. Lily had actually thrown her former life away, flinging her prized modelling portfolio off a bridge in Amsterdam, along with other mementos. I couldn't believe she'd done that, and not just because it was canal littering. If I had access to all that glamour I would keep it close to me for ever, I thought, wrap myself in it like a stole.

I always thought the age gap made no difference to us, twinned as we were at some pre-being stage. And it was mostly true, though there were a few small ways our developmental stages announced their difference. I liked watching deranged internet cartoons, or playing aggressive hip hop in every room of the house. She was more into yoga. I'd often find her peacefully knotted on the rug, knees vicing neck, arms arranged cat's cradle. 'I'll save you!' I'd shout, diving to untangle her, looking as she did like a trussed-up victim at a sick crime scene. Buddhism and meditation were daily practice, and other incomprehensible activities such as drinking aloe vera, which looked and tasted like a medical sample.

I was less excited by this side to her, the side that wanted something gentler from life, that said thank you to bus drivers and smiled at our south London neighbours. These were mainly hardbitten immigrants, elderly people with spines like shelf brackets, and an assortment of shuffling chaotics who I suspected ate dog food behind closed doors.

'Why do you bother?' I asked her. 'They never smile back.'

'That's why,' she said.

Then I enrolled at Drama Centre. From the very beginning, my days were colonised in the ways she knew they would be. Suddenly I was not at home, or when I was, my brain was not. So close to the beginning was seeded the possibility of an end.

'Fall in love every day,' had been one of the former principal's advice. This would be the place to do it, a cracked church full of heavenly bodies, and me ready to fall to my knees. Newly liberated from the sexual torments of my past, I started to wonder what else was possible, if I could turn myself inside out. Could I bury my old body, and be born again? Could I become someone else? Someone possessed of his own power, desirable? It was surely well past time to introduce a little funk. I decided to become a Casanova.

It was a tall order. As far as I could see, there was nothing about me to make women weak at the knees, other than my reluctance to give up a seat on the bus. But I was at a school whose entire creed was one of physical transformation. Impossible feats were required of us as a matter of course: roles that required us to look taller, or fatter, or younger. 'Height is a perception,' James Kemp scolded us by way of example, 'concerning posture and ownership of space. How do you organise your body to make others see what you want them to?' This was a blazing new idea to me. But it was demonstrably true. A plain actor could hold themselves in a way that made it impossible to look away. They could be expressive in ways that would convince you a coquette or a god was in the room. Emotional openness, willingness to play, the ability to listen; these were hallmarks of the well-trained, versatile actor, we were repeatedly told. Standing at the holy text, I realised – a wisp of corruption in my nose – that they would work as well on an audience of one. Or a succession of ones.

Of course if an audience saw the strings being pulled, it was curtains for the enterprise. This took a while for me to learn. The Wetherspoons pub closest to the school, on a Friday night, was the dark church where I practised the murky arts. That's where I could always be seen, leaning against brick arches, the slope of my shoulders making it clear *I was a bad boy, who knew how to take his time*. This was only a lie by omission – I was bad at communicating, and erectile dysfunction does take up a lot of time – but you don't put all the stock in the shop window.

I was clumsy at first, a levitating skunk clutching a cartoon rose. 'I'm a bad boy,' I'd murmur huskily, in case the message hadn't got through. *You're funny*, the ladies would often respond, which was confusing but still broadly positive. More effective was pretending to be scandalised after they confessed some minor indiscretion, such as stealing a colleague's yoghurt. '*You're* bad,' I'd gasp, and they'd giggle, amused by the flimsiness of the patter. We were all young idiots, giving each other permission.

It helped that I was surrounded by other acting students, appreciating their own new powers, slopping charisma around like slatterns.* When we were pushed out of the Wetherspoons nest, venturing into the world around, we realised we had wings. There were bestial, last-days-of-Rome bacchanalia, parties on rooftops and boats; it didn't matter who had originally been invited. When one of us found an opening, the rest would pour in, like ants formicating over the counters. A thrum of libidinality was the accepted tenor of our socialising. Coupling unpredictably and frequently, one-offs, threesomes and four-ways, atomic compounds, ionic bonds. *Everyone wants to be like this*, I thought. On a night out, I'd expect to kiss three strangers, and go home with one. Once, having broken into a club event for Young Conservatives, a cockney rascal I knew left with an heiress for her flat nearby. An hour later they returned, and he repeated the trick with another. I stared at him in admiration, a raccoon let loose among Siamese cats.

I'd grown up with the cultural indoctrination that men wanted sex, and women wanted an argument in IKEA. They bartered sex to access DIY, or a scatter cushion with a picture of a baby on it. I was surprised and delighted now to be around scandalous women who announced

---

* I use the term in the gender-neutral sense.

their desires as if the world were a bathroom mirror in a club. I'd unexpectedly grown to be friends with Vicki, the low-born Scottish gum-chewer, due to us both being put in a lot of the same classes. Moonlighting as a stripper, she lived an aggressively liberated life. Red-lipped and dark-eyed, feline of feature and carriage, she enjoyed the power of her beauty. When we went out socially, she would select her targets – male or female, it was all the same – and wrap herself around them like a silk scarf. It was wonderful to watch them melt under her attention. I loved the frank pleasure she took in bodies: describing the way she liked to run her fingernail down a man's inguinal crease, the lip-biting thrill of hard thighs. How her favourite torso was muscular yet overlaid with 'light blubber', indicating the owner possessed a naturally broad frame, but not the vanity to maintain it. She had her own class-perverse *faiblesse* for full-lipped English public schoolboys. If she ever came across one, floppy of fringe and cruel of streak, she'd yowl with the memory for months like a tuft-eared lynx, calling her mate across vast distance.

One night, a tall girl I had known only to be stooping and shy, hanging at the edge of groups, mildly invited me back to her place, which I assumed would be the attic room of a library or orphanage. I was shocked by the change that came over her behind closed doors. 'You can put anything anywhere,' she said, an instruction I had previously heard only in relation to coats and bags at a dinner party. Who was this person? She had a hand in my trousers, trying to start me like an outboard motor.

'Do you ever think, fuck everyone's expectations?' I thought about it, and said no. She seemed to find this annoying, breath catching with impatience. She was behind me now, a mouth pressed against my ear, speaking at conversation volume. It was uncomfortably loud, like the voice of God, or mental illness. 'What would happen if you totally, completely let go?'

'Do you mean like . . . piss myself?' She gave up, putting my hands on her. From the very first touch, she started emitting a high-pitched keening, and squirmed like an otter. I felt a dimly risen discomfort, somewhere about my knees. It crept over me as we proceeded to what must have been, to her, entirely vanilla atrocities. A bad boy would have known what to do, or how to respond to her messages that followed in the week.

tell me what to do . . .

how do you mean

tell me do something, maybe I will

like what

She pulled me aside at a party a few days later, still half-wearing her shyness, like a costume with buttons missing. Her short, bobbed hair had changed colour. The point was, she hissed, to take control. Be strict. Make her do things, even difficult things. I was a keen student, if not a bright one.

> *change your phone tariff*
>
> *huh?*
>
> *quit your job do it now*
>
> *your stupid*

She broke things off via text too, after I'd told her to report her debit card as stolen. I couldn't get the hang of her desire, which made no sense to me. It was fascinating, though, the private ocean of desire that lived in other people. No one really knows anyone, I remember thinking. It was thrilling to break the surface of the water, dive into all these worlds. One girl made animal noises in bed, mostly feline, occasionally bovine, not at all unpleasant. There was the bohemian girl in a squat, reckless and full of something so that when she kissed me, my lips turned numb. A hippie in a glowing neon basement actually enjoyed the fact that I was Indian, and talked glowingly to me about the connectedness of all living things.

'If we're all a unified consciousness, why do I find other people so annoying?' I asked. 'Isn't that like my leg not getting on with my elbow?'

Another night, a friend and I found ourselves unexpectedly together in the street. Inclining our heads for a first kiss in the same direction, we both switched the other way, then back again. I waggled my head like a dashboard toy. We both laughed, and moved on to find other people without a word passing between us. It was funny, how much of this money we had to spend, knowing we could print more.

New language widens our world, and this was the language of physical joy, no less. The curve of a calf, theatrical curtain raise of a lifted skirt, the summer fruit of someone's thighs, these spoke to me like nothing else. Promethean, all this stolen electricity, grounding me as it flashed through the body of another. Finally, vital. Each encounter felt like coming home, gazing into the eyes of another and seeing life, indivisibly there. I had found an identity. Something I was good at. Does the songbird stand mute for his drab feathers, wishing he were a peacock? No, he opens his beak for all who have ears, and lets the motherfucking angels out.

Yet desire, often caricatured as a blunt instrument, is no simple thing. It began to dawn on me that the girls I liked were overwhelmingly white. Factor 50, TED-talk, skiing-holiday white. To this day I appreciate pale women, regardless of whether they're interesting, and am knocked into concussion by most redheads. I worry that I'm wanting to be absolved of my own darkness. I wonder what swims below the surface of their attraction too, if there might be some counterpart. The latent desire to have what has been historically denied. Sexuality is a winding journey, and I can only shake my head at the narrowness of my desire back then, blind to beauty in cinnamon, caramel, chocolate and a hundred other tones that don't sound like Starbucks extras. I love these skins now, the ones close to my own, that have absorbed a quarter-century of summers, and radiate it back out. All that loveliness I chose to not see, the absence of imagination. Horrible, to understand I was a perpetrator of the same system that annihilated me.

It was not only the acts committed that were wrong. Acts withheld could be a betrayal too. I would come to realise, after this explosion of liberation, that sex was not the thing I wanted. What I wanted was acceptance, which I could not give myself. To see the sign of it with my own eyes: a message on a phone, a beckoning finger, a secret glance. That was the magic I was after. I didn't need to follow through – once I had the affirmation I needed, more often than not I'd drop the flirting and move on. It's hardly as if they could complain. No one had signed a contract. I hadn't promised anything. Flirting and bully-ing have this in common: at their most sophisticated they operate without trace or accountability.

I'm not proud of any of this time. It's as if having realised all good sex has a little transgression in it, I mis-takenly concluded that all transgression is good. I flirted with people who had partners, authority figures, friends. It didn't matter how many hours of others' time I wasted, or feelings I bruised. Something someone observed in me years later – this was, inconceivably, after I had calmed down – 'It's like you're trying to make the whole world love you, one person at a time.' There was no admiration in it. What's worse than a taxi with its light on who won't take anyone home?

Because of course, I had someone at home. The way I found enough comfort in my body to finally start using it was through the love of a partner, who offered somewhere to live, words of encouragement, a hundred loving actions a day. Who said I was beautiful and capable. She was the reason my attitude to my body changed, my attitude to myself. I liked who I was around her, and kept that confidence with me. More than a school, or the passage of time, it was a person who saved me. Lily showed me the safety of a bed, and the unfolding possibilities of a body that stayed. I took that gift and scattered it.

I was immature, full of arrogance and self-loathing, not ready for a relationship. I don't know why I had to disprove my own theory about the connection between love and sex. I only succeeded in making myself smaller. I could have been more honest about where I was, at the beginning of that winding path. Lily was wise and non-judgemental; she loved me with an open palm. I had once told her I couldn't promise to be faithful. Later, it emerged she thought this meant for acting training exercises – she knew what kind of a place Drama Centre was, how extreme its commitment to the work. But that's not what I was up to, and I offer no defence. In the end, it's not the unfaithful acts that are the biggest betrayal. It's the mental compartmentalisation that allows them, the splitting and hiding. That's what's unfair, becoming half a person to the one who sees you, to whom you owe the most. Pleasure passes, and reckoning remains. I'll always be the person that did those things, and it's hard to live with. Not Casanova, but a coward.

I never paused for thought when I was rounding those bases, trying to break free of the past. Making others responsible for my self-esteem was to enlist them in an unwinnable war. I don't believe promiscuity is anything negative at certain periods of one's life – to be honest, I think it's quite wonderful. Every want is a single bud on the many branches of desire, all of which connect to our central libido: a desire for life. But I should have been braver. I should have tried valuing others as much as myself, to see how that might affect my sense of worth.

The only salvageable good is an old lesson: self-worth starts within. This means abandoning stories about ourselves others have asked us to carry. Let's finally drop the old beauty myths, which we've been saddled with a long time. They're too heavy and far, far too boring. There is no value on our foreheads, placed there according to the colour of our skin or the shape of our nose or the size of our chest. Regardless of what I believed then, beauty does not determine our fate. We are not objects with a specific utility, like a sixteen-millimetre wrench. We are not the split-flap display of a railway board, clacking through the preordained arrivals and departures of our days.

I've also come to realise that attraction is not the property of those labelled beautiful; it's largely the reverse. Beauty is what we project onto the attractive, anyone we find interesting, whose spirit speaks to ours, confident in itself. It is a lustre the gaze adds, noticing what is already there. We are dazzling lights, the envy of the universe, given temporary form so we can watch each other dance. I also know, hoping it's not too late, that excitement and respect are not enemies but bedfellows, and the best of physical mischief comes from this place too. That's why good sex is never just about sex. It is us becoming porous, and empty and full and forgiven, and it is green shoots and everything that is alive. Hoping to keep that feeling, that's what I want. Swinging for the fences from here on out. Trying to run that diamond complete.

Letter to the girl I didn't save

It looked like he was going to hit you, and that's when, contrary to my personality, I intervened. At Charing Cross concourse, everyone ignoring the guy shouting at his girlfriend, punching the wall next to her head. The scariest part was that no one was doing anything, so at least I did something, though it really shouldn't have been me. I was a snack for fists. Don't be unnecessary, dude, I think I said. Something like that, odd-sounding. Like I was denouncing his alter ego, Unnecessary Dude.

He looked at me the way a whale looks at krill. Perplexed at being addressed, by our difference in size. Awkward more than anything else. But he came to, and stormed off. Cursed us like a departing hag – suck his cock then and fuck you both – but punching neither of us, to his credit. We were both drunk, so I bought us tea in Pizza Hut, which is not a tea place. I tried to find out what had happened, but you had a better idea. Let's go out. Even though it was late, and there was no way I could miss the last train back to south London where I lived with my parents. Show me where you grew up then. And then you kissed me.

You were a few years older, Australian, and beautiful in an Australian sort of way. I couldn't believe it. I had called a man out, and was kissing his girl. Saloon doors flapping at the back of my mind. We kissed kneeling on the floor of the station

142

as you tried to find your travelcard, and we fumbled on the train and we kissed more at my home station, and in the park, and I showed you my old school and we broke in, and lay down on the ground there. Pure adventure — the sexy uprush heroes get after escaping the beast. Monsters can be matchmakers.

I used to think I was the hero of that story, but not any more. The bad guy was clearly cast, but there are other ways for people to fail each other. I know you didn't want to discuss your circumstances, and maybe that's why you gave us an easy way out. I should have done more to know for sure; I couldn't understand why, hours later, after we had made our escape, after we had an adventure, cuddling on kerbs, laughing and playing at outlaws, you went back, on the first bus of the morning. To the house you lived in, the boyfriend with serious problems, to the life that might have been bad, but was at least real. I didn't help, didn't offer you a real way out. We didn't have to be teenagers sneaking around. We could have found people to give you practical advice. We could have figured it out. I rang the next day and you sounded tired, inconvenienced. You said you'd call me back but didn't, and I was confused and left it at that. I never thought about how you might have to explain yourself.

Maybe it's fine, and you just wanted adventure. But that isn't always the answer. Maybe that relationship ended safely, and you found someone better. But I don't know, and I'll never know. Kissing mouths aren't talking mouths. Next time I'd choose better, for both of us. I still think about you. I hope you're okay.

6

How to Grieve

My father and I didn't talk, and that's a familiar story. What is this gift men pass on to each other? A tobacco-y silence wrapped in burlap, left in the hollow of an oak, the co-ordinates of which can only be communicated via wrestling. The widely held belief is that sons learn these ancient skills from their fathers. Since before we can talk, our fathers are teaching us not to externalise our emotions. Men express feelings in their actions instead, we're told. Pay attention to the way he tightens the wing nut on the cistern, because he is telling you he cares. Do you see him flicking fennel seed out of the dishwasher filter? His heart is full.

In fact, I'm not sure my silence came from my father. Silence might have been preferable. *Stop shouting*, was what I remember pleading from the top of the stairs, the patterned carpet writhing with infantile dread. Unjust to characterise him that way, I suppose. He was married to my mother, a woman who could not leave the house for a short chore without falling down a manhole cover* or returning home with five magic beans. And he was my father, a bad job to have; you'd get more thanks on a firing squad. It must have been hard, locked inside what he vexedly described as a madhouse, but not in a fun way.

It's not quite right to say we didn't talk; I didn't let him talk to me. I can't pinpoint an incident, just a slow growing away over years. Perhaps I felt unprotected. No one could have escaped the electrical storm that was building in me as a teen, a fury ready to destroy things. I guarded my privacy, let my parents know nothing that was going on at school, none of the contents of my inner life. When I went out, I didn't tell them where I was going, made no promises about when I would be back. When I spoke it was in tense, broken sentences, barely English really, that seemed to mock my parents. He was older than the other boys' fathers, which I would never forgive him for. The older I got, the harder we found it to get along. He would get frustrated at my not doing what I was told, or doing what I was told not to – drawing on the walls, bringing strange dogs home, repeatedly blasting a football through his flower beds, snapping freesias and peonies off at the stem – and I would meet his anger with aggressive muteness or sudden, unannounced screaming, which enraged

* 'I did fall down a manhole cover!' she says now. 'But that was in Bombay, and they left them open as a flood defence system. What a thing to do.'

him further until he called me mad, and one of us would leave. *Pagla chele.* I don't know much Bengali, but I put that one together. Crazy boy. 'Why don't you have a chest?' he asked another time. Looking back he was confused by my desire to starve myself, to not develop, but my skin was thin, or non-existent, and his disappointment crushed me. '*SPEAK NORMALLY!*' he exploded one day. I decided never to speak again.

Unless we train ourselves to look through the anger of others, we don't see it as pain. I did get a glimpse at what lay beneath one day, years later. I can't remember what I had done but I will never forget his response. *Why won't you talk? I know we've had difficulties, but that's all in the past now.* He was by then in his seventies, softened by age, wanting to make up a little of what he had lost with his son. Believing it was never too late. I felt the clench in my stomach, knowing this was our moment. The clench moved up, constricting throat and vocal cords, freezing thought or feeling. I ran from the room, leaving him there.

Sooner or later we all get a call, and once you realise that, you're done for. At least mine wasn't the worst kind. A nurse, waking me from a nap, telling me it was a good idea to come in and see my father, today. Never having had the call before, I didn't know the code. I grudgingly pulled on trousers, traipsed up the road in the January air, through the park, over the two bridges, towards the handsome new wing of Lewisham Hospital that my father had watched being constructed day by day, as he took his morning walk. The walk that was meant to keep him out of there. At dinner, he would talk about the progress they were making, joists and poured cement and rainbow cladding and blinds. He'd be one of the first to see those rooms; they would be the last things he saw. Ironic, I suppose, but again, not in a fun way.

He'd gone in a few weeks before, the first time. I couldn't say for what, but no one could. I hadn't paid much attention. Hospital was just a place older people liked going, I thought, like the post office or library. When I visited him, I felt bored, depressed by the strip lights and bland sandwiches in the canteen. The canteen was always playing the Commodores. *Know it sounds funny, but I just can't stand the pain.* What the fuck, Lionel? I thought. That doesn't sound funny at all. Perhaps because not caring was my speciality, I was alarmed at how little the attending nurse seemed to care either. She'd slow-sway her round with bovine placidity, not making eye contact, nor listening when he tried to ask for something. I'd never seen him reduced like that. I pretended not to watch, silent and unnerved. They couldn't find anything wrong, they said. Had they looked? What had they even tried? Dusting him for fingerprints? Examining him by periscope?

In the absence of diagnosis, he'd been sent home for the Samadder family holidays: a not-quite-right, broken-biscuit, Christmas-shaped set piece. My mother would always cook something off-kilter such as chicken à la figs, or omelette in a croissant.

'Smoked Halifax,' she'd announce.

'Do you mean . . . *haddock*? This is a HADDOCK!' he would shout in exasperation. Her favourite experiment was 'medley', in which a succession of pricey desserts – Portugese custard tart, Cadbury's Mini Egg, Angel Delight and Space Invaders would be tumbled together in a bowl, like a disaster at sea. 'Would you like a medleeeeey?' she would sing with self-delight. My father, the most serious man I ever met, would sit at the table wearing a yellow paper crown, looking like a man who'd been sent to death row for a traffic offence.

Nowadays when I'm there, I understand. It is a house with madness in it. A hoarder's paradise, full of boxes of tapes and bags of bags, sagging shelves of books. My mother's old room piled high with fabrics on the floor like crowded termite colonies, past one's waist, while the top bunk bed – right next to the ceiling because it's a small room – has a junior drum kit on it. Cuckoo clocks with broken mechanisms hiss at you in the night. The light switches turn on and off in the opposite ways you expect, the taps are backwards. Everything cockamamie. I can see it as he saw it, a man who climbed uphill his whole life, an intellectual man shouting 'This is a HADDOCK!' in his own home. I can see that to someone houseproud, the tall dresser cabinet in the front room, stuffed with Kinder Egg toys, is not a crowning glory. The kitchen drawer reserved for the plastic sporks from pasta tubs is chaotic. His wife and son liked it looking like this, like Santa's grotto turned over by the cops. I think we're both seeing it differently now. The refrigerators and sofas in the neighbour's garden bow the wire link fence, and foxes pad brazenly through the jungle, right by the house. When he was alive, that narrow garden was his refuge of order, a tended place of season and sense. Cherry and pear trees, a lawn and shed, even a tiny rockery. When he left, we let the shrubs grow out like green Afros, and the trees grew as tall as the house. The squirrels eat the cherries.

When the new year rolled in, so did something else. Announced its presence by pushing up the floorboards, as if it had been there all along. He'd gone back to the hospital, and they were worried this time, if none the wiser. I'd missed a lot of holiday TV to visit him in hospital the first time around, so now I mostly stayed where I was, at Lily's or 'looking after the house'. My mother was at his bedside. Home alone, I had turned the corridor into an obstacle-course football pitch, and was perfecting my masterpiece, the Ham Bra. This involved grilling two circles of ham on toast so the edges curled upward, forming perfect pink bowls, into each of which I'd crack an egg. The dish was ahead of its time, and still is, but breaking ground is tiring, and I was sleeping a lot. The call came, and woke me up.

In hospitals there is so much floor. Fathoms of it, crested with white beds and swelled with rippling green screens. In my memory the floors are always blue, rivers of blue that carry you down like a dream. I floated to him, crossing a channel, traced a tributary to his bedside, where he lay in starchy sheets, against a vertical white cliff of pillow.

I so rarely saw him relax. Immigrants never relax. Once we went to the seaside and he wore a suit jacket and some sort of business short, and I was mortified by his inability to dress down. He wore hats easily, trilbies in autumn and winter, panamas for summer and spring. I never realised what a skill that is until I grew older. I can't wear hats. If I ever do, I look like Bugsy Malone. I suppose I wanted him to wear untucked shirts and chinos like the other dads, the safety of being beige squared. But no: always full tie, overcoat, tinted glasses. My mother and I were fragile and birdlike, but he was handsome and solid, in a Muammar Gaddafi kind of way, with thick hair swept back. I'm pretty sure he gardened in spats.

I'm not sure he felt free most of the time. Most of what I remember was the tiny study next to the living room that he would hunker down in, how that room was all desk, a citadel of papers and him at the heart of it all, worrying. I had the sense he was always preparing for a Worst Case Scenario. I know he had health problems, and they were the reason for this restricted diet and curtailed social life. Diabetes and a triple bypass evidenced by a dragon scratch on his sternum, and many lancets lying around the house, as if legions of tiny knights had been lost in battle. As a child, I would test the point of them on my finger and recoil, wondering how he could stand to draw blood every single day. I tried to imagine what it is like to live with bombs rigged inside you. Maybe I'll find out, if that's another chamber of my inheritance chest.

His fears about what would happen to us had probable cause. My mother and I were both too . . . silly to be safe. She once stepped off the top of the bunk bed she'd taken to sleeping in, in the middle of the night, to confront burglars, who had crossed over from her dream to steal her collection of Kinder Eggs. She sailed through six feet of air until her chin connected with the edge of the cabinet and split apart. As for me, I liked crawling on my hands and knees well into adolescence. I'd descend the stairs on my belly, working my limbs gecko-style and wondering if my body would adapt over time. I was probably seven when I crawled onto the head of a screw that had worked its way two centimetres clear of the threshold strip. It punctured my knee, leaving me in agony, and with a scar in the shape of Abraham Lincoln, livid for thirty years. I would crash my bike all the time, into bridges and post-boxes and lampposts. *Don't think about crashing*, I would think to myself, until I could think of nothing but. But more than this physical disposition to disaster, it was our oddness that caused him anxiety. The fact that my mother would frequently walk past the front door, having forgotten where she lived. My preference for silence and my own company to socialising with other children. The way

I would run from the front door if ever someone knocked on it, slithering up the stairs like a lizard. We all knew my father was our dam against the world, and without him we'd be washed away in hours.

He did later relax a little, after retiring from local council work, allowing himself the *'Allo 'Allo!* and *Poirot* years, and I would join him in that front room, sitting mute. Watching him, watching them. Englishmen playing Frenchmen and Belgians, I owe you. Also Frank Spencer from *Some Mothers Do 'Ave 'Em*, a milksop constantly roller-skating under buses and falling into bins. It's unclear how Frank fitted into this continental canon, but he did wear a beret. It wasn't that Kamalesh Samadder had no silliness; it was that Aparajita and Amurtarhik had a surfeit of the stuff, and someone had to keep the lights on. I loved hearing my father laugh, I realise now. That sudden weightlessness, as if gravity and the body could be shrugged off, just like that.

When I reached him, his head was gently moving, a buoy on lazy water. His eyes took me in, as if he wanted to tell me something. But he couldn't. Whatever it was they didn't know had got worse, and he had lost the ability to speak. Why does this happen at the end? At this point, a clean-shaven, handsome-for-grandmas doctor mentioned pancreatic cancer as a possibility. It was plausible, the way one writes 'Fleetwood Mac' in a pub quiz, if you don't know the actual answer. Hard to detect. Fast-moving. The

Learjet of cancers, though he didn't describe it as that. Or a severe case of gastric something, hard to know. Later, a nurse told me that if it was cancer, it could already have spread to his brain, killing the part responsible for speech.

If he couldn't talk, it was up to me.

'The roads in Lewisham are bad, for roadworks,' I managed, as if I were standing up in my second-ever English class. 'But I came through the park.' I followed up with questions about the food, which he couldn't eat, and some remarks concerning the weather ('It is not raining'). I asked a passing nurse why he kept moving his head like that, like he wanted to look out the window, or jump out of it. Did he need something, or was I making terrible conversation? She smiled at me.

'The boiler . . . is working properly,' I said to him with feeling. The old model, on its last legs, had been repeatedly failing over the holiday, leaving the house freezing. Fed up with things breaking, I'd somehow interested myself in boiler engineering, and petitioned my mother to ask for a superior replacement, a condensing combi-model with frost protection and keyless filling tank . . . the details aren't important. It was a good boiler. It was expensive too, but my father, weakened, had agreed. In his absence, it had fallen to me to oversee the installation, a masterful performance. So sibilant were my inhalations, so plausibly wide my stance, the plumbers must have been confused that we had never met before, or hung out socially. I was actually proud of myself, for getting us out of a spot, and was looking forward to him seeing it. 'Hot water fine. No problems there.' I wondered if it were possible I might bore us both to death before the mystery illness staked its claim.

Strangely, death hadn't much been in my thoughts, either before Christmas or now, here in the place where it was daily reality. Some inversion of perspective had made it harder to see. That is, until the clean-shaven doctor, who really did look a hell of a lot like a young Cliff Richard, appeared. After performing some checks with increasing speed and seriousness, his face taut with the effort of revealing nothing, he invited us into a dimly lit private room. The room came from a different dimension to usual hospital business, a TARDIS that materialised in times of emergency. I appreciated this parallel space. A little place to honour the words a heart could only hear so many times. Or maybe it existed to protect the still-living from those words.

'I'm afraid his organs are shutting down,' Cliff said, dividing his attention with equality between my mother and me. 'We could try to prolong that, but it could cause further suffering, and at this stage the process is irreversible. He's approaching the end.'

My father was wired, but not for sound. Mouth obscured by a ventilator, so we could see his breath made visible, and then less so. I felt something huge swell up inside me, sticking in my throat. I didn't want to say goodbye, I didn't want to let go. I wasn't ready; there was supposed to be a time, for the past to unknot itself, for me to come home. I wanted us to see each other, for me to stop being wrapped up in my own pain. I didn't know if he was in pain now. I had wondered about death so long and here it was, and I was pierced by the loneliness of it, that he couldn't share what was happening. I sat in a chair opposite, so he could see me. Ma by his side, until the last. My words had run out too. We had waited until the end to speak, and now neither of us could. *I'm here now* was all I could think as I sat opposite him, hoping the presence registered, that he knew we were holding him. His eyes were beginning to defocus. How could this be happening so quickly, after all these years?

Perhaps we had another hour with him, perhaps less. Time is an illusion in these situations. Before the last, though, a moment, which will be with me for ever. My father looked at me, even and clear, as if there was something he wanted me to know. I looked back, and we saw each other at last. He nodded. Just that, directly into my eyes, so reassuring, wanting me to know he was okay, and not to be afraid. I nodded back. To tell him I was okay too, and it was okay to go. Satisfied, he started to scan around, as if he was somewhere else already, and it was all new to him. Then his eyes rolled back, and the obscure animation of spirit, that made him him, my father, my creator, was gone.

He was pronounced; and I was a child, I was instantly a child. A howl escaped, before I had time to strangle it.

His tense changed, in that moment, and now there was nothing to do or be done. The nurse let us know we could take as much time as we needed with the body. His co-creator, my mother, was processing things her way, taking pictures of his body on her cameraphone like he was the Golden Gate Bridge. *People will think it's strange*, I thought, and wondered why I cared about that, as my mind reeled and puckered and gasped. I began wailing and trying to swallow the wail at the same time, an accordion in the key of grief. Or does grief begin later? What are the parameters? I was suffused with thoughts, involuting and vomiting other thoughts, chief of which was the sense that we would be washed away within the hour, carried down that river after him.

But then I was given a second gift. In the midst of her own shock, my mother stepped to me, putting my face on her hip as if she knew that reality was too much, the light was too much, that I needed darkness and oblivion and safety. She spoke into my hair. *I'll look after you, everything will be okay. I'll look after you.* Having turned twenty-six a few days ago, I was experiencing profound, explicit parenting. I decided my mother's probationary period was over, and that she could have the job full time. With unpaid overtime, as it turned out.

We waited a few weeks before having the funeral, which we were told was unusual. How quickly was this all supposed to happen? Who can think about plastic cups and finger food when they've been kicked in the eyes? We couldn't believe the price of the coffins, and couldn't afford them, so we cremated his body in a plain cardboard coffin. Actually, that's not true. It arrived plain, and my mother took it home. When I saw it again she had covered every inch with brightly coloured waves and petals, acrylic paint and poetry and photographs of happy memories. Highly unorthodox, and perfect for us. She had created a vessel for his transformation, a newer and more purposeful body than the one I visited at the undertaker's.

That body was always too mysterious, too closed to me. I wasn't even sure what he had died of, because even the way this had been revealed was absurd. A voicemail, weeks later, in which the message had broken into static over the crucial word. *Good afternoon, we have the results of your husband's post-mortem. We can confirm he died of Zuy-SSHTRfssHG.* Good old Zuysshtrfsshg, the silent killer. Probably with added complications caused by *Pwyssshyrgh*. We hadn't called back to find out more. If we weren't meant to know, so be it. No point making waves. In a way it was strangely apt and perfect, this final miscommunication. Hadn't that always been the problem?

It would be over a year before the loss hit me at its fullest. I should have been grieving after the funeral but I mostly recall cruelly admin-heavy days, interminable months of sorting out life insurance paperwork, closing the innumerable bank accounts he'd spent his time managing, most of which contained a few pounds at most, as if he'd been burying nuts in scattered locations to see us through the winter. He'd kept minute, detailed records of everything, on the backs of envelopes and receipts and anything else, in handwriting so small it was illegible. For when the catastrophe came. His hats seemed to bear the most intimate trace of him, panamas and trilbies that read 'Dunn & Co. of Piccadilly', inner band padded with the pages of a 1967 *Telegraph*. The whole business drained me, but I assumed grief had taken its worst. I didn't want to be held back. I was still discovering life, so returned as soon as I could to my adventures with Lilith, as if nothing had changed. Everything had changed. I know because I have few memories of the rest of that year. It was the static of absence, a whistling freefall that lasted so long I forgot the ground existed.

I have a friend named Tabby, a forthright doctor who never voluntarily smiles. This makes her, de facto, one of the funniest people you'll ever meet, and the worst teacher I know. She can't understand why people struggle with things that come so easily to her.

'Making cheesecake is a one-step recipe,' she'll say, frowning at a cookbook. 'Step one. *Make a cheesecake*. That's it.' Same with performing an emergency tracheotomy, or landing a man on the moon. I think there's something to her theory. When people ask me how I had a breakdown, I tell them something similar. You just have one. There's really nothing easier than letting go of some personal hygiene, most communication, and all responsibility.

The worst Hollywood thinks a breakdown gets is sitting down in the shower. Mine took a long time to arrive, and when it did, looked nothing like that. It actually started in Paradise – or Bali, which is the same idea in fewer letters. Lily had taken nearly a month away from work, planned a trip to restore us to ourselves. It had been more than a year since my father's funeral, which we'd held on her birthday. I think she quite liked that. Intuiting we could both do with letting off steam, she brought us to a country dedicated to relaxation. Four-handed massages, pink drinks in coconut shells sipped at sunken bars, palms with green arms that ushered you along, as if every road was lined with doormen. We wore sarongs and ate banana cake every day. Watched lizards, fat ones and flat ones, bustle around as if conducting structural surveys of the buildings. Inland at Ubud, we spent a week living in a forest, stopping dead at snakes in our path, but even these felt benign, weaving around like drunks on their way home. Golden sunshine bathed us, and home felt like a photograph of the past.

In the aftermath of the 2005 terrorist bombings, tourism in Bali had dwindled to nothing, which had been catastrophic for the national economy. You're not meant to put phrases like 'terrorist bombing' and 'silver lining' in the same sentence, but the fact was we had the place to ourselves. We ate up the VIP treatment for weeks, then headed for the coast. Empty beaches, unbroken seas. Luxury steeped my bones, and I didn't feel the sliver of coldness deeper within. Something immune to gold, biding its time.

All was fine. I was swimming as much as I could, snorkel breaking the surface, water folding around my back like wings. It was inexplicably healing, the other world down there, laid out like a neon feast, a Vegas strip. The solitude of being out of one's element, ears blocked to the human world. A humming fantasia of electric blue and yellow and zebra, coral ornaments lit from within, sea fans and feathered stars, quark-like creatures that slipped in and out of existence.

I would swim further out each afternoon, losing track of time. Intoxicating, the dynamism of flippers, translating every tiny twitch to forward thrust, the feeling of extension and power. How could anyone not grow addicted to the sensation? One day I saw clearly that I was an angel flying, with the world turning below me. Below me, the boulders were sprouting with hair that swayed to a musical breeze, and the whole sea sung with it. It drew me on, told me to keep going. Heaven is the absence of horizon, the blood in my ears told me, pulling me through the diffuse light. I streamed forwards, until a kind of inkiness introduced itself in the water. The scale of the rocks below seemed to grow. There'd been no neon fish for a while, I realised, no less mesmerised by this starker beauty. How far out was I? The snorkel started to feel a touch narrower, the mouthpiece uncomfortable. Without warning, a shelf dropped away far below me. The dimly seen landscape was swallowed up, and became nothing at all. I had swum over the continental shelf, and was now staring at the abyssal plain of the ocean. The water turned cold as a dropped mask. Freedom turned to fear.

Chest clenching, a moan trapped in the tube of the snorkel, the feeling of falling. I was having a panic attack. I stared into the bottomless black, pitiless and sucking. Suddenly I thought of the funeral home, the last place I had seen my father. The coldness of the skin when I held his hand, the only time I could remember touching him. Why was I now reliving this memory, which I hadn't allowed myself for a year? The things I had whispered in that dark room. Thin and small, and too late, for he wasn't there. Where was he?

A rope of water rushed down the snorkel and into my lungs. Eyes closed, body snatching in panic, I turned away and broke the surface, gasping. And suddenly I was being . . . burned? Bitten? I cried out in pain, the snorkel jumping out of my mouth and carried away. I dove beneath again, trying to break free of an attacker I could not see. Not knowing which direction I had come from, I kicked and choked and prayed. After some time, the burning increasing – needles in my muscles? – I could make out land, and pushed harder.

The rocky bed rose to meet my feet but, attempting to stand and walk, the flippers caught the water, and dumped me on my arse. I had to inch towards the shore backwards, sitting down the wrong way, water flowing over the flippers. Hardly Daniel Craig-like, this shuffling out of the sea backwards, with cuts to the buttocks. Still, it got me back to shore, where I regarded my arm in horror. Tentacles of ectoplasmic blobs with electric-blue centres radiated up the bicep, into the armpit. The pain was almost unbearable. I was a long way from where I had started, but recognised a few abandoned huts and started running weakly.

My mistress was sitting at the bar reading a book about mass hysteria in Mormons, with her fourteenth cocktail. The barman frowned as he looked at me, joining the dots. Jellyfish didn't usually appear close to shore this time of year, he explained. I think that's what he was indicating. Because of the language barrier, he was fluttering his fingers a lot and shaking his head, like charades. I didn't understand the point. I guess he was telling me I was unlucky, as if that was news. Maybe he thought aliens had laid eggs on me. I tried to charade that I could feel muscle paralysis creeping from my armpit across my chest, and when it reached my heart I would die. But that's hard with only one arm.

'Shall I piss on you?' said Lily.

'You just saw him wash the stings with rum,' I replied.

'It's my holiday too.' She was not, at that point in life, a healthcare professional. I removed myself from the scene, flopping down on the sand and staring at the water, keeping my arm raised as instructed. As I waited to die in the failing light, bleeding at the arse and stinking of rum, an old doubt stirred. The wind picked up, gusting away my only company, a small yellow bird with a ring of white around its eye. *I should know more about birds*, I thought, watching that piece of buttery popcorn on the wind. The sliver of nothingness started drawing strength, and then it began to speak to me.

The next day, over an ice-cream sundae on the beach, Lily asked me if we were a good match. She spoke the words distantly, like someone musing on whether an extra armchair might unbalance a room. Like someone whose partner had been pulling away a long time, and she had stopped expecting more. The truth was obvious and unthinkable. *I want to be alone*, I told her. *I'm sorry.*

She seemed to know this had been coming, that it was right, which made it no less piercing. I had wrongly believed magic was enough, and that in meeting, our work was over. I wasn't attending to her the way she deserved, in the way my soul called to hers. *I lost you*, she cried, tears starting to run down her face, but it wasn't true. She had found me, and loved me openly. I took care of the losing.

I thought of the exquisite things her creativity had brought into the world: an ungraspable snarl of briar thorns wound into a crown, primal figures pulling themselves into existence from cold clay. To me she was an exemplar of the possibilities of creative transformation. More than this, there was the simple, shining heartbreak that she had loved me, and I her. We were twinned, and would always be there if the other needed. But I needed to strike out alone as she had.

The chosen grief echoed with another, unchosen. I hadn't mourned my father. The anniversary of his death had passed unmarked by me. I had pushed away all thoughts of him, believing this would make him less dead, but it achieved the opposite. I didn't want to face the pain of words unspoken. I'd tried to run from grief, as if I didn't carry it in my belly. Perhaps if I went through the process alone, I thought, the lack of comfort would serve as some atonement.

I needed to go; but I also needed to be driven. Having avoided learning to operate a car, when I moved back to my mother's, it was with my belongings piled high in the back of Lily's cab. 'I don't understand why this is happening,' she said, staring at the road to keep it together. I didn't have an answer, sat on the passenger side, mute and stone and sorry for myself. As my mother received the bin bags of clothes I sensed the silent sympathy passing between them.

Newly single, I dove into my little black book like Scrooge McDuck into a valley of coins, still running, chasing the feeling of being alive. But here was no refuge from the feelings. You can only blot pain with bodies for so long. Eventually the pain seeps through, turning those bodies dark and deliquescent. After a few encounters a grossness began to creep inside my nose again, the particularity of sweat, vinegariness of scalp and product, the whole human genital situation when looked at with any objectivity. Looking down at those lusted-after attributes muddled me with the sense I was a grave robber, collecting parts. Soon I couldn't bear to be near another person.

Over the previous year I'd been in correspondence with Vicki, the Scotch strumpet with a heart of gold. We emailed every few days, which was initially a surprise. I wasn't 100 per cent convinced she had ever held a pen, at least one that wasn't topped by a fuzzy pom pom. But I needed a friend, and she'd been one. I was intrigued by the way she was rebranding herself. She was beginning to hold opinions about smoked cheese, and once claimed her favourite entertainment to be Restoration comedy. I suppose she was growing up. She did me a kindness by keeping things normal, at least our version of it. The pitying, avoidant pattern other acquaintances established after the funeral made me feel so leprous, I had to count my fingers.

> *Where have you gone? People that NEVER NORMALLY TALK TO ME are getting in touch to ask where you've gone. When did I become your keeper? If I was your keeper I would give you a fish every day. Or scallops. Kind of a crap fish, doesn't even have a shell. Just a squidgy blob. Miss you Xxx*
>
> *P.S. Don't call Scottish people Scotch.*
>
> *P.P.S. Don't call me Vicki. I'm Victoria now.*

Looking back at my replies, there are clues as to my state of mind.

The thickness of everyone on Facebook is bringing me down. So little gets written that's worth the time reading. Spent four minutes trying to bring up the home page, and then trawled through the shit like a convict looking for a nail-file. It's slowly killing me. I don't know what the point of living is. All I'm doing is waiting for the next person to die. We lose everything eventually, it's all a big joke.

P.S. Scallops have shells.

I stopped replying to Vicki for what she later told me was nine months. I deactivated, logged out and let contact drift in every direction. I stopped responding to the temp agency who had been giving me work. Grunting to let it be understood she could leave meals outside my closed door, I barely interacted with my mother. I can't really say what I was doing at this time, apart from staring at the walls. Oh, and Disney films. When geologists plumb my strata they will find a primary-coloured seam that is forever *The Little Mermaid*. I struggled to concentrate; reading was impossible. But I could spend days weeping at gorgeous tapestries of whole new worlds, that were not real or possible. I was an Amerindian princess and a clownfish and a sexy robber fox. Most of all it was Pride Rock and 'Hakuna Matata' and an incredibly rendered sunrise, the nobility of the lions a deep ache inside me. I would never gaze out from that cliff face, though. There would be no Mufasa with swishing tail, explaining destiny and inheritance. In any case, what could he have said to a hyena like me? *One day, everything that is covered by shadow will be yours?*

Darkness rolled through the valleys and the dells and alleys and suburbs, and it covered the people and the houses and there were no stars. I would sit in the bath in the dark, trying to drown the black mass in my head. People talk about losing your mind when you let go like this, but the world is the only thing you lose. Your mind is all that remains, leagues of it. I couldn't have normal thoughts. *I am living in a body that will die. Time is an illusion. I am inside a dead body*, I thought at night, lost in the polystyrene, labyrinthine ceiling tiles of my child-hood room, leaving my body behind. Unable to move, possessed of an ancient weight, I merged with the earth, left myself under it, as the seasons arced overhead.

When I started to leave the house again, after months, I was sliced open and unhealed, a mess of guts spilling before me as I walked. Grief is a bone-rattling loneliness. I was ashamed of my rawness, how uncomfortable it made others. A thing of spines, in a room of balloons. I had a sudden, unsettling need to go to Tesco, and punch all the loaves.

I was seeing ghosts. Indian men of a certain age, wear-ing olive coats, started to appear in the world. I'd see them and wouldn't think it strange, I would just think, *oh, there he is*. But it was always a different face close up, not the one I was looking for. I would never see that again. He was gone, though I felt his presence, the way one can for a time see the shadows of autumn leaves burned into the winter pavement.

On the other hand. Loss of this magnitude was a useful alibi. When people asked what was wrong, I now had an answer. Depression's nagging illegitimacy can, perversely enough, be remedied by catastrophic events.

That ratcheting, explosive force that had been gathering since childhood now consumed me in flame. Before I left Lily's, I took a poker and smashed my phone to dust, swinging the metal again and again, until the fascia disintegrated, showing dirty green and gold, and the poker was flinting off the fireplace floor. At my mother's, I destroyed the freezer, kicking out the shelves so metal rods dented then flew off, and sprays of ice hissed at me. Probably because she was out of Mini Milks. Kicking a freezer to death is one of those acts which details only make more stupid. I had to stop because my foot got cold. At a railway station I kicked in a ticket barrier, until I was apprehended by a guard, a man I'd often seen, but never spoken to. *You're not one of those bad boys*, he said. I was relieved he didn't press charges, which probably proves his point. He asked me to get help.

I avoided the station and started stepping out in front of cars instead. In my defence, I would do it at zebra crossings with pedestrian right of way, to cars who refused to slow down. *If driving like a prick is so important to you, have the courage to take a life* would be the last thought I had. I developed a consuming intolerance of motorcyclists, especially the teen variety who sawed off their exhausts, ripping the sky apart with their amplified revs. Everyone else was shit to these arseholes as far as I could see, these fucknuggets who denied anyone in ten postcodes the right to not hear them. I stuck my middle finger up at them as they roared past, spewing rants of a towering improvisatory quality. *Do everyone a favour and crash now, not later, you nutless dickprune*, I would curse, though they were gone, and I was inhaling only fumes. *I hope you get run over by your best friend and fall into a coma and due to legal technicality your family gets sued, and lose the case the day before you die.*

Eventually I was left rambling in the streets, completely directionless and cursing God. Calling him out, telling the coward to show himself. Every day felt like another humiliation. *What are you waiting for? If you want me dead, just do it.* A latter-day Job, bellowing outside Poundland. Ironically, I didn't have a job. I would challenge any gawkers, knowing, absolutely knowing, that if anyone reflected the aggression back, I would go straight through them, holding nothing back, no instinct for preservation. My body was on the line, ready to be turned entirely to violence, and men twice my size – which is every man – turned away, and that's when I knew I had gone mad.

One day, a crocodile of schoolchildren crossed the road

ahead and started to file past me. I was trapped in the gauntlet of their fidgeting bodies and the wall of a church. A corridor of stick-together and all-ahead and hope. Tears sprung to my eyes, the need to hide my face. I didn't want them to see what a man could become. They trooped past, with their big little open faces, because they hadn't learned to look away. Their eyes carried no fear or judgement. Maybe they hadn't learned those yet either.

I wish I'd known that violence can be uncoupled from anger, that I didn't have to turn into something I despised. Anger isn't bad. It is nothing more than a body yearning for rightness, for moral balance. The existence of anger tells us we are creatures who are meant to live together, under conditions of justice. The problem is, no one balances the scale. The universe doesn't give a fig for human fairness. At the cosmic scale, there are no figs given.

Death is the ultimate injustice, the most egregious wrong. It is unfair we can lose people we love, and ones we haven't yet learned to love properly. It is unfair that so much of grief is gone through alone, a mirror process of the dying itself. It is unfair we do not have more time. Wrong that life goes on. It often feels as if death is meted out unfairly, that some families are more in its sights than others. 'How old were you when your father died?' a writer once asked, a woman decades older than me, whose parents were still living, in part thanks to very private health care. Twenty-six, I told her. 'Oh, so you weren't *that* young,' she considered to herself, knocking me down the ranking of some internal chart of sympathy owing, or interest worth. *How young would you have liked me to be?* I thought, with a molten flash. But this is where I need to remember that although death owes no debt to fairness, they are not strangers either. Mortality is nothing if not fair. Senseless to quibble over years. Eventually the curtain falls, no matter who we are, and in the scheme of things, it happens in the blink of an eye. Death bats her lashes at all of us.

Not that I'm advocating stoicism, as nice as it sounds. Anger and guilt corrode us, but cannot be avoided. They will have their due. Something that helped me move on from anger, slowly, is to have the injustice of a situation seen and named and admitted. Death is devastating and lowering; it burns our bridges. And it cannot be undone. Guilt would prove much harder to let go, the root of regret being proximity to the path not taken.

When the certificate of death arrived, it read 'myocardial infarction', words which appear on the majority of certificates of this type, being essentially medical speak for *To be honest, he died*. It didn't tell a whole story, but that wasn't the story I needed filling in. With a slow letting go, it became obvious my anger was nothing to do with the hospital. I should have been trying to find out who my father was as a man, so I could honour him, and finally open myself to his lesson. I've been thinking about what it would have been like to arrive in a country in 1965, with three pounds in your pocket, and start life over. The way you might dress to prove you're making an effort. If things were bad for me, it's unimaginable what the seventies must have been like, how he would have had to fight for what was his, and later for a wife and child with feathery brains and shining eyes. What it must take to protect a family above all else, to put your body on the line.

I remember coming home with tears in my eyes after that brick had been thrown at me, and my father asking what had happened, the way he flew out of the house. *Bastards!* he shouted in the street, scaring me. But I now remember that it wasn't always anger, that there is more to hold onto. As I recall, he actually grew fond of the dogs that followed me home, persuading the police to let us keep them until the owners were located. I remember too, walking through this park, to school, and him being at my side. Funny how I remember so little of what went on at school, but these walks to and from it are evergreen. I was maybe ten, ready to play the lead in a school play for the first time. A hydrochloric anxiety had dripped through my brain for weeks, through the entire rehearsal process, until in desperation I shared them with my daddy on that walk: what would people say when they saw the play, and saw me? Peter Pan is meant to be white. The things parents have to hear. The leaves were a blur on the ground as he spoke, but the air was clear. *Neverland isn't a place on Earth, so Peter Pan can look like anything,* he told me. *You can be anyone you want.*

He released me, and I loved doing that play in the end. Being king of the Lost Boys, who goes looking for his shadow. The one who needs his shadow, in order that he may keep looking. Loved the flying, crouching on windowsills and sword fighting with Hook. And I have an indelible memory of the crocodile: Jimmy Chester lying on his belly on a skateboard, inside a papier-mâché torpedo he could not control. Many times his size, it was lined up from the wings and rolled on, and we'd improvise around where he ended up. It took him many minutes to leave, trundling blind, sticky-out claws snagged on a background cut-out, and you'd see that green felt frame *vibrating* with controlled panic, then a deliberate reversing to dislodge himself, like a Transit van at a loading bay. So palpable, his little sweating, paddling hands on the parquet floor. And onstage I'd be staring at this eight-foot crocodile, thunderous in its attempt to be discreet, and realising that if I looked, everyone looked, and learning what comedy was while waiting for my turn to speak.

But my relationship to that production has altered. The drama I think about now was in the audience. Watching me sitting alone, centre stage on a cardboard rock, lights down low and all life far away, fronting that *to die will be an awfully big adventure*. So many lines of sight. So much dialogue unwritten. Monologues and inner obstacles, playing out there in the dark, in the hearts of those wondering how long they would be okay, and if their children were going to be okay, and what was going to happen.

Letter to Daddy

I think the boiler was a metaphor. Took me ten years to realise, to stop beating myself up for ruining our final hour. I was trying to speak your language. Not Bengali, I never learned that and didn't know why it was so important to you, when all I wanted was to blend in here. To be invisible, I suppose. I know it was hard for us, not having the language to talk to each other in. Maybe you became a parent when that stuff wasn't really done. More likely I shut down the possibility of anything smooth between us, because I needed things to be jagged.

I'm sad I never asked you about what it was like when the Beatles . . . well, when the Beatles. Or England winning the World Cup. And maybe you wouldn't have had good answers, but it could have paved the way towards asking what it was like to be you. Because I think you're an interesting person, and I should have been braver. Ma told me you moved here to escape Indian caste hierarchies. When she arrived, you told her to free herself of the old ways, to live free. I found the workers' rights pamphlets of your youth in your study. In later days, you were working for an Aids awareness charity for black and minority ethnic sufferers, the people most left behind. You didn't waste your days.

Now that you're gone, I understand how much it takes to keep the wheels in motion. How did you do it? You kept us going, Ma and me, dug out a life big enough for us. It must have been bare hands in winter earth. Every brick of the house, every penny of education, every money worry and health difficulty I was shielded from was an act of protection that weighs far more than words.

But words are all I have, which Ma says I inherited from you. The further we get from each other in time, the more I see you. Anxiety, bunker mentality, I have those. The determination to make a place, too. I found it hard without you, and I know you wouldn't have wanted to leave us alone, but it's okay. If I was the last thing you saw, it's as if you placed some part of yourself in me, a final gift. Like Columbo always says, One more thing.

Everything you did showed you wanted me to live free too and I never had time to say thank you, and I never said I loved you. What I talked about when I talked about the boiler, what I meant, was that we were going to be okay. We're warm and watered and the winter can't get in. We had a magnetic filter fitted, to keep the rads clear of sediment, and there's a lifetime guarantee. Also we had to get a new freezer, but I guess you don't know about that. Don't worry about it.

It's a really good boiler.

I love you.

7

How to Be Alone

I was at my lowest ebb when Eliza found me, next to a bonfire I was considering throwing myself on. Yeah, I'm that guy.[*] Despite our attraction, I decided to prepare the ground for a while, so our relationship would progress organically from a solid base of friendship. It wasn't that it took over a year to persuade her to fancy me. You mustn't think that.

We met when she was twenty-two and I was nearly thirty. Then, despite my best efforts, I did turn thirty, disappearing across the globe with my mother for nearly a month, on what turned out to be the trip of a lifetime. I returned changed, without a job or many friends or possessions, newly open to life. We were a decade into a new millennium, in the teeth of a recession, but my spirits were on a perverse upswing, and meeting Eliza felt meaningful. We were both back living in our childhood homes, which I'd been doing since before it was cool, when it was still

---

[*] A fireworks-night joke, where you least expected one!

considered a mortifying failure. Eliza was impatient for life to begin too, and decided something had to be done.

She gave me a job, playing one of the witches in Macbeth in a large ensemble she was directing – after every show, other home-seeking theatrical waifs would sit around our great director in the pub, while she spun stories about how one day we would all live together in a big house. It was romantic. What was surprising was that she followed through – checking out property listings, visiting houses daily until she found one big enough to take in six, with a garden for us all to run around in. She was den mother, the youngest of us but also the bossiest, I noted with a concupiscent eye.

She drew up cleaning rotas, organised a bank account for rent, ordered us to weed and mow the lawn. Many tasks. Comb the streets until you find a clothes-drying stand. Look into steam cleaners. Introduce yourselves to the neighbours. All onerous to me, though it would later grow clear that her real work was us. She knew such acts would help us take psychological ownership of our precariously rented new home. She would imagineer surprise birthday parties, throw ad hoc award ceremonies and attempt to turn the outhouse into the world's smallest poetry salon. She was not a woman, but the doodling cone of a tornado. A hod carrier, laying bricks of pure positivity.

To her, The Way Things Were Done was an instruction manual, to enable anyone to build a ladder to their dreams. An incomparable Can-Do attitude, to counter my

Will-Die certainty. I'd never met anyone so optimistic that I didn't immediately wish to strike in the pumpkin. She was an ideas factory, perpetually brainstorming. *A cat-sitters' network, staffed by refugees*, she'd say apropos of nothing, or *what about a public holiday where everyone does anonymous good deeds? Like* The Purge *but reversed*. She wouldn't even check if anyone was listening. For all I know she was striding into rooms devoid of people, babbling away, an algorithm gone rogue. Her ideas were all about helping people and making the world better, things I stood passionately against. Yet there was something between us.

The heat of it flared up the summer night that London erupted into riots. We were alone on the sofa watching the news. A fancy-dress shop was on fire, which sounded like an obscure punchline. The TV was playing the clip every seventy seconds, insinuating London was burning down, painting a vision of hell with a single mosaic tile. Almost everyone we knew was in Edinburgh, at the Fringe Festival, and many of their liberal values had been lost in transit, judging by the number of Facebook updates they were posting that contained phrases like *water cannons* and *tried as adults*. There was an absurdity to the rolling news and the furious improv troupes and the looting of Foot Locker.

'You want to go looking for it, don't you?'

'This is our Woodstock!' I shouted, up and out the door. We didn't find any hot blood, at least not in the deserted streets strewn with empty shoeboxes. We walked the wreckage, and saw it as a beginning. Our city burning but also not burning, looking for a riot and finding only peace. One thinks these connections arrive in a look, a melding of gazes, but it was more like the magnetic poles inside us turned to face each other, and our bodies knew before we did. Our first kiss came a week later, at a working men's club, in an atmosphere electric as guitars. She led me to a room in the basement, clad in memorials to the 1914 conflict, and urged me to consider the war dead. Love landed on us, fat as a bluebottle bumping off the window.

There was nothing similar about us. Our minds ran on opposing tracks. When she woke in the morning, she would raise her fist in the air, exclaiming something like 'Porridge exists!' or 'Anything is possible!' She thrilled to get on top of 'personal admin', a phrase I'd never heard before and thought wild. Wilder, certainly, than the hedgerow of tax bills and jury summons and court orders I let grow about me. 'If you're feeling listless, it's good to make a list!' she would exult, like Mary Poppins the Younger. I'd stare at her the way one might regard a chess-playing computer, or a prison, wondering what went on inside. There was no reason on paper for us to work as a couple – I know this because she actually wrote down the pros and cons of us as a potential couple before we proceeded. Unhelpfully, it was an even split, though gut instinct told her things would end badly. I ignored her intuition, because I was ready to be better, determined not to make the same mistakes again. Here are some reasons I loved her, construed in the only literary form she sanctioned, the list; bulleted not numbered, because hierarchy is patriarchy.

- I have never met another person who whistled as they worked, outside of the films that reminded me of darker times. Not even any of the workmen pals I'd ever contracted did it. The sound of whistling is one of forced ease, and inherently suspicious. The air in the house was baubled with these notes, the sound of someone leaving a murder scene at a controlled pace. Annoying if I was trying to concentrate, which luckily I rarely was, at least at first.

- When we played the superpowers game, she dismissed the standards – flying and invisibility – and chose the ability to get by without sleep, so she could get more done. Arguably she had misunderstood the game, but was unarguably in possession of an iron She-EO mentality.

- The baffling sticky note she left herself that I intercepted, which read 'Lunch – USB and screwdrivers', the most disgusting meal deal ever conceived.

- After we returned from a trip to Bombay with my mother, Eliza vowed to eat only with her

hands 'like real people'. I would watch her
over my knife and fork, scooping vindaloo and
thumbing rice balls into her mouth. She was a
star attraction in curry houses, but at Jamie's
Fifteen there was confusion, and some
judgement.

I'd never encountered this level of organisation. Sitting
on the sofa, she might casually ask if I wanted to share a
rice pudding after the TV show we were watching had
finished. No sooner than I'd murmured agreement, a little
box would pop up on my phone: a calendar invitation
labelled 'rice pudding'. I hadn't even seen her move. Was
she interfacing with my email using . . . her mind? Later,
our attitudes to planning would be more of a problem. My
dissolute friends would text at the last minute, suggesting
we catch a train to Brighton to play in the arcades, and
I'd have to admit my next eight weekends were booked.
'I'm visiting a cousin of someone who was at school with
Eliza's . . . I want to say niece?'

Family was a big thing for Eliza, and hers was very
big. A constantly communicating net of aunts and grand-
mothers and godparents. Hours were spent explaining
to me what a great-nephew was, how "twice removed"
worked. There were many weddings. I'd always disdained
weddings, particularly staid English ones full of dead
ceremony and decorum, prematurely aged young couples
avowing their intention to muddle through together.

People were far warmer to me now than I invited or deserved. Every concert or exhibition or christening, I was embraced by people I didn't know, eagerly brought in, validated just by being hers. It was strange. 'Do you want to go to all these birthdays all the time?' I asked.

'It's family,' she said, and I never knew if that meant yes or no.

'Why don't you wear high heels more often?' I'd ask, if things ever got too peaceful.

'Because why don't you go fuck yourself?' she'd reply. Feminism and education were her passions and I teased relentlessly, but the truth was I felt a raw admiration for this, more plugged into the world in her company. My father would have liked her. She had a radar for power imbalance and undisclosed privilege, which made her a curiosity for her Victorian industrialist family, who were fond of Spitfire fly-bys and ham. There'd clearly been money in the family at some point, but it seemed to have dissipated by the time I got to them. Had Eliza funnelled it all into NGOs?

She was particularly sensitive to racial imbalance, often lapsing into a sullen patois when we took a seaside break. 'Too many crackers up here,' she'd glower, staring down a salty promenade of people who looked exactly like her.

'What do you mean?'

'White. Folk. Everywhere.'

'That's because they're terrific,' I said, wondering if we could find one of those machines that flattens pennies.

We didn't have money, so took Groupon getaways like this whenever we could, to suicide-y bed and breakfasts on the outskirts of market towns, trundling our mini-suitcase up the side of dual carriageways on foot. Eliza decided it would be good if we learned to drive, for road trips. We both signed up but I was scared, stopped going to the lessons I'd paid for, would spend the hour in a café eating falafel instead. So she took the wheel, driving us through the nearest bits of map that were green, belting out her own baffling version of 'Thong Song' by Sisqó. A bizarrely overconfident trait this: her insistence that she could predict any lyric in any song, due to English's branching syntax, which narrowed possibility with every word. In reality she was all over the place, even on songs she'd heard a thousand times before. Classics with a twist, these, from the Beach Boys' 'I'm Picking Up Goodbye Rations' to the lesser-known Simon and Garfunkel ballad 'Are You Going to Starve Your Au Pair?' What would Carole King have made of Eliza's fruity tribute, '(You Make Me Peel Like) an Actual Lemon'? I'm fairly sure that's what she was singing. *Ac-tu-al lemooooon.*

When the money ran out or the weather turned we stayed in, dancing in the kitchen, eating jerk and jollof and fufu, while our four other housemates found ways to be out. I would leave her little love notes, and sign them from Anthéa Turner, a dementedly cheerful ex-*Blue Peter* presenter, which we both found to be funny.

After two years of spicy looks exchanged over rice and peas, Eliza decided we needed to find a new home. The campsite thrill of sharing a room had begun to pall, we were ready for our own place, and Eliza asked where I'd like to live next. *A home with room to manoeuvre*, I thought. *A special room, just for my manoeuvres. I'd manoeuvre in the morning, I'd manoeuvre in the evening. All over this land.* Despite the city being all I'd known – or because of it – I yearned to live somewhere remote, with space for day-dreaming, and not much talking.

'Anywhere far away from people,' I said.

I'd loved being alone since childhood. Bliss, to close one's eyes against the sun, with no need to translate the swim of feeling into words. Perhaps it came from being an only child, who had learned to do without company, and then couldn't bear it for very long. My favourite memories were all of being alone. Once I put on boots and waded up the river in the park, the Ravensbourne, all day, far beyond any place I knew, until it grew high concrete walls and became too deep to pass. I thought I was Huckleberry Finn, though I knew the black leeches on my legs when I climbed out were slugs. My imagination was a personal spacecraft with which I could leave the world at will. I grew close to animals, with whom one didn't have to talk. I was never lonely. I spent entire weekends at the bottom of the stairs, throwing a tennis ball up to the top. I knew the ball would descend in regular bounces, until it unpredictably struck the lip of a step, and would shoot towards me at speed. I had to sharpen my reflexes to avoid being smacked in the face: penalty practice. I made myself goalkeeper, the most thankless position, out of a desire to save, or penalise, myself, I don't know.

I'd guarded my solitude at all costs as I grew up, needing space around me, and privacy within. I defended it at all costs, lashing out if anyone tried to get too close – there'd been one violent incident at school for which I was lucky not to have been expelled. As I grew into a teen, my extreme attachment to solitude and interiority had blossomed into a strange prejudice against relationships. I thought people entered couples and made themselves half a person. Their concerns became banal. *People are scared to be alone*, I thought, *because they are weak.* The fact that at that age no one was interested in being in one with me was immaterial. I would remain above them, I decided, seen only from a distance, wreathed in holy light. *Noli me tangere.*

Incredibly, Eliza found us a place to live that had all the solitude I'd dreamed of. On an upper floor overlooking a park, no shared walls with neighbours, a terrace that looked out onto the tops of trees. It had light every hour of the day, domed by an expanse of sky. Every evening, this limitless heaven would catch fire in the most extraordinary sunsets imaginable, a drowning field of nuclear salmon. We could only scrape a way to afford the rent, 90 per cent of our combined income, because it was located in a transport dead spot, a Bermuda triangle of train stations, in which commuters could get lost and be later found feral. We had no money, but everything we needed. I didn't have to be anywhere on a daily basis, and Eliza took it as a chance to rediscover cycling, being involved in only a handful of accidents during our entire time there. Life was perfect.

What's that saying – if you want to make God laugh, tell him your plans? God has an incredibly niche sense of humour. He would have had a rib-tickling time living with Eliza, though. Never has anyone shared so many details of their day, in such breadth and microscopic detail. How many segments of her chocolate bar she had saved that day, the place her mother's iPad had been the whole time, what the rain on the roof of her shared office space sounded like. The plot, we called it. All the things that happened in a day. They didn't have to be interesting, they were just the things that happened.

I could finally see the gifts of difference. There were benefits to relationship I hadn't imagined from my judgemental teen perspective. We filled in each other's missing spots and felt expanded, a fortified team to take on the world. You think you know a person, and then one day she bleeds a radiator like she was born to it, and you realise it's not her first time. On the other hand, we had radically different needs regarding space. It's hard living and working in a one-bed flat. One of the advantages of wealth must be space, physical and mental, the freedom to set one's own boundaries. How did people do it without money, crammed in on top of one another? Although she did not share this hang-up around space, Eliza noticed the fly in the ointment. For my birthday, she bought a subscription to a flotation tank compound, so I could float naked in absolute darkness whenever I wanted. The skin-temperature saline let me lose my extremities, disembodied and isolated and infinite, like God's first good idea.

She worried it wouldn't be enough. I loved our life and our home, yet in small ways had begun to placate my unexpressed need for mental quiet by growing emotionally distant. There is a causeway between our fantasies and fears, perhaps. Despite a deep longing to feel at home, I'd always been romantically attached to the notion of drifting in and out of people's lives, rootless and unknown. Or something even more drastic. 'I wish I could start over, move far away and leave everyone I know behind,' I mused to Eliza one day, as we walked to the engagement party of a friend. 'Maybe I'll see something terrible, and be put in witness protection. Do we have that in this country?' I didn't understand why she had started to cry until it was too late.

Another occasion we were riding the bus and I started to intone the words to 'Get Lucky' by Daft Punk in a gratingly robotic monotone, because I was bored.

'You're not making any friends on the top deck,' Eliza pointed out. Some pressure in me was uncorked by the knock, volcanically fizzing over.

'YOU WANT ME TO BE NORMAL,' I screeched, starting to hyperventilate. She rubbed my back, attentive as a nurse.

'Just breathe,' she said. 'You're having an overreaction.'

Peculiar pleasure, to be managed. To have one's temperatures known so intimately, to be an object for whom someone has a knack. Eliza and Lily both had known when a downward spiral was beginning to manifest, and when I just needed a bun, or to undo a button on my trousers. I pity anyone who has never known the brush of a nurturing briskness. I could see the mathematics of supervision playing over Eliza's face every time I had a headache, and made my usual point of refusing paracetamol.

'No, I need to feel this. It's telling me something.' She'd stand there a beat with the pills in hand, unsure whether to let me make my own mistakes, or save time. 'I think the body articulates feelings that our thoughts—'

'You are chatting absolute shit.'

If you live with someone you find inspiring and do not attend to your love, they can grow as unseen as the trees. Or annoying, like a loose button. Having found someone who did not baulk at my negativity, I started to push it. I was jealous of how much attention her work took away from me. Having quit theatre when we got together, she was now running her own company, managing her own staff. The company produced nutritional advice flyers for primary schoolchildren, which she said was a way to counter racism in the curriculum; I wondered if she just wanted to go back to a time when everyone got gold stars for sitting up straight, and sharing. Yet when I did see her, I would be dismissive. Returning from work, she'd find me in underpants and track shoes eating yum yums, reading a medical textbook as soft sugar drifted onto my belly and legs. 'This is not a picture of mental well health,' she'd sing, taking a second to appreciate her own phrasing. She'd ask how my day was, as she always did. *Loves the plot*, I'd have to remind myself. When I worked, it was as an office temp, sifting emails and processing payments. More usually I was home alone, waiting for the phone to ring with an audition, half-hoping it wouldn't. How could anyone want to hear about the mundanities of my day?

'Same as yesterday,' I'd snap. 'Aren't you going out? When are you leaving?'

I thought love banished depression, and that was a miscalculation. It had started to come back, a multiplying cell feeding on itself. I could feel that pressure building in me again, and there was someone I cared about in the blast radius, but I didn't know how to stop it. My insomnia was making me miserable, and I wondered if the extra heat in the bed was to blame, or being made to follow a night-time routine that wasn't my own.

'You haven't slept? Oh no. Can I help?' she said groggily at 4 a.m. one night, woken by the huffing and fidgeting. I wanted to tell her that my soul was sick again. But I couldn't talk. In any case, speech would have pulled me further from the possibility of sleep. Making contact would be a wrench. And how could she possibly help? What a stupid thing to say. I brushed off her arm, and turned away.

A few months later she asked if I wanted to go back on antidepressants.

'I've felt you closing a door on me, shutting me out,' she said with immense sadness one evening, over a scratch dinner. That was what we called the hodgepodge meals we cooked with whatever was unused in the fridge, to put off buying more food. Potato waffles and walnuts, pizza base and spinach, celeriac chips and a cup of stock. Fusion is what the gastro-set would call it, my mother knew it as medley, but it tasted quite a lot like poverty. If I didn't believe in aspirin, there was no way I was taking SSRIs, I thought, though failing to meet her eye did nothing to disguise my look of contempt. 'You're ill. It doesn't need to be like this,' she pleaded, absorbing my irritation. She asked if I would consider seeing a therapist. I had been made to go to counselling as an adolescent, due to behavioural problems, and I'd seen a few therapists over the years. But I'd stopped going after Eliza and I got together, figuring there was nothing she couldn't fix.

'I don't want to talk about it,' I said, which was almost witty.

Besides, she knew I couldn't afford it. I never exempted Eliza, the woman who saved me, from my suspicion that the world was constantly trying to screw me over. As money anxiety became crippling, I grew convinced I was being taken for a ride, paying more than my share in our loose arrangement. Eliza tried to allay my fears, showing me an app in which we could individually catalogue our spending as we went along, to be fair about who owed what. That system didn't work. To my dismay, the list was populated with household items I'd never heard of and which were too boring to focus on, thick bleach and rinse aid, printer ink and a box file she'd bought, to teach me how to do my tax returns. The list made it appear I was the one not pulling my weight. Awful, how technology dictates our lives.

'We'll find a way to afford it,' she said. 'Or you can go on an NHS list. It's a long wait, but they're good at keeping in touch while you wait.' She knew about all this because cracks had been appearing in her too, and she'd gone looking for answers. Starting a company is hard. I'd made it clear I couldn't help her, as I had no money and business talk made me sleepy. The fire for her work had ebbed, as she'd been carrying us. Uncertainty, pleading, consoling, cajoling . . . this is heavy emotional work. But there wasn't room for her struggle; that was my speciality. In relationships, unlike the real world, walls are easier to put up than knock down. Some of my worldview had started to rub off, and she no longer thought everything was possible. I'd broken Mary Poppins.

'I don't want to talk about it,' I said again. I couldn't stand it when she kept bringing this up. I heard what was really going on, the disappointment in me, and wasted potential. She must have hated coming back to find me always at home, getting fatter and sadder and older, as months unspooled like ribbon. I was worthless and poor and unable to achieve my goals, because I didn't have any. Of course, I didn't want to admit any of that. I never wanted to open my mouth again. I hung my head, and waited for her to leave me alone.

'If you sat in this room for the rest of your life, I'd still love you,' she said, and something splintered in me.

Ambivalence about family returned to play its part too. Children represented an unimaginable burden to me. Who had the strength? Life was already fragile, economically precarious, and noisy. Childcare cost £600 an hour. Parenthood ate your dreams and spat them out. As far as I could see, children were puke- and debt-spewing little Churchills who required you to transcend your own ego and never sleep again. They stayed eighteen months old for the rest of time, beyond the point their haggard owners longed to be put down. Eliza liked kids, and wanted them, so that was pretty much that.

A failure of imagination, my tendency to regard the future as a black hole. Not wanting children is an ecologically responsible choice, but I had grown into a cliché of doubting masculinity, egotistical, someone who assumed women weren't equally terrified of having children, though they had far more reason to be. My behaviour was childish. Shown a photograph of a friend's baby, I'd clamp the muscles of my face so no positive emotion could leak through. If we passed a stroller, I'd run into the road, in case the surge of hormones caused Eliza to leap on my back and impregnate me. Men can enjoy this luxury of doubt into their fifties, sixties, and then change their mind, but even that comes with a price. You can't keep a good woman hanging on.*

After nearly six years, we decided to break up. There wasn't any other way out. We wanted different things from the future, and all I could seem to want was to be alone, and not dragging somebody down with me. Cruelly, a possible new career in journalism had by then started to take off for me, thanks to Eliza's constantly flaying me with encouragement and energy, her heavy-handed cat-o'-nine-praises. I was still at home, but working all the time suddenly, my mind everywhere but where it should have been.

As she loaded up a car to drive her things away, I looked at how little space needed emptying of her. Half of one rail of the shoe rack, a quarter of a clothes rail. Squeezed into the smallest possible space in the home she had found, then pushed out altogether. She returned one last time to leave the keys, turning to me with a face that hadn't been dry for months, eyes brimming with the sadness I had introduced her to.

---

* Legal disclaimer: you can't keep bad or middling women hanging on either.

'I wanted to keep you safe,' she said, and every cell I had reached back to her. But I said nothing. Safety is a solitary figure, any number divided by itself.

When she was gone, I sat on the floor with all the space around me that I wanted, shaking, sobbing vocally for the first time since my father's death. A shock, how comforting it was to hear a noise at all in that dead air. I cried out from the shock, but from pain too. Was this what I had craved: total isolation so I could cry out loud, heard by no one? Just as when I was out of a relationship I couldn't imagine entering one, when I was in one, I couldn't bear to see it end. I felt like I could die. How did people endure break-ups every few years? The grief of separation amplified every other loss I'd stored, the clamour of it threatening to drive me mad.

For longer than a year, I knew true loneliness. Not a handsomely enigmatic, acoustic-guitar kind of loneliness, but a series of abject, surreally isolated images. A freezer exclusively stocked with bread, for one. I couldn't finish a loaf on my own before it got mouldy, so was always buying more, forgetting I already had a freezer full, and having to add it to the pile. A man talking to mice that had begun to infest the flat, growing so bold, or concerned, that they tugged the hem of my tracksuit bottoms with their teeth as I sat motionless in my chair. The lumpy outline of a body under the covers of the bed – a body that would never wake up. I had started stuffing the lonely half of the bed with pillows, to trick my body into believing someone else was there. In the awful silence of night, I would play music from a phone wrapped inside the pillowcase, muffled and small, and pretend someone was singing to me. Embarrassing, how much comfort I found in the trembling of the tiny sound wave upon the sheets, in the bedsprings, how much my loneliness amplified that movement of air into a loving touch.

It wasn't that I never saw people. I even took a holiday to Spain. But the nights were hard, and no matter where I went, there I was. When the end of the year came around, I spent that alone too. Despite my big talk of loving solitude, I'd always defaulted to socialising at New Year like everyone else, worried that to be on my own would be boring or lonely. This year would be different, I decided, I would be braver. And so I cooked a meal and watched the fireworks. I listened to the cheers of my neighbours, so close by, and truly *sat* with myself, and came to a realisation. It was even more boring than I'd imagined.

For weeks I watched those sunsets alone, astonished at how harrowing the colour pink can be. I didn't sleep. How to feel the grief, without breaking down? It was not going to be easy, with all this time for thinking. Regrets piled up. I thought about how, when some piece of good fortune fell my way, Eliza's eyes would light up, and she would feel elated for me. Every one of Eliza's successes, by contrast – whether passing a driving test with only one minor, or landing thousands of pounds of investment – had left me stricken, convinced I was being left behind, that my own inability to succeed was now set in stone. I'd been treating our relationship as a zero-sum game, and building my own gallows.

I'd been here before, I realised, and would be again. I took energetic, beautiful women, made them my nurse, and then resented the change. How could I stop this pattern of recruiting strong women to fix me? It began to dawn that if I genuinely wanted a partner, I had to adjust my conception of love from a transcendental experience received, to a working one shared. In admiring these bright-burning goddesses and their abilities, I stopped trying to improve myself or valuing my own. Low self-esteem was stopping me fulfilling my end of the love contract. It feels immodest, to be diagnostic about what you offer a partner. But if you can't identify it, you can't check in on it, and get better.

'Do you realise how much you laugh in your sleep?' Lily had said to me one morning. I rarely remembered my dreams, which I assumed were full of sinkholes and submarines and skeletons pointing bony fingers. In fact, I'd been chuckling away throughout the night, waking her up. I was horrified by the revelation, but she'd been weirdly delighted. 'You spend all day wrestling the dark, but at night, you're an absolute buffoon.' These were intelligent women, who had chosen me for a reason. There was still good in me, waiting to be recognised. Despite all my unhappiness, there was a side to my character unafraid of joy. A person who liked to dance, and kiss, and talk for hours. Who wanted to nurture, and disrupt, and tease and adore. I hoped that if I learned to look beyond my pain, there was a person who could be truly happy for others, truly loving. It was a chance worth changing for.

A relationship is transformative and terrifying. It comes in more shapes than ever now, though the old ones haven't outlived their usefulness, I think. Most of us get a few chances at a five-year coupling, or ten. But you only get one chance at forty years of unfolding, and I'm curious what's inside there. Chris told me how recently he convinced our friend Ella that Dwayne Johnson and The Rock were twins, *for two whole days*. The fact Ella is his wife makes the story so much funnier.

Then again, there is no right arrangement in which to spend our lives, no guarantees on how long things will last. The only certainty is that no one person has the power to unlock all that is good in you, scatter all your devils. To be a person I liked in a relationship, I needed to stop looking for one who would save me. I had to save myself.

My happiest memories aren't of being alone, really, no matter what I tell myself. It's just easier to be alone than to learn how to ask for what you want. I was wrong to think coupling invariably creates two half-people. A good relationship lets you be yourself completely, and bears witness. My happiest memories are a car journey, with the driver crooning *O Danny Boyle, this pie, this pie's appalling*, after describing a flapjack she ate last Thursday. Or the breathing of someone trusting themselves to sleep, with a hand on my chest in the dark. Or being gently woken by a high cheekbone pressed under mine, as I lay dozing in the sun. The perfect tessellation of two oddities. A treat, meant just for me.

Letter to Shane, the boy I sat next to at school

*We chose our tables every class, and you always chose mine,
and when I moved, you'd follow. Everyone had stopped asking
me to share a desk; they knew I wanted to sit alone. But
not you. You'd come back, repeatedly, always excited about
something: your haircut that cost eight pounds, an action figure
of Aquaman, a video of* The Best Goals. *I thought you were
a stupid kid, and had other things on my mind. I didn't want
to talk to anyone.*

*One maths class I warned that if you followed me, I would
stab you. It looks pretty mad now I've written it. You know
what happened after. I remember you smelled of roast chicken
crisps, and I hated it. I don't know why. I'm not trying to
paint myself as some cut-price Camus* L'etranger, *but that
was the final indignity, to be continually subject to the
roast-chicken-crisp smell, and I took my compass in my fist
and hammered it deep in your belly button. You didn't make
any noise, apart from a funny breath, a breath with a vault
halfway through, a breath that had realised something big
about itself. Your mouth was open, and blood started to blot
your white shirt, drawing grain lines in the cotton. I was
shocked too. It spread, growing light pink, like spilled Ribena.
I don't remember exactly what you said about me, but you
weren't wrong. And you didn't sit next to me again.*

The lesson is clear: maths needs to be banned in the classroom.

I was so confused as to why you always sat and talked with me. I gave nothing back. Did you just like my company? Strange that the possibility never occurred to me. I didn't even realise I had problems until it was spelled out in that blot. The sight changed something, and my revulsion was instructive. I wouldn't spill anyone else's blood after that.

I'm sorry I did that. I truly hope you weren't left with scars of any kind. To be honest, I think what I really want to say is thanks for not telling the teacher. My problems could have got a lot worse if you had, and incidents like that can change the course of a childhood. You had no reason to protect me, but you did anyway, even after I rejected and cut you, and you remained a better person. Not such a stupid kid after all.

If you ever read this, let's have a drink sometime.

One of many...[faded ghost text from previous/next page bleeding through]

8

How to Let Go

Sorry, but do you know who I am? Do you know who you're speaking to? I am the face of Arla Dairy milk, or was for a time, at least in the Bangladesh territory. At least, I think I was. I never actually saw that advert. A friend texted me once to say it was airing on the Asian network, when they were at their parents' house. Unless that was Tolly Boy Rice, who had hired me to play a father of four. The casting prompted a little existential crisis once I realised that, given my age, it wasn't unreasonable. Jealousy too, when I saw how much attention the rice was getting on set. Personal make-up artists, plural, tweaking the position of individual grains with tweezers, jewelling the pile with morsels of red pepper. Even a personal steamer, directing a hose of vapour over the bowl before every take.

Like the rice, I'd been hot once too. I achieved the ideal acting career, but in reverse: taking to the field with great acclaim, before descending into journeyman roles, and ultimately playing second fiddle to a biryani. Straight out of drama school, I'd signed with one of the most powerful agents in the business, who operated out of a gymnasium-sized office fringed with hanging plants and succulents. I'd pop in every now and then just to steal the toilet paper, which was enriched with natural butters. We'd have meetings the only purpose of which was to tell me how great I was, and ask what I wanted to do. I'd take my shoes off and put my feet up, wanting to be at home in the feeling.

Within a few months, I landed my first job. A lead role with the Royal Shakespeare Company is a dream gig for an actor at any point in their career. *The Indian Boy* was a uniquely brilliant new play, a modern retelling of Shakespeare's *A Midsummer Night's Dream*, focused on the changeling who is fought over by the king and queen of the fairies. The play placed this feral child, literally raised by animals, in a psychiatric unit as doctors try to socialise him. Rona Munro's script was a wonderful, layered exploration of what it means to be human, and from the title page I visualised it as a giant finger crooked from the heavens, ready to hoist me skyward. *I am a changeling boy*, I thought.

From the first page it was apparent I had to make the boy mine, and a few minutes into the audition, I knew I would succeed. The lack of confidence elsewhere in my life melted away, as I swapped out my central nervous system for his, and looked out through his eyes. It helped that the character was displaced, mistrustful and mostly mute. The back of the set was a monumental cage wall, on which I clambered and perched and slithered on all fours like a gecko, more at home than I was on the ground. Prowling, the stamp of hooves, tilt of a curious bird's neck, I understood all these things, and howling too. The boy was out of his element, shrinking in the light. He could only be at ease when left alone, whispering in a way that would strike outsiders as gibberish.

When we opened, I was so in control of the character that little control was needed. It was a tap, and, turning it on, I'd feel the creature stealing over my bones. Staring out from a wave of hair grown long again for the part, it was as if I were possessed. In some strange way it was nothing to do with me, being only the steward of this very particular consciousness, though it nonetheless needed me in order to be seen. Onstage for the play's entirety, I knew I had the audience rapt, could flick thoughts into their head with the smallest gesture, or by simply shifting my attention. For once I was not scattered. I had pride in myself, and the work, and being seen.

The reviews were uniformly ecstatic. The show sold out. A magnetic field, the one that surrounds anyone in control of their career, thrummed around me. It was the Samadder CV at the top of the pile; I was being invited to the advent-calendar version of life, with a chocolate behind every door. My agent lined up meetings with influential casting directors and producers. The future yawned and touched the horizon, and for the first time looked inviting. *Acting is easy*, I thought.

The Indian Boy played in November, at Stratford-upon-Avon, Shakespeare's home town. In December, my father checked into hospital, and before January was over he was dead.

The blast took me out, caught not in my habitual crouch, but unfurled a little, ready to stand, believing everything might be okay.

Actors occupy a tragic place within the arts, in that they cannot practise their craft alone. They cannot sing to themselves, or retreat to a rose garden with a canvas. There is no joy to be had in practising monologues. They need other actors, and an audience. They exist in the minds of others or not at all, and I was exploring the second option. Flat on my back, and not getting up for anybody. It is said that in a major city you're never more than six feet away from an actor, and if you listen closely, you can hear the scuffle of their claws against the skirting. Every day they're hustling, hustling.

I was doing nothing, nothing, writing to nobody, not picking up the phone. After a full year of rumours that *The Indian Boy* might transfer to London, I accepted that it wouldn't. Too difficult to move the cage, apparently. It didn't help that I hated every other job I was sent up for, the majority of which were terrorist dramas. They differed only superficially. All had been plucked from the same script tombola, stuffed with tickets reading *sister, honour, paradise, cell, vest, mosque, mobile, detonate*. Of all the motives that teem within the human drama, revenge against the kuffar was low on my list. The fixation with intercepted text messages and glass-walled rooms bored me, the kind of boredom that is actually anger in costume. I was furious at the double standard, and people telling me it was a good time to be an Asian actor. It was hard to explain without sounding ungrateful, which doesn't mean I was wrong. What would it be like if every time a white English actor received a script, it always concerned the 1846 repeal of the Corn Laws? *You'll be playing an extremist farmer, hell-bent on reviving the Napoleonic Wars in order to push up wheat prices.* Every single one. You'd understand if their habitual response was, *This again?*

'There's enough room for everyone at the table!' people told me, which was objectively false. There were four good parts a year written for Asians, and three of them involved knowing the Urdu words for "bridge" and "midnight". I got down to the last two for a lot of jobs, but I'm not convinced this isn't something agents tell all their clients, to lower the suicide rate. You'd have a fantastic meeting about a fantastic project, hear nothing until eight months later, when you'd see it on TV, with another actor in the lead. Strategically, I decided to play possum: I would abandon hope for a while, stop trying, but only until Riz Ahmed was too famous to be going up for the same parts as me, at which point I'd swing back into the game. Which I did, only to start losing them to Dev Patel. My agent dropped me and removed my photo from their website. This didn't hurt my pride, as I had none of that left. It was, though, a blow to my ego, in the literal sense that I didn't know who I was without their initials underwriting my name.

I started to grow bitter, believing myself more talented than my peers, as the supporting evidence grew more scarce. Okay, Riz was clearly better, but why let that get in the way of the story I was telling myself? I started looking out for Danny Boyle on television or in print. He would always repeat the same anecdote about *Slumdog Millionaire*, which I'd gone up for. About how it had been impossible to find any Asian actors who weren't Bollywood beefcake types, until his daughter recommended a skinny unknown from her favourite teen drama. 'WHY ARE YOU LYING, DANNY BOYLE?' I would shout in the newsagent as I was erased from the narrative. Stupid Dev Patel. Why was he given so many chances, and allowed to improve on the job?

I'd moved back in with my mother, for a much-needed 'pit stop' of about fourteen months, in which I took the opportunity to 'recharge my battery'.* Despondency mouldered to resentfulness and desperation. I registered with every casting website going, checking every box in the skills section: unicycle, rat-trapping, playing the spoons, I was skydive-certified and spoke Swahili. I'd take any audition, just get me in the door.

Having transferred to a more boutique agency, I told

---

* See entries on: breakdown, punching bread in supermarkets.

them I didn't want to go up for any more shows with bombs in them. They did their best, and there were some roles. I landed parts as a pick-up artist in *Doctors*, a smooth suitor in *Emmerdale*, a doctor in *Coronation Street*. I took a picture of myself on set at the latter, outside its iconic pub, the Rovers Return. They serve real beer there, which apparently tastes better than any in the whole country, because they clean the taps once a week.* But none of it was enough to survive on, and the fact that I was temperamentally not suited to any of this was becoming harder to ignore.

'Find a job you love, and you'll never work a day in your life' had started to sound extremely ominous. I was already working less than a month a year. For many, following that career path means temping on reception desks, working fringe shows evenings and weekends unpaid, for the exposure. It means never allowing yourself a holiday on the off-chance your agent calls because there is a schools tour of *Treasure Island* workshopping at short notice, and apparently you play the Northumbrian smallpipe, or so it says on Spotlight.

Hitting rock bottom can have a certain nobility, but my lowest points in acting were so absurd I was denied even this. That's what struck me as I stood in a cluttered room near Euston that was apparently functioning as a theatre

---

* I didn't taste it though. I'm keeping my body pure, so when jihad comes for the infidel, I can get out of the way quicker.

bar, box office, foyer and props storage. The barman –
who I'm strongly convinced was also the building's artistic
director and janitor – wordlessly directed me to a narrow
flight of stairs leading downwards through the doorway
behind him. It had been fitted out as a cupboard front,
which was disorienting. Hard to feel positive about auditions accessed via a cupboard staircase, as if success here
were Narnia-shaped.

I landed in a cold, low-ceilinged room with damp
flowering across the walls and a good collection of mops
strutted in corners.

'Coo-ee!' a voice assailed me. Coo-ee? A bulbous
woman with a sprig of spiked hair was tipping towards
me. 'I'm Harper,' she said in a breathless but perky
Canadian accent, 'won't you come on in?' There was
something about her of the onion. There was no way to
come in any more than I was, the basement being an undi-
vided floor, akin to a deserted car park. Set arbitrarily in
the space was a school table, to which Harper ushered me,
introducing a woman with her hair pulled in a tight bun.
'Anastasia is my other hand.'

'Let's hear your piece,' said Anastasia, who clearly had a
policy about small talk. I was anxious to make a good
impression. I can't remember if this audition had come
about via my trawler net of lies, or a chain of tip-offs,
recommendations from friends unable to take the job
themselves, but it certainly didn't feel like a sure thing.
They never did any more. Like others before me, I'd taken

to referring to these try-outs as "meetings", to kid myself I had some status, that I was an equal player, here to hammer out a deal.

It's hard not to be your own worst enemy in this business. Having landed a single line in a film, you stay up nights wondering how to deliver it with such magnetism that any producers watching will be whiplashed by the raw charisma of Man with Cup. You're in a similar bind when choosing audition pieces: torn between playing safe and meeting the director's expectations, or revolutionising the form. That's why I was second-guessing myself, standing in a lower Camden basement, limbering up an interpretive-gesture adaptation of Walt Whitman's 'Scented Herbage of My Breast'. It had felt right when I did it in my bedroom. But that shouldn't be anyone's guiding philosophy.

'Leaves from you I yield, I write, to be perused best afterwards,' I warbled, a sweep of the arms inviting my audience to consider their relationship to time. In this I was successful, as it became quickly apparent they were in a rush.

'That's just great,' Harper decided in the first brief pause. 'We've only got twenty minutes, so shall we dive in with the puppets?' Apparently, I'd missed a meeting.

'I don't remember any mention of puppets. I'm certain I would have remembered that.'

'Yah! A mix of musical and puppetry, full-body to sock. Shall we dive in?'

'We're forty per cent there with the funding, but we're booking the tour now to keep momentum going,' Anastasia added, seeing that I was lost. 'Six venues in west Scotland, driving back to Cumbernauld each night. Could be a tough crowd, so the politics won't be overt, but the aim is to push buttons. How do you feel about puppet nudity?' It was not something I'd ever considered.

'It's not something I've ever considered.'

'Great! Let's get you a partner. Would you like to choose?' offered Harper, introducing a mound of over-sized grotesques.

I thrust my hand into the miscellaneous clump and pulled something out. Unchosen puppets tumbled down either side. These were unconventional puppets, I could see that. There was a Playboy bunny, a radish with a mouth but no eyes, one that looked like Hitler. Gazing up at me from the floor, with its squashed approximation of a face, was a felt cock. This was a minefield. Wondering how to avoid the contempt payments that would surely be sought by the Whitman estate if they got wind of this, I settled on a monumental sea clam. Its umber body was corrugated with dun fur, parted by wavy lips and a vivid red interior.

'A man who's up for a challenge. We like!' bubbled Harper, senselessly. 'Let's hear your piece again, this time from Esmerelda.'

There really is no ceiling to the indignities most performers endure, being perpetually youngish and in need of the money. I remember earlier years in this profession, living in Eliza's house of theatrical waifs and strays. She was working as a director, and in addition to me there was another actor, a designer and a playwright. All of us earning less than a living wage, not claiming benefits, because our jobs were a social luxury. Persuading letting agents to take us on was an uphill task. We were each other's references, impersonating previous landlords, employers, Dickensian benefactors, anything to keep a clawhold on the bottom rung. So much is bearable in youth. The thrill of newness, of taking possession of our lives, can lend hardship and prosperity alike a not-dissimilar flush. Our electricity ran off a meter which we could often only afford to charge by fifty pence each time. You might as well feed a car a thimble of petrol every mile. Blackouts were frequent, so we learned to navigate by the light of our phones like miners, tipping coins out on the table by candlelight. Heating was an unaffordable extravagance, although the large house was so cold our breath would steam as we lay in bed, as if the souls were leaving our bodies. Every morning I awoke to a face full of the bobble hat Eliza slept in, assuming for an alarming moment that I was spooning a homeless person. One bone-crinkling winter, we calculated that if we shared pasta, the house could afford two hours of heating twice a week, for which everyone had to be in. Christmas they were, those four non-consecutive hours.

I turned Esmerelda over, finding an operational cleft

on her base, marked by an elasticated collar. I billed my hand and went in. I don't know if you've ever attempted, under pressure, to ventriloquise a clam the size of your head in front of strangers in the service of an unorthodox reading of *Leaves of Grass*.

'Really try to punch the comedy,' advised Anastasia, unhelpfully.

The hard part wasn't locating bankable gags in Whitman's transcendental elegy. It was moving the clam's mouth. The lips were spongy, neither fully closed nor open. I rubbed my thumb and fingers, like a cartoon gangster demanding payment. I quacked my hand, turned it sideways. The overall effect was of something unspeakable, struggling to be born.

'Death is beautiful from you,' I started. Esmerelda gurned and mashed her gum. 'What indeed is finally beautiful except Death and Love?'

'Concentrate more on closing the mouth than opening,' Harper advised. 'Also, don't move so much. Let Esme – she's the one we're interested in.'

'Comedy!' reminded Anastasia. I spun the mental Rolodex, imagining how a sea clam would talk. All I could think of was Davy Crockett, but had no idea what he sounded like, or even who he was really. A pirate?

'*Arrrrr,* how solemn it grows, to ascend to the atmosphere of *lubbers,*' I growled, sounding like an Irish alcoholic. At least Harper was smiling.

'Punch the double entendres, anywhere you can,' Anastasia commanded. Was this really what I was doing with my life? If people spoke of me in my absence, wondering what I was up to, would I be happy for this moment to come up? It dawned on me that nobody spoke of me in my absence.

'I am determin'd to unbaaare this breast of mine.' I winked, accent slipping, as if we were now auditioning *Carry On Up the West Country*. 'Spring away from the conceal'd heart,' I yelped, trying to make it sound like 'fart.' This was almost physically painful.

'Let Esme! Let Esme!' yelped Harper, as if someone had stuck her with an epi pen.

'You're not funny – she's funny,' reminded Anastasia.

'Do not fold yourself so in your pink-tinged roots!' What was this, Larry Grayson at the hairdresser's? How long would they let this go on? 'Oh *burning* and *throbbing*,' I groaned, hoisting my fist like a rampant phallus. 'I will raise *immortal reverberations . . .*'

'That's so great,' cooed Harper kindly. 'The Lady Garden is tricky to get the hang of.'

Lady Garden? What did that mean? My brain felt like stretched-out putty. I saw, so obvious and yet too late, that I had my hand inside an anatomically exaggerated vagina. It didn't impact much on my reading, more or less set by now.

'It does not *laaast* so very long,' I finished, in the voice of a sad, horny pirate. My fist had wilted, Esmerelda staring at me utterly disassociated.

Falling out of love with acting had been a slow process of estrangement. Difficult to know when to leave, but fairly straightforward to know that I should. It boiled down to one question, I realised. How does this make me feel, most of the time? The career's limitations that I once found charming beyond reason now struck me as simply unreasonable. My thoughts grew painfully widescreen: I couldn't live my life like this. When an actor has this realisation, as many will, there is no other option. She will spend at least another seven years struggling by, because doing what is best is agonising.

A performer never stops wanting to perform – the connection, elevation of the moment and search for emotional truth make them feel alive like nothing else. A dangerous predicament, in a career where 90 per cent of the workforce is out of a job, feeling unconnected, un-alive. Actors are, at heart, fun-aholics.

After the break-up with Eliza, I started to wonder about other things I thought I couldn't lose. Top of the list was acting. I loved it, but it didn't look after me. It broke my heart a different way every month. How would it feel to let a vocation fall away? It was impossible to imagine, but we often have to do things we can't imagine. Imagination is not necessarily a criterion of growth. I wondered how my stars were aligned. Were they up there, smashing lumps out of each other, breaking into magnetic dust? How did astrology work, exactly? What if this career dissatisfaction was a rush of blood, one impulse to self-sabotage following another? If only there was a sign.

'Got a meeting, vee hush hush. Can't say what it is!' my agent whispered, which was a problem, as that was literally her job. 'All right – it's Take That!'

'What is?'

'They were a boyband in the nineties. Gary Barlow—'

'No, I know who they are. What's it to me?'

'They're looking for dancers, but you don't need to be able to dance.' This was the sort of cryptic briefing you'd get a lot. *They're looking for singers, but not singers. They want someone beautiful, but not so you'd notice.*

For fuck's sake, I thought, striding along the upper floor of a dance academy. The long, panelled corridors streamed with seven-year-old girls in pink satin, like a cruise ship being flooded with breast-cancer awareness. So many noticeboards. I found the room. It was palatial, with a small group standing against the mirror on the far wall, very far away, like Live Aid. Casting directors have made up their mind within three seconds of your walking in the door, we'd always been told. There may be more disempowering workplace truisms, but that one was definitely down there. In theory, I could have lost the job seven times before I made it over to them. When I eventually arrived, I was instructed to sit in the lotus position on the floor, and mime playing sitar to a Beatles track. Ahhh. So that's why I was here. To add Indian flavour to a number on tour. They were going to have dancers emerging from an elephant and, I don't know, throwing mango chutney around.

When the track started, I plucked abjectly at an imaginary sitar and wondered whether all the wrong turns I'd made in life would be enough to fill a quarry, and how big a quarry was.

'Wait until the sitar part starts,' one of the men instructed, with slight impatience.

'But I'm not actually playing anything,' I said. For some reason, I was also not playing it quite badly. To prove I knew that sitars were very big I was miming something the length of a grandfather clock, which I couldn't control. Splayed fingers struggling to reach strings, me toppling under the weight. The men were looking at me in great confusion. They didn't ask why, when asked to imagine an instrument, I imagined one I couldn't play. I didn't explain to them that I was very, very bored. 'You're welcome,' I said, before they had thanked me for my time.

My agent rang a few days later. Actually, her assistant, asking if I could print more colour headshots and send them over. I told her I was quitting acting, which sounded like an overreaction. I was scared of my agent, and thought the news would be best if it didn't come from me. I could hear the colour draining from the other end of the line, and sometimes picture the follow-up conversation. *Did he say when to expect the pictures? No, he said he was leaving and never to call him again.*

It wasn't the bravest way out, but I'd never been good at goodbyes. I was terrified of such a definitive break. Unsure how to support myself, though the fear ran deeper than the material. Who would I be now? Was I going to have another breakdown? At that moment, a perfect capsule of memory returned to me. Something Lily had said, a decade ago, as we watched the chrysalises hanging from their twigs. Inside, she told me, the caterpillar's body was dying. That form had to die, and there would be a time when it was reduced to liquid, possessing no solidity at all. Yet from this absolute breakdown, this total dissolution, a new body would be built, one that had dominion over the air.

It was unthinkable to leave behind what I thought I would be doing for the rest of my life. Yet equally unimaginable, the relief of taking a step to free myself. I wanted to perform, but I wanted to be respected more. The industry was not a kind one, I suffered in it, and I needed that to be over. It made sense to me finally, how you could let an old life flutter down, and be carried away by the water. I could perhaps now intuit what Lily did on the Amsterdam bridge when she threw her portfolio into the canal, realising that jobs or people or lifestyles that suit us better are trying to finding their way to us, but first we have to clear the space.

I texted Amish Tom, asking if I could fly out to visit him in Spain. I had no plan, only a desperate need to get away, to mark this year of tumultuous change. I was also wondering if travel was the answer everyone said it was. Tedious types, who wore scarves indoors, were always gumming on about how they had found themselves at an ashram in Pune. It always struck me as a surprising place to have left oneself. I rarely left the city, never travelled alone for its own sake. Perhaps the tonic to this period of letting go was wanderlust. There was also the possibility that for the first time in my life, I was scared to be alone.

The plane wasn't due to take off until the afternoon, so I passed the day running laps of the park, hoping constant motion could switch off my worried brain. I ran twenty-five kilometres, which took all morning, and I only managed to catch the budget flight because it was delayed. More than a half-marathon, I explained to Amish Tom when I touched down in Gibraltar. 'Why did you do that?' was all he could say, and I could not summon a response. We were men, after a fashion, and did not speak easily about emotional catastrophe, or demented physical exertions suggestive of it.

From the air, Gibraltar looked like a giant monitor lizard crawling out of the sea, getting ready to hump the mainland. Amish had been out here for months, teaching English to Spanish children. I believe he was teaching them English from old Chartist pamphlets, but it made no odds, the way he described it. The six-year-olds in his

class would listen politely to anything, as long as he promised to play Ed Sheeran songs off his mobile phone in
the breaks. Recounting this, he wore the expression of
someone passing a gallstone. Those kids clearly had him
wrapped around their jammy little fingers.[*]

He was searching for a path too. He'd quit his job in
the UK, and was looking for something new, to which this
was just a stopgap, or would be once he'd figured out the
next step. He looked frazzled, his thinking more scram-
bled than I'd known it to be.

'Someone was telling me Gibraltar is called the Rock
after the actor Dwayne Johnson,' Amish told me. 'Which
doesn't sound accurate. Dwayne "Gibraltar" Johnson? Is
that his real name?'

He was living and working just opposite the island, on
the mainland in Algeciras. I'd envisioned warm, scented
nights, sharing velvety red wine by candlelight with local
señoritas. But Algeciras is a port city, and most people we
encountered were grown-ups who worked haulage. There
wasn't much to do in the evenings, Amish admitted, and
it rained a lot. His best friend on the island was an ex-pat
conspiracy theorist who believed 9/11 was 'probably an
inside job, but also a distraction from what's really going
on'. The whole place reeked with the kind of maleness
I had sworn to avoid. It touched a particular horror in
me, this depressing atmosphere of straight men without

---

[*] They don't have jam in Spain though. Quince paste, perhaps.

partners, virile years behind them, with only each other for company. Looking for novelty, we climbed the mountainous steps of the fort on Gibraltar, overrun by wild Barbary macaques, who didn't stir or even blink as we passed, except to make unpredictable lunges at our bags. They reminded me of aggressive, depressed old men, even the lady monkeys. It felt like *The Island of Doctor Moreau*, as if the place itself had gone mad, left out in the sun. At the top of the Rock, we looked out at the broad horizon and glittering water, the Korean cargo ships hanging there like barracuda. The shipping company had gone bankrupt, Amish explained, and these abandoned vessels now lurked off the coasts of many countries, like ghosts, with no purpose, and no one to claim them. I knew how they felt.

It was clear I needed a change of scene, and the next week Amish informed me he'd booked us tickets to somewhere more postcard-worthy. He was as good as his word. On a glorious sunburst of an afternoon, we sped north by train. In the lemon trees and bougainvillea, swallows bombed from bough to bough, and the air through the small window smelled of oranges. I had the backwards seat, each pleasing sight rushing by, rapidly receding from view as soon as it had appeared, demanding to be let go. I began to unclench a little. Amish and I gossiped about our university friend Chris, who was preparing for his marriage, already on his second or third child, we couldn't keep track. Chris's grown-up commitments stood in stark relief to the paths we'd taken, so I suppose we were really talking about ourselves.

I realised Amish probably didn't know why my long-term relationship had ended, and we would probably never talk about it. Equally, I knew nothing about why he hadn't chosen a partner all these years, though every girl we knew was in love with him and his stupid Panama hat. I began to grasp the possible benefit of male company, a sort of safety valve. Mates happy to overlook the hole in the centre of your chest, the one you could see clean through. But maybe our friendship was capable of more.

'Do you want a family?' I asked. Amish stiffened.

'Maybe. Do you?' I had never been asked this, except in conversations with extremely high stakes. I tried to think down, beyond my instinctive rejection.

'What if I had a child and . . . it thought like me?' I'd never formulated this anxiety, even to myself. Discomfited by the confessional turn, Amish battled himself to give me a straight answer.

'It would be half you and half someone else. And it would also be its own person,' he reminded me. 'You don't know how these things turn out.'

'What if it looked like me?'

'What if it did? You're not *that* ugly,' he said. It was very moving.

It really is about the journey, not the destination. Ronda was a stunning place, a town bridging a precipitous gorge. Buildings sat flush to the brink of the cliff, hovering over disaster, and all the more breathtaking for it. Hemingway had arrived here as a journalist at the outbreak of the Spanish Civil War, and described it as the perfect honeymoon town. I walked its streets with my old friend, neither of us knowing what the next year held for us, let alone our lives. For that evening, it was okay not to know. We rambled without a map, pausing to let a long stream of cyclists pass, ducking when the mood took us into tiny bars for wine and vegetarian tapas, which is basically potato salad. It felt far away, the uncertainty and mess. That didn't feel completely like a good thing. I wanted to take ownership of the losses, make space for the future. Maybe travelling was what everyone said it was, but I needed to go home.

I'd always been paralysed by big decisions. I lived with the never-ending suspicion that Disaster lived next door, and was sharpening her knives through the night. I fretted constantly, dealing in counterfactuals and what-ifs and hidden costs, feeling trapped by my own life, trying to chart its perfect course. I know others do the same, longing for versions of themselves they were never able to give birth to: the one who has children or the one who doesn't, who stays or goes, who does this job or that. But we can never know how things would have turned out. Those other lives are weightless. We'll never know where those paths would lead, or if those other versions are any happier. We don't know where our current path is leading either.

The best thing I could do for my depression, much of which sprung from existential anxiety, was commit to my decisions, I was realising. Give up the what-if game. It's okay to change one's mind, leave relationships and careers behind, to let things go that once meant everything. The only course to avoid is passive regret, feeling life has been done to you, or that you made the wrong choice, and must always bear the cost. There is no right path, only how you walk it.

Back home, I picked up my phone, and made two calls. The first to a therapist, whom I asked for an appointment. It was ten years nearly to the day since my father had died. I'd been using guilt as a way to keep him alive, and he wouldn't have wanted that and it was making me very sad. I wanted to separate my grief from my regret, and honour him in better ways. I meditated on the months after his death, when I was heading for a major depression and believed the world had nothing left to show me but pain. In that same time, I saw a woman on Peckham Rye check a shopping receipt then screw it up, chuck it into the air and try to head it into a bin. Just like a schoolboy, except she was an elderly Ghanaian woman.* A ludicrous sight, and I started laughing – the kind of laugh that gets throttled in your nose and has to explode

---

* I had to report her to the council because she actually missed, and it constituted littering.

out of your mouth, and every other orifice. I'd felt so treacherous for the laugh, as if sorrow could be shrugged off, just like that. Yet my father had never stopped appreciating absurdity in the midst of seriousness, though I blocked us from sharing that. It could be how I remembered him now.

The second call was to Eliza. I'd finally come around to her way of thinking.

Eliza had come up with this plan about forty-eight hours into our break-up, and the idea had her stamp all over it: one third brilliant, two thirds crazy. 'We'll invite our families – okay, my family, plus your mum, and everyone we know, and ceremonially separate. I think it will be helpful for us to properly say goodbye to each other.' I wasn't keen; it sounded like it would involve a lot of talking. 'There will be *so* much talking,' confirmed Eliza. 'And everyone will cry.'

The novelty of this emotionally virgin territory was appealing. But it also sounded overwhelming and threatening, and I'd dragged my heels at the time. Did she want to denounce me? Had I been so terrible? Isn't it every girl's dream, to be turned into their partner's mother, then have the Oedipal drama of separation played out in their relationship? But no, she was sincere and open. She talked about how the language around break-ups and being dumped always sounded violent or one-sided, which didn't reflect our experience. Was it possible to honour what had been, she'd been thinking, to symbolically transition out of coupledom in a healthy way, and convince everyone it wasn't weird? That last would be the hardest part. The spectre of Gwyneth Paltrow hung over the idea, like a mist of reiki-infused delusion. Still, even a stopped clock, and all that. We hadn't seen each other or communicated in months. We still felt connected, but separate and robust enough to see this through.

Many were unsure why we'd want to see it through. The invitations met a mixed response, some people being sceptical, others outright wondering if we'd been inducted into a cult. *Is someone making you cut ties with your family too? Blink your left eye if you need help.* Eliza explained to them that it would be a sort of anti-wedding, the ceremony we never got to have, but instead of a cake, everybody would leave with a heightened sense of loss. She was so persuasive, everyone eventually bought this as a good thing.

It was nice for me to spend this time with her again, planning the event and shopping it around. Living alone, my heart had been snagging on items of hers and breaking all over again, like stitches that couldn't heal. There was also relief, in no longer being the cause of her pain. Looking at Eliza as she spoke to Ellie, the friend who would act as our officiant, I realised I wanted only good things for her, even without me. In achieving everything it was obviously she would, I would be left behind, and I realised with a jolt that I didn't mind. I'd grown a new dimension of loving. It was like going to the shoe shop as a child and discovering you'd gone up a size since last time.

'What do you want from the ceremony?' Ellie was asking, over a turmeric latte equidistant between our homes. She was an engineer who danced, and perfect for this groundbreaking ceremony of emotional innovention.

'I'd like to thank everyone who supported me through the months when I didn't think I'd make it,' replied Eliza. 'And to ask Rhik's friends to keep helping him.' I pushed down a squash ball that had announced itself in my throat. I was already tightening up, wondering if this was a mistake.

'And you, what do you want?' asked Ellie, turning to me.

'I want everyone to leave promptly. No hangers-on.' They were looking at me with relief, as if a hard decision had been proven right.

There wasn't a cloud in the sky on the day we did it. Thirty guests crowded the flat, spilling out onto the terrace with glasses and olive tapenade in hand. Mostly Eliza's friends at first. Vicki – sorry, Victoria now – did show up eventually, but almost immediately sliced herself open cutting a baguette into coins. She was dripping blood all over the floor, and in the hummus. I decided not to interpret this metaphorically. Kate – formerly Chris's childhood sweetheart, but now a delinquent adult and friend in her own right – showed up extremely late, having woken up on a stranger's sofa in Edmonton forty minutes before the start. Despite her barrelling in reeking of vodka and apology, it was touching she'd made the journey, as she'd no doubt been medically dead an hour ago. My mother was there too, sitting on a chair in the corner. An awkward presence for me, who was not used to sharing any of my life with her. Luckily there was so much else to do, attending to other guests' plates, slipping in between people, swimming upstream, going down to check the gate was still wedged open. Eventually I went over to her and gruffly asked if she wanted anything.

'I want you to sit here and say hello to me,' she said. There wasn't time, I told her.

I went over to see the Scottish Nancy Sykes instead. She'd had her wound dressed now, and was turning the chinaware over to peer at the backstamps.

'This is reproduction Spode, so you know.' I didn't, and whatever she was talking about sounded gynaecological.

I was strung out on the weirdness of what was about to happen, and exactly what it was we were asking our friends to witness. Was it right to celebrate this ending, which was another station on my campaign to be left behind? People younger than me owned homes and pushed buggies, while I was still figuring out what I wanted. I was worried too, about speaking my feelings in front of these people that knew me best. Worried about so many of them in the flat, worried about how it would feel when they left.

'Would you ever get married?' I asked Victoria, knowing the answer, but needing some solidarity.

'Yeah,' she said, after considering. Not the answer I'd

anticipated from the garter queen of Edinburgh. I looked at her, in her vintage serge trousers, the eighteen-year-old girl who was now somehow in her thirties. She'd got out of acting sooner than me, realising that to stay was self-destructive. She now had some sort of actual job involving words and design, which exercised her brain and let her travel, with responsibility and colleagues. She had a long-term partner, and a penchant for novellas about spoilt, *fin-de-siècle* lesbians. I'd spent so many tormented hours wondering if it was possible to ever really change, and here was my beautiful friend, showing me it was impossible for a person not to.

'Isn't it a woman-as-property, bourgeois system that kind of only exists to fund tax breaks for, like, so the government can keep us indoors?' My words were a sucked mint, rolling around the floor picking up dust and hair.

'I think it would be romantic,' she replied, sucking an olive off a skewer.

'Guess I hadn't thought of that.'

The ceremony began with a speech from Ellie that I can barely remember because I started crying as soon as she opened her mouth.

'The worst feeling isn't pain,' she said to everyone present, 'but the loneliness that accompanies it.' *Jesus Christ*, I thought. The intensity was only slightly remitted when a courier let himself in to watch a portion of the ceremony, holding a kilo of penny sweets I'd ordered online, at a low point the previous night. The delivery turnover was shorter than I'd anticipated. Too short really.

Eliza addressed her family and friends, thanked them for helping her through the last few months. The little future that was snuffed out affected them too. The sun beat down, though it was early in the year, and people hid behind sunglasses, poking fingers under frames. The fact there was no convention around this type of event, no comfortable tradition, raised its aliveness. I suppose they were thinking of their own obscure losses, lesser witnessed. Sadness glinted the air like a dewed web.

As she spoke, I thought of the time that sorrow had lifted, when I met this slight girl with untameable curls, and an untameable urge to fix things. I remembered one evening when we were returning from a night out, running through the rain. Skipping in front of an oncoming car in front of our block of flats, we saw a snail – in fact two – crushed on the tarmac, jagged shards pressed through their flesh. Looking back at the pavement, a strange sight – around thirty more snails on the pavement, a caravan of mysterious purpose. Emerging from the park, summoned by the drumbeat of droplets. Pushing their heads out and silvering forwards, they were heading for the road, where, every few seconds cars were careening past. Eliza had looked at me through sodden hair, streetlight reflecting off her wet face.

'We have to save them,' she said, already rushing back across. Fifteen minutes in the deluge plucking the snails from the tarmac, from which they unstuck reluctantly, like suction-cupped bath toys. Starting at the kerb edge and working back to the fence in shifts, with soaking feet, we returned the escargatoire to the park, through the entrance thirty feet away, one by one, turning them in the opposite direction to danger. *Be safe*, she called to them. What I felt for her was larger than life itself.

On the terrace, my face was soaked again, this time clear for everyone to see. Eliza was speaking to me now, though it was almost impossible for us to make eye contact. My mother was sitting on the ground, in purple sunglasses, thinking.

'I'm not the same person I was when I went into this relationship, you know,' Eliza said. I stiffened, couldn't help it. Waited to hear that I was ruinous, had cracked her good heart, wasted her time. I raised my eyes to hers. 'I have a foundation in me now which feels solid and strong and is built of your love.' Her words were one more way to save me, one last time. Without bitterness, she lifted the burden of being the bad guy from my shoulders, because she knew I couldn't carry it. 'I will always be thankful that, for a time, we spent our lives together.'

I made a largely unintelligible speech in response, and signed for the penny sweets. We asked forgiveness for any hurt caused, and gave it, and wished each other happiness to come. No score-keeping any more. There was a ceremonial untwining of a braid, the separate strings of which we wore as bracelets. (A few days later I was to burn mine, as well as my eyelashes, chest and head hair, in a propane backdraft. But I chose not to interpret this metaphorically.) When it was done, Ellie announced that everyone had to leave, Eliza's friends to one pub, mine to another, where I could join them if I wished. She strongly advised that I did.

Through baguette blood, sun sweat and lethally dehydrating quantities of tears, we let each other go. Although my loneliness would take a lot longer to soften, I felt the jaws unmesh. In an alienated, technological time, it feels important to hang on to the ones who really see us. Being 'friends with your ex' isn't always possible or advisable. But where affection beats in any form, and pardon is at all possible, I'd urge you to seek it. There's no such thing as the perfect relationship, but I'm proud of the one we had, for the distance travelled together, even for the journey's end.

That's how it can be with letting go, the best we can ask. We do it so our hands are open to receive the new. We don't know what shape it will take, or what it will require of us, weary of the starting again, knowing only that our hands must be open. We must stay open.

The day after the event, picking my way through the pregnant, particular silence of a room cleared of a crowd, I noticed someone had watered the neglected basil plant on the sill, and I think I know who. What had been dying already showed new green, and perfume. I'm choosing to interpret this metaphorically.

Letter to Eliza

*When we broke up, it was like someone had ripped the soles
from my shoes. Suddenly I could feel everything the ground
gave me, except stability. Every stone, bump and needle,
every step.*

*I miss you and all the things you did for me, talking
me off a ledge twice a day, knocking the wrong opinions out.
You taught me there was such a thing as the future, and to be
less afraid of it. I learned how to be a little more kind. I also
learned that if a person buys another person top-of-the-range
headphones as a gift, and they routinely ignore the signature
noise-cancelling feature – the only reason to buy that
particular pair of headphones – that is their business and
I should let it go.*

*More than those things, I miss being so close I could see
and honour the tiny facets that made an Eliza. I miss cooking
for her and making her laugh. It was nice being that person,
though I wasn't all the time. I'm sorry for all the horrible
mistakes I made, the times you cried, and felt unwelcome in
your own home. It's too late now, and you wouldn't want
me to, but I punish myself for that all the time.*

*You once said you were worried you held no mystery for
me. That there was nothing in reserve. And it's true you'd
laid out your mind comprehensively within the first forty-eight
hours of our meeting. But I didn't know how to tell you that*

you are and will always be a bottomless mystery to me.
(Should probably rephrase that. Your bottom is nice.) What
I mean is that the goodness of you, the goodness that runs
straight through and shines from you, I could never get tired
of trying to understand where it comes from. I thought
everyone was like me: scaled beneath the skin. But no – you
are the funniest, wisest person that ever paired a dress with
Converse. You should know that you're still my hero.

I'm sorry I wasn't able to give you everything you want.
I hope you can forgive the hurt, and that what will last is
love. And I promise, you will have everything you want from
this life: a house, laughter, pets, the satisfaction of seeing things
get better. And a family. You are a force of nature. God knows
why I deserved to have you blow into my life and start moving
the furniture around, but I will always be grateful. And so,
so proud of you.

Anthea Turner

9

How to Work

Back in my mother's bed, but this time with gangster rapper Ice Cube.

'Fuck you.'

'That's the *worst* thing anyone's ever said to you?'

'There's nothing worse, man.' Ice Cube spoke slowly, being cool, or stoned, or both. Or maybe he was confused by my interview technique, which involved only asking super-intense questions of a generally negative bent.

'How often do you cry?'

He wasn't answering in full or supplying details. After each gnomic reply, I was left circling my hands, as if wafting the aroma of soup, willing him to keep talking. I hate doing these things over the phone. It's the only reason I was in my mother's house, as she has a landline, with better reception. 'What makes you cry, Cube?'

'Something that makes me sad.'

'Right,' I said, wondering how this exchange was going to look in print.

'Or happy. You can cry from happiness.'

'I never cry from happiness,' I said sceptically. 'What's the closest you've come to death?' He recounted the story of being hit by an ice-cream truck when he was five. I was expecting a description of cold metal in the Compton rain, which says more about me than him, but at least I was finally having an effect. He was on the first day of a holiday in Maui, but from the sound of his voice, also possibly the last.

'I guess I worry about not providing for my family. I'm only one man, and I don't want what I've made to die with me.' Bingo.

This is why I got into this work, to meet celebrities, and leave them feeling sad. It's a tough job but . . . well, nobody's got to do it, but I choose to. I look back at my scribbled notes, and realise the questions are too miserable to be printed. I ask instead if he has any life advice. Cube considers, and brightens. 'Don't be a pussy all your life. Sometimes you gotta be a dick, and you gotta get hard.'

Totally unprintable, but there was a poetry to it. And that was enough for me.

I'd never planned on being a journalist, if that's what I am, which I'm not. Newspapers weren't consumed much in our house as far as I recall.* I never saw journalists in their

---

* I remember the TV news, back when the news was boring, like listening to someone describe long division. Nowadays it's *Mad Max* in suits.

natural habitat until my second year of drama school. Drama Centre had moved buildings at that point, setting up on the upper floors of a converted print factory in Farringdon, with long windows that looked into a news-room opposite. During ballet classes, swinging a studious thigh through a *battement en cloche*, I'd stare through the long, mullioned windows at the people in that office. Frowning at computers, or jabbing flapjacks at each other during walk-and-talks, they were the epitome of grown-ups. Anyone not wearing a leotard looked like a grown-up to me.

I thought no more about it until it became clear that acting didn't pay the rent with the regularity my landlord liked. If only I'd worked on my *pas des chats* until it was perfect. I took temp work wherever I could get it, sitting on reception, cleaning toilets, handing out ice-cream samples, though not all on the same day. Saying yes to everything, because I had to. When I was given a day's work on the switchboard of a newspaper, the address was familiar.

It was a new kind of thrill, walking up to the reception desk of the *Guardian*, asking to be let in. My father had died, but I was not yet at breakdown. I could still function. I was sent to work alongside middle-aged women in a room that had the air of a World War II code-breaking bunker, ranks of permed WRENs cryptoanalysing German weather reports. I liked that job, as far as jobs go. An unctuousness entered me when I picked up the receiver. A new sound came purring up from my chest, the words a cream top scraped off a column of smarm. *Goodmorninguardianandobserver*, I would murmur. I'd often dreamed of being a butler, and this was not dissimilar. I liked attaching myself to the prestigious name, feeling its mantle settle around my shoulders, becoming the oracle. A kind of acting, but isn't everything? The feeling of being solid and capable was not one I'd felt in a while.

I wasn't actually capable: repeatedly disconnecting calls, or putting messages for the foreign desk through to the maintenance department, but that hardly mattered; they could call back and get someone better. Besides, a massive proportion of the calls were about how the government was spreading paedophilia via genetically modified pollen, or hiding spies on the moon, and I figured it would be good for these sideways-sounding people to have a cup of tea, and reconsider their story.

When my day was up, I asked the temp agency if they could find me more work at the *Guardian*. The atmosphere of the building felt strangely familiar, with its backstage air of hushed bustle, urgent conversations conducted in low voices. Unlike acting, a realm of make-believe, this was real-world high stakes. While it wasn't my calling, I was curious.

The agency did find me work, this time in the newsroom of the *Observer*, the *Guardian*'s Sunday sister. A few days here and there, covering one or other of the quietly competent administrators, who paid writers and booked train travel and kept the place running. They were also mascots of a sort, sitting encouragingly beside the editors, who were the important people, identifiable from the rosaceous streaks of their much-rubbed foreheads. I was neither quiet nor competent, and did this job for a long time, becoming known as 'a useless temp'. That's a derogatory term, with structural prejudice beneath it. The technical handover required for me to learn any important responsibilities wouldn't be worth the time it took, since I was only ever working a desk for a few days at a time. It was simply more efficient to suspend those responsibilities for a few days, until the job's owner returned, to sort everything out in one annoyed morning. I did go through a phase of cleaning desks and making tea, throwing piles of crumbling old newspaper that littered the place into the recycling skips, until I was informed I'd destroyed a decade's worth of archive material. The consensus was I should make less effort.

In my heart, I didn't believe there should be any such thing as a job. I remember classmates in school breaks obsessively discussing computer games they'd poured their weekends into, which sounded suspiciously like trial runs for actual work. A football-management game, in which the object was to buy and sell players, adjust formations and deal with injuries, while balancing the books. I asked when they actually got to play the matches, and they told me in irritation that they just got given the results, before returning to the discussion of transfer windows and consolidated debt. Town-planning games, in which the idea was to keep a city functioning in the face of zoning regulations, insurance problems, problems with sewer maintenance, issues arising from traffic control and God knows what else. 'Do you get to enjoy stress-related early retirement?' I didn't make friends easily, and still don't understand. There was one game a few years ago in which you played a border-control officer, checking immigrants' supporting papers, keeping abreast of complex and ever-changing government rules. The aim is to earn a daily wage, with which to support your virtual family. Don't kids realise that shit is coming for them anyway?

My fecklessness was a separate but related issue. I'd lost nearly every job I'd had, or been called into disciplinary meetings, or simply stopped showing up. Back at university, Chris and I had both started working at Senate House Library at the same time. That was another impressive edifice, a Fritz Lang-looking building which would have apparently been Hitler's HQ had he successfully invaded Britain. Once you're familiar with the colonnade of the building, you recognise it being used as a location in films all the time; a marbled, senatorial slab of power, Art Deco luxuriousness and historical moment. The grass outside was where I had fallen asleep and lost all my coursework two weeks before finals, but there's no plaque about that.

That job crystallised our differences. We were both initially tasked with replacing books in the tall, deep library shelves once they'd been returned. Turning the trolley sideways, I'd barricade myself into one of the less visited aisles and, using the wheeled footstep as a seat, catch up on the sleep I hadn't got at night, my face pushed up against an almanac of Austronesian root-crop cultivars. It was a good system, which worked on and off for months. Within the same span of time, Chris was promoted and promoted again. He landed the sought-after photocopy-room gig, where the honeys hung out, then the checkout desk, before finally being entrusted with the archive stacks at the top of the building. This was very restricted access, and they knew Chris wouldn't put any of it in the recycling. By contrast, one day my supervisor approached to say he'd been watching me sleep for forty-five minutes. It was only on the walk home that I realised he can't have achieved much either, for three quarters of an hour. At least I achieved a nap.

The university years had proved I was not clever, which many jobs still discriminate against. It's disgusting. I considered becoming a career criminal, but what I lacked in book smarts, I also lacked in street smarts, so that was a non-starter. Besides, the point was I didn't want a career of any kind. Even the word makes me drowsy.

The Fourth Estate was not an obvious place for me to make a home. As a child I'd assumed newspapers were boring printouts of reality; now, seeing their headlines side by side, they struck me as diverse and terrifying sorcerers struggling for control of a collective hallucination. News, in particular, is little more than anxiety ticker tape, and I find it draining to keep up; it feels like cracking a sluice gate, and allowing the evil of what men do to cascade out, until your eyes are gummed up with the hell of it all. It was an opportunity to work alongside unusual colleagues though; a chance to have colleagues at all. *Colleagues*. A smoking-jacket sort of a word, which I wanted to try on.

And so I made tea and snappy banter, wondering how I would *alienate my colleagues*. Because it was an itch waiting to be scratched, this angsty utopia of moral uprightness. Every other day, I'd read company-wide email arguments about cultural appropriation in the cafeteria menu, or advocating the possibility of cycle lanes inside the building. It was overwhelming, the urge to write 'ISIS' against the religious checkbox on the equal-opps questionnaires, or show up wearing an *FBI: Female Boob Inspector* T-shirt. They were such good people, and it made me nervous.

After a lot of not very hard work over a number of years, I eventually earned a downward promotion. The *Guardian* had moved offices, to several floors of an imposing building in King's Cross, a wavy glass structure that looked like someone had set seawater into jelly. Like you could dip a net into it from above and scoop out the news you needed. I was tasked with walking the floors every hour, checking which chairs were occupied, and marking the fact on a set of blueprints. I was a bank robber, casing the joint. Fascinating, to walk every part of a company, a microbe taking a tour of the body. Red-soled high heels and stiff leather bags in the legal department; whiteboards and prosecco down in sales. My favourite, editorial, had book stacks for supporting walls, and while you rarely saw a full tray of cake out, you could always see the crumbs. It became a joke, everyone running back to their desks as I approached, as if I were taking a register. Everyone asking what I was up to. A Kafka-esque joke, because I didn't even know. 'I assume you're all going to lose your jobs,' I said.

I cased the joint for eight days, every hour, until I began to lose my senses. The walkaround itself took less than ten minutes, with the remaining fifty passed in a think pod, a windowless, solitary computer cubicle for one, with a door behind my back, and no windows. You'd think I'd have loved it, but blank walls close to the face make a man come up against himself. I'd been alive for more than thirty years, with what to show for it? Working a menial job at the newspaper that had given me a great review a few years ago. By now the few auditions I got were ludicrous. And so I was here more often, because the rent was relentless, and staying home all day was affecting my relationship. Hard to feel my life was on track. Had I followed my dreams, or just crossed the road? By some strange jockeying of fate, Drama Centre had by then also moved to King's Cross, setting up two hundred metres away. I pictured the two institutions as disappointed parents.

There's a pressure to lock in achievements before you turn thirty, to have found a fulfilling job, marriage, a ladder that progressively allows you to earn more than your age. It's arbitrary, but hard to think outside that framework. Similar to the fresh-bread smell they pump into supermarkets – knowing it isn't real doesn't stop you getting hungry. Once I'd passed thirty, it was a great relief; the way I imagine it feels to clip a pedestrian on a driving exam. *Pfft*, and the pressure lifts. Nothing to worry about anymore. You failed.

I didn't want conventional things. But I had never pinned down what it was I did want. I tried to think about it now, in the airless pod. What did I want? The halogen light flickered. Maybe I wanted a donkey, I thought. One I could walk in the park every day. The chatter of the newsroom receded. Over time, it would become less clear who was leading whom. We'd sprawl a perimeter of shade under the same tree, and when he grew old I would carry him; restitution for the ass who bore the burden of the unborn Christ. We'd eat sprouts and alfalfa, and when we slept, dream the same dream. Someone tapped on the door, needing to use the computer. Goddammit.

I woke up the screen, and logged into the work account. Without thinking about why, my hands opened up a new email window, and wrote in the global address, the one that would send a message to everyone in the company. *I'm the guy who's counting everyone*, I wrote. *A lot of you have asked what the hell I'm doing*. Was this a good idea? I let my hands keep moving, and saw with interest that they were now writing up an animal story I'd recently heard, about a snake that escaped its vivarium every night, stretching out next to its owner in the warmth of her bed. In short, she finds this behaviour strange but cute, and lets the snuggling continue, only mentioning it in passing to a vet friend; he immediately tells her the snake has to be put down. It's not snuggling you, he says, *it's measuring you*. What a great story. Too good to be true, but good enough to jeopardise my only source of income. I pressed send.

If you're ever invited into an empty boardroom, it's probably either because you're being confirmed as a new company CEO, or you are about to get canned. When your previous job has been counting chairs, one of these outcomes is more likely than the other.

'This is a severe misuse of the communication channel,' said the visibly nervous supervisor who had given me the job. He looked even paler than usual, and it was the slight tremor in his voice that started worrying me. 'For your sake, I hope this breach doesn't make it out of the building.'

It got out. '*Private Eye*, you little rooster!' exclaimed Paul, walking out of the security gates in the lobby, past a large screen of scrolling headlines. An unpredictable editor of one of the edgier supplements, he'd been amused by the kamikaze round-robin email. He opened up a page in the satirical magazine, which I rarely read because I only understood the cartoons. They'd reprinted the email and taken it as damning evidence regarding the paper's future, which was inaccurate. It was damning evidence about my mental health and bad choices. The worst thing was, they'd referred to me as a 'dogsbody'.

'We should find the mole,' said Paul, striding ahead. I thought for a second he was tasking me with actual pest control, which made sense given my trajectory. Where would I end up next? Selling lemonade in the lobby, or jerrycans of petrol I'd sucked out of people's cars? Paul asked if I'd ever written. Always a scheme in the air around him, I'd noticed. He was tall and fast-talking, dashing in a sort of pickpocket-y way. When he said hello, it sounded like a preamble to asking if he could keep a horse in your house for a few days, or if you knew how to keep a secret. But I had nothing to lose and no friends. On the one hand, I had no writing experience; looked at another way, who doesn't? Clearly, I wrote emails. I wrote my name. Filling out IKEA order slips with the tiny pencil: that had to count for something.

He gave me odd little pieces, reviewing a Christmas ad here, a grime single there. They were bad but they were game, which Paul found a more interesting commodity. He started setting me more outré challenges, following hedonistic DJs on tour, or staying up to watch a conspiracy theory channel for forty-eight hours non-stop, to see if I lost my mind. I said yes to everything, because I needed to, and because I wanted to. We both got off on the gonzo aspect of these missions, intentional on his part. I simply didn't know what I was doing. Fun though, this dousing for adventure, in a way that acting hadn't been for too long. One day Paul asked if I had a passport – I waited to hear if he was going to sell me one, or needed to borrow mine for a few days, but he was actually sending me to the Mojave Desert, to watch a man bury himself alive in a coffin filled with snakes. I'd never flown alone before, and in that moment, I decided to become a journalist. Reclining on that miraculous silver machine a few days later, a time traveller with longitudes rippling through him, I thought, *now* this *is a job*.

'YO STAG,' a voice would ring out in the *Guardian* corridor, loud, and Paul would be moving towards me in an exaggerated lope, rapping the word "swag" on every step. He was potentially bad news. When other editors heard this unpredictable maverick was my patron, this loud man of the newspaper, always scrunching and dunking galley proofs in the wastepaper bin, their brows darkened, suggesting I'd fallen in with a bad crowd, as had been foreseen.

Stag, up for a club tonite? It's a Dollop dollop nite

I'd stare at my phone for forty minutes, wondering if this was how it felt to have a stroke.

Nah had a big one last night, boss

I'd eventually reply, which sounded more acceptable than saying I was in my thirties, and wanted to stay indoors with a lasagne I'd been thinking about all week. It struck me that everyone now noticing my writing, or me generally, thought I was younger than I was. A new kid on the block. They didn't realise I'd been in and out of the building more than five years, stealing toilet paper when times were bad. It was a stab at my fantasy, a chance to wipe out the wasted breakdown years. I let people assume I was a decade younger than I was.

Strangely, I had less imposter anxiety about the journalism itself, because I genuinely was an imposter, with no experience. It was true I shouldn't have been there, and still is. Nor should anyone of my ilk. It's my firm belief newspapers should consist of raw data, statistics and the occasional pie chart on a Sunday. No features, no humour, no glossy photographs of ex-cricketers. If I were in charge, there would be *at most* one charcoal sketch of the chancellor a week, seated at a desk doing the economy. Having been an actor, and counting them my closest friends, I also recommend we stop asking their opinion about anything. They only want to be liked.

Lack of confidence and qualifications weren't the only reasons I felt precarious. Having been gifted a golden ticket to the upper echelons of the media, I realised how out of place I was. I would never belong here either. Journalism appeared to me to be a reserved paddock for the well-to-do. People who had access to homes in the country, and had spent their childhoods travelling, eating za'atar and knowing someone's uncle. Wannabe influencers who spent their time taking pictures of hot drinks, or pseudo-philosophers who published pieces about wandering the Yukután for three months, collecting their thoughts. They could afford to live off perks alone.

How are they paying the rent? became an obsessive question for me when I met other writers, many of whom were
becoming my friends. I couldn't understand how they
made this work. I had nothing left after rent. I regarded
'Hot thirty under thirty' lists with my *how-do-they-pay-the-*
rent glasses on, and in time learned I was being naïve. A lot
of the time, they weren't paying rent. Sometimes, they
weren't even paying off a mortgage. Cursory googling
revealing that there was usually banking in the family,
or a famous father, a peerage on the mother's side. Rank
bitterness wasn't my best look, but Eliza supported the
preoccupation, as she believed the entire media was
Masonic propaganda anyway. I think she may have called
up about it, once or twice.

There was something disingenuous to my jealousy,
though. Clinging to outsider status was another way to
mask fear. I was terrified by old inadequacies. My new
peers were sophisticated, well-read polymaths; I couldn't
have told you the Greek messenger god was called Herpes
without looking it up first. I struggled to generate ideas,
write quickly and hold interesting opinions. Disordered
thinking meant straightforward arguments were beyond
me. I was also not a real person, and a recovering basket
case. How could I write a round-up of the best walks in
the Lake District when I was convinced reality was a collective hallucination? There was something in this work I
wanted, but I wasn't sure what, or how long I could afford
to take to find out. Scariest of all: people were offering me

opportunities and support, and the chance to improve on the job. If I failed to find a way out now, there would be no excuses left.

'They're flying me business class to Beverly Hills to interview Matt Dillon . . .'s brother, Kevin!'

'Sounds like a waste of the planet's finite resources, but I'm happy you're happy,' Eliza would reply, flashing a thumbs-up. I was getting more commissions, and had arrived at the point I could choose the jobs I took, a privilege I'd never known. Unsurprisingly, I oriented myself to the ones with the most air miles and biggest freebies. Here, finally, was a champagne bowl of my own, everything I wanted. Hampers of crockery, algae-enriched moisturisers, PR hospitality that would have delighted an Old Testament king. There was always somewhere exciting to be – catered events, film previews, open-bar parties. The opportunity to be around celebrities, even feel noticed by them sometimes. All of which made it harder when I eventually checked in, as I had learned, to ask myself: *how does this make me feel?* There was an inconvenient emptiness under the glitter. When my depression started to reassert itself it was too easy to distract myself with superficialities. I was meeting my heroes, and not attending to my relationship. I was on top of my emails but, my God, at what cost?

It was only over time that I grasped the potential of the job, and what it was that agreed with me. Writing. I remembered Lily and her studio. Writing was work that suited my temperament exactly – the obsessive need to be left alone, yet also connect. It's good for my head, making use of my thoughts, while the generative act itself – transforming a blankness of space via the word – carries no small amount of divine pretension. I had a surprising patience for the Rubik's Cube-ness of revision, I found: turning a sentence this way, a paragraph that, until the colours lined up and my hands knew it was done. Order singing from chaos, briefly, miraculously.

It was a shock to me that work, of all things, could make me feel stronger, healthier: the same person, but more defined, as if I'd traced around my edges. When Eliza and I parted ways, having something to do was what held me together. It was still work – and as such an abomination – but there's work and there's work, and this was the latter. Hey, I can't line up the colours all the time. I liked it, is what I'm saying.

The person I loved most at the *Guardian* was, weirdly enough, a strong and independent woman who made a concerted effort to change my life for the better. Susan Smillie, the food and drink editor I'd sat opposite on my very first day outside of the switchboard.

We got on immediately as, despite her name, she was the most unsmiling person I'd ever met. It wasn't as if she was depressed. More like they just didn't have cheerfulness where she was from, and she didn't care to acquire a taste for it at this stage. She lived alone on a boat, giving her a rugged authenticity quite inappropriate for an office environment. If you asked how her weekend was, she'd reel off meteorological data without looking up from her screen. Secret Santa was a spectacle when she was involved: you'd watch some unfortunate unwrapping a box of snap shackles and carbine hooks, along with a length of general-purpose rope, having to pantomime delight, surprise and innocence, all at once.

'That's from me,' Susan would interject in deep Scots. 'Entry level, but it's good kit.'

She liked me too, because I didn't make small talk or pretend to be happy. Nevertheless, it was a shock when she approached me by the coffee machine no one used, asking if I wanted to write a column. 'What are ye interested in?'

'Nothing.'

'Okay, what are ye good at?'

'. . . Nothing,' I said, thinking on my feet not being on the list. She squinted, as if trying to second-guess a large fish. There were mysterious cuts on her nose.

'What about reviewing stuff outae catalogues? But crap. Kitchen gadgets and that.' I said yes, then went home to think about it. The *Guardian* had to be the only paper on Earth that would give a cooking-related column to a mentally ill anorexic, in fact insist on it. On a related point, the column would be a lightning rod to the this-isn't-news brigade, who hung out under everything I wrote. As with any website that allows public interaction, articles on the *Guardian* website were appended with numerous pages of psychopathic insults.

Ill-informed, unfunny and irrelevant would be an
improvement over whatever this is

Wish I could unlearn English so I could unread this.
Shouldn't be possible to unlearn English, but judging by
this I'd be the second person to manage

The article is so bad it has made me seek a divorce

So dark were the insults I almost admired them, as a type of modern art. More civil put-downs, of the *not my sort of thing* or *are you work experience?* type now struck me as antiquities from a gentleman's age of the internet. The inevitability of baroque abuse was a clear danger to my mental health, and from the very beginning, had killed in the shell any pleasure at being published. No sooner had a piece gone up, no matter how harmless, than some *éminence grise* would rush to the keyboard to throw dogshit over your baby, and you. I knew other writers felt the same way, that we were just clay pigeons. But it still hurt.

I got some insight into the strange world of internet comments when an actor friend of mine mentioned he frequently commented on my articles. He's very funny, and has a lovely big head – as in a sizeable skull, the sign of a really good actor. I knew he had a dark sense of humour though, because he was given to making remarks such as 'Ebola, a helium balloon and a shotgun would make the perfect murder' while you were hanging out at a country fair. I cautiously asked what kind of comments.

'Stirring shit up, you know. Say something negative, some people agree, others defend you, gets a pile-on going.' He observed this without emotion. 'I've got several accounts. Sometimes I'll start arguing with myself.' I wondered how it was I had come to befriend the Unabomber, and said nothing to him, but privately spent weeks debating whether the time had come to fill the internet in, and sow a lawn on top. He would never have said a word to hurt me in person, but online, we don't see people. The solidity of a byline made me appear more robust to him, as if nothing could dent me. Meanwhile I mistook his anonymity for ubiquity, assuming everyone in the world wanted to transport my limbs in different directions. The fact was, no one really cared. The moral I took from this? Don't read the comments.

There was one excellent reason to take the gadget column, which was that it made no sense. Gadgets were a male domain, a world of boys and their toys, a world I had defined myself against. But the contradiction made it funny. Perhaps there was a way to subvert tech-talk, refashion and reveal it for the silliness it was. A weekly column in a national paper about kitchen gadgets, the most banal objects in a home, was an idea so enticing it may as well have been covered in confectioner's sugar. Susan gave me total licence, occasionally stepping in to save me from saying something illegal, and for three years I got to write unfettered. Sushi bazookas, bacon suitcases, selfie toasters, banana stuffers, cheese guns and radish shapers. Even better – and entirely unexpectedly – it was popular. The comments were appreciative and supportive, sometimes filthy. It was revelatory to me that there were other people in receipt of the secret message. Hundreds of thousands more, in the case of one of the early columns.

The Egg Master was a vertical grill, housed in a rubber tube, into which you could crack eggs. For various reasons – the smell of the device in use, the pops and squeals it emitted, its sex-toy design, and the fact that when ready, a log of cooked egg would rise from the device unaided, and flop over one side, like a net-caught manatee – I was unable to give the device a thumbs-up. It was a turd, laid by one of the Four Horsemen of the Apocalypse. Not the horse; the *man*, whomsoever was of them the largest, and in diet most foul.

The analytics team told me the original article was shared 70,000 times, but individual elements of it had a readership of many magnitudes higher, which couldn't be captured by their software. A video of the device, and a picture lifted from the article, of me licking an egg lollipop and feeling sick, had separate lives. They were memed all over Reddit, the oceanic portion of the internet, as opposed to the minority landmass of respectable news. Somehow, base metal had been turned into baser metal. I would be featured on American news, approached to film TV pilots.

A bastard kind of fame came knocking, and I opened the door in a nightie. This was the dream of anyone with low self-esteem, to be approached in the street, as I now was.

'You're definitely one of the . . . things of the internet,' a man with a tattoo of a UFO hovering above the White House told me, in line for a falafel wrap. 'Like those girls with the cup, and the dude who loves Britney. He does porn now.'

I was no one's idea of a good celebrity spot, though, and people invariably left these encounters undazzled, even confused. They'd come up while I was standing outside Sainsbury's, looking homeless, having just had an argument.

'Sorry, but it's you, isn't it? The egg guy!'

'Yeah. Can I ask you something – if a friend invites you round and says to pick up waffles, pak choi and flowers, that's not coming over for lunch, is it?'

'I dunno. Can we get a selfie?'

'That's doing their shopping,' I'd say, a dog with a bone. 'I could stay at home and cook the ingredients myself, and not have to make conversation.'

'. . . I think that's meant to be the nice part?' They'd look at the picture, frown, decide not to bother with a retake.

The compliments from strangers were enjoyable, but I noticed how, emotionally, I discounted them. This homeopathic dose of fame was enough to show me that everything people said about that particular state of being was true. It was as if there were a hologram of me out there, someone else people were pleased to see, of whom I was but a lookalike. Only I could see myself for what I really was. The extra attention only complicated my existential malaise.

On the other hand: I loved it.

People write to leave some black on white that will outlast them, some scrap of profundity for the ages. It has become clear that I'll never write anything more popular than a negative review of a steaming log of chicken protein. Still, that's a weirdly luxurious predicament. Comparisons to 'the egg thing' appear under everything I write now, which is better than strangers requesting my hands be chopped off. I picture a blue plaque when I'm gone, a backlog of the souls I touched, underneath which someone will have scrawled *not as good as the egg thing*. Rather than be the ageing rocker who scored one hit in the seventies and spends fifty years refusing to play it, I've accepted this preposterous legacy. If the alternative is 'he does porno now', I'll take it with gravy.

Having forgotten so much, I don't think it's an accident I spend all my time writing things down. This life fits me, and I've called a truce with work. I'd been thinking of it in the wrong terms. In nurturing gifts, learning new skills and feeling our capabilities, there can be a satisfaction in work, and satisfaction has little to do with pleasure. Art has an indirect relationship to pleasure too, and I think higher of it as a result. Work is also an opportunity to be useful, something I understand in theory.

Sometimes we don't know the real value of our work in the moment either. When I think about acting, I think about my father's face when he came to Stratford-upon-Avon, and saw that I had made something good. A simple happiness. I think he allowed himself to leave in faith that, though I had chosen a difficult road, I would be all right. I wouldn't be all right, but that's not the point. When he left, my mother stuck a photo taken of that very moment onto his hand-decorated coffin. Not every job can give you a gift like that.

Writing has helped me find my way in the world, in ways that go beyond paying rent. But I hesitate to say it is what has saved me. This is a practical reservation, because while we will always need writers, circumstances might make such a life untenable. Reports of its death are exaggerated, but print journalism isn't in its salad days. Maybe I'll have to move on again. Besides, creative work isn't the answer for everyone. We put a lot of expectations on employment to fulfil our deepest needs. But finding work you love isn't necessarily practical, and perhaps your work – the activities your talents most uniquely suit you to – isn't located in a job at all. We should dispense less pressurising advice in this area. Something like: look for a job you're good at and like well enough, especially if it can be tailored to your interests over time. Leave space for the rest of life to have a go with you too. That's a safe route to well-being, though it doesn't fit on a fridge magnet.

Sometimes my phone lights up, and it's a picture message. A hurricane of seagulls, a sunrise at the dawn of the world, a dead dolphin floating fin-side up, like an aquatic rotisserie Jesus. They're all from Susan, who left her position at the top of the tree to sail around Sardinia and Western Sahara and Skye, writing, taking pictures. She just left, having kept her life simple so she wouldn't have to work for money. It seems unbelievable we met indoors, and know each other through work. 'Just live in a van with birds,' is her advice to me. I like knowing it's an option.

Before the inevitable van years – being still unable to drive, these will be stationary years, with grass poking through wheel rims – I have a strange faith that I'll be able to keep going if the catastrophe comes, that it'll be okay. Starting again isn't starting from nothing, because you take the person you are with you. I took the lazy philosopher into acting, and the underemployed actor into writing, and I'll take the fatalistic writer into whatever comes next. I learned a new skill, and it opened up a new self, and possibilities I didn't know existed. The fact of this remains a grain of faith that has worked its way into my circuitry, shorting out my usual thinking.

Shocking, how the things we want can change so drastically over time. I remember being invited to cover the

BAFTAs once, the glitziest awards I'd ever been to, the glitziest anything, really. The invitation filled me with stress. 'What does "black tie" actually mean?' I wondered. I google-image searched 'BAFTA' and it threw up a picture of Eddie Redmayne essentially dressed as Rupert the Bear, which didn't help. A workable definition of fame is a group of people that don't carry their own bags, so would there even be a cloakroom? And how would I get to the Royal Albert Hall? 'Practice,' one of my unhelpful friends advised.

Arriving at the BAFTAs on my own was like going to any party where you don't know anyone, except that everyone there was the most elegant person I'd ever seen in my sordid life. I awkwardly stepped over the exquisite long gowns, gazed up at tall men. I felt like David Attenborough examining a rare colony, peopled exclusively by birds of paradise and emperor penguins. There was no cloakroom. But quite a long way into the show, there was someone who looked like me. Dev Patel, winning an award for his beautiful work on the film *Lion*. I watched as he thanked his people, who had worked tirelessly to help 'a noodle with wonky teeth and a lazy eye trying to get work in this really hard industry. I'm overwhelmed,' he stuttered. 'I'm terrible at this and it means so much.' I found myself feeling happy for him, this talented man who had come from little and risen so high.

After an astonishing dinner, the ballroom at the Grosvenor opened for the after-party. I pushed in line to be served a cocktail inside a real pitcher plant plucked from a vine, smoking at its brim. I felt like Alice in Wonderland, drunk on the occasion. Flicking greedy eyes over people's shoulders as I talked to them, wondering where Meryl Streep was sitting, suppressing a feeling of not liking myself. With help from a far more connected journalist, I scored an invitation to Harvey Weinstein's party at the Rosewood Hotel, which might as well have been Mount Olympus. I was scared to blink, wanting to hold onto every moment. Finally, I had gained entrance to the innermost circle. The curtains would be parted. I might even meet the wizard. Inside were mirrors and marble surfaces, darkness. A room at the back was made up as a French patisserie, with macarons, millefeuilles and opera cakes stacked on shelves for the taking. The chocolate fountains came in milk or white, possibly in response to calls for greater diversity at awards shows. The concatenation of stars was ludicrous. Just walking in, I pushed past Casey Affleck, J. K. Rowling, Riz Ahmed. Every banquette contained a celebrity or model. I was mingling at perhaps the most exclusive party in the world that night, yet absurdly there was a smaller VIP section in the middle of the room, with the artists and all the famous people I recognised *outside* it. As far as I could make out, Harvey Weinstein was one of about five people in it, and no one was smiling. What was the need for another velvet rope? Was there a danger Isabelle Huppert might get rowdy after too many pitcher plants? Or was it because status anxiety and control of bodies were the cornerstones of this church I worshipped at? There was something perverse at the heart of the party. The champagne still bubbled, but I had the sense it was time to go home.

Of course I stayed too late, but I'm not sorry about that. As the night was winding down I found Dev Patel, standing at the bottom of the stairs, still looking overwhelmed. I told him it was nice to see a fellow brown man up on that stage, holding his own. It was a relief to realise I still meant it. 'Thanks, brother,' he replied, smiling. I think that's the moment I'll hold onto.

Not as good as the egg thing.

Letter to Paul

MUSK OX

  What's the hap, swaggy man? Heard it's popping off east tonight, big, big damage.

  I have very rarely understood what it is you are talking about, and have always been full of anxiety about how to talk to you, especially when we first met. But you did something for me that changed my life; I mean you showed an interest. You gave me a confidence I'd never had. I think you probably hate talk like this, so I'll just say thank you, and hope you know I mean it.

  Or maybe I should be braver. I got an email a while back from a charity I volunteer for. Shortly after, it was followed by another email, asking me to delete the first one, as due to human error it contained the email addresses of all their other volunteers. I can't talk about the volunteer work for confidentiality reasons, which is annoying because it makes me sound terrific. But as I forensically scanned the list of names, I came across one I never expected to see: yours. And an email address I'd only ever associated with JPEGs of rappers and all-caps banter.

  And so, I think I sold you short with my worries. I worried about what people said about you. I worried you were only helping because you thought I was something I wasn't, who I had to then pretend to be. In the end, I think it was you

who always saw me clearly, and I wasn't able to do the same.
You're a good person, and generous, and I'm so grateful our
paths crossed, every hour, for more than a week. It honestly
was a crossroads.

I don't know if this is out of line, but I have this sense
you're looking for something, and I hope you find it. I hope
you can find someone or something who can be what you
have been for me.

PEACE! SNOOOGES
Sorry. Old habit.

10

How to Be Free

So how do you solve a problem like Rhik Samadder? In the final months with Eliza, my depression and her anxiety were interacting badly, her pushing and me pulling away, our spiralling little two-step. We'd both hit our coping point and were starting to lose it.

'I'm going to write some thoughts in my anxiety journal,' she said over her shoulder as she ran out of the room, 'so I can think about them later, in Worry Time.' I never asked her if that worked, though it had to be more effective than the healing gong bath we'd taken the week before, in which they'd rolled us up in carpets. We'd been learning about mindfulness too, cultivating awareness of one's immediate surroundings as a way to quiet brain chatter. *Try practising mindfulness every time you sit down, or have a cup of tea*, the video had said. I think it's the way these meditation people talk, mindfully, like they're slipping under anaesthetic, that I find distracting. I end up confusing mindfulness with slowness, doing everything quarter-speed like a wind-up toy that's winding down. I would take thirty seconds to lower myself into a chair, as if I were ninety, and once there I'd be too late to enjoy the cup of tea I'd let go cold. *A rag infused with essential oil can be a good sensory focus, as can concentrating on a single object.* I stared at the bottle of Radox left on the counter from our shopping trip, until the letters on the label started to spin and rearrange themselves. Radox. Rain Dogs. Botox. Give Up. *This is madness*, I thought to myself. *This is more madness than the madness I'm trying to get rid of.*

But I'm at peace now with the fact that I'm not going to get rid of anything. After all this time, I know the darkness isn't going anywhere; it will still roll around like clockwork. The difference now is that I know the light will too. Philosophy tells me there's no reason to trust the sun's rise each morning, but it's never let me down. It's hard to get through life without a little faith, even if it's just in this.

Once I'm out of bed, there are any number of barmy things to try. I've tried them all, and when they come up with new ideas, I'll try them too. I've become interested in it for its own sake now, this business of getting traction on my mood. It's so revealingly personal, what works and what doesn't, that there are bound to be missteps, and this can be discouraging. The pursuit of mental well health is courageous and important and often very boring. Embarrassing too. I once saw a counsellor who asked me to list good things about myself, and it took four awful, silent minutes to arrive at 'I'm usually the first to detect rain.'

She wasn't sure that even counted, and only accepted 'I don't overfill hot-water bottles' because we were running low on time.

Still, it's good to try a range of solutions. Recently, a CBT therapist showed me how to keep an activity log, a daily record of the things I did and who I was with and where.

10.30 a.m.   Did work at home, alone.

1 p.m.   Had burrito, enjoyed. Home, alone.

5 p.m.   Tidied up, home, alone.

5.30 p.m.   Went to visit geese in the park. Park, geese.

7 p.m.   Watched *Captain Phillips*, ate paella.
             Good film.

I asked if it was okay to stop keeping the diary, because it was depressing me. I'd enjoyed my day until I saw its particularities set down, under a fluorescent tube. That's the worry, that looking closely reveals the flaw that hadn't bothered you before. That asking yourself if you're okay, too many times, will start to generate the negative response the question is looking for.

Then she told me the other part of the homework, which was to give each activity two ratings, one for enjoyment, one for achievement. All the things I liked, Tom Hanks films and world food and hissing birds, scored as highly enjoyable, but were hardly achievements. Things

I couldn't stand – tidying, washing, drying – were valuable achievements, the screws that kept the wheels on the bus going round and round. She told me to look out for golden activities like cooking, which might score highly as enjoyment and achievement. It was good to aim for a balance of both in the day, she said. Too much of one at the expense of the other brings us down.

I think I twitched my nose. This was what I was paying for? Actually it was the NHS, so I wasn't, but someone must have been. It sounded insultingly basic. I waited for her to tell me it's good to wrap up warm when it's cold out, and for a growing boy to eat his vegetables. Still, she asked me to try, so I did, and was dismayed to discover it had a huge effect. Recognising the value of achievements, even small ones, made me feel a little bit of pride. And it let me enjoy the things I liked doing more, because they had value too. I took it further: started recognising my achievements out loud, even patting myself on the back. The value of keeping the boat afloat, of making appointments and unblocking the sink, proving one can look after oneself; these are things of immense satisfaction, which for most people go unremarked. But they are remarkable. Especially for someone like me, who formerly would burn the woodshed down sooner than sweep up the shavings. 'I am the captain now,' I whisper to myself, as I put away the laundry.

It's an affirmation, of a sort. Affirmations are the worst. I've tried them. How can anyone take themselves seriously, declaring the person in the mirror is a big winner, deserving of a wheatgrass shot? But privately, very, very privately, I find it affecting to hear a voice telling me something good about myself. Speaking externalises thought, a bit like writing. Sifts good ones from the chaotic swirl, giving them shape, and physical vibration. Lets them enter you from outside. It's all laughably earnest at first, or nervously ironic, like suggesting getting out the Ouija board. But then you try speaking to the part of you that has always been underfed, addressing some ancient wound, and your voice will shake and you will find it hard, and that's when you know you've hit something.

There are still bad times when I can't trust any voice, especially my own. An acid mentality that believes even an ounce of happiness is a delusory state. This is one of depression's most macho manoeuvres, a voice that tells you it is the sole lens on reality, unfettered by sentimentality. A voice that is suspicious of all advice on happiness. When a beaming celebrity appears, delivering an inspirational message about following your dreams, the dry heaves come upon me. Of course you're feeling positive, I'll think. Everything worked out for you. What's that got to do with me?

I've spent a long time battling fears that have the talent of resurrection. I'm afraid that I cannot outrun my own mind, and the ways in which it goes wrong. That I will get worse, not better. That one day something truly awful will happen. At these times, when the mercury is low and the wind gathering, I reach for a bottle of the hard stuff, a little moonshine of my own making. When I know I will kick against any positivity, I remind myself of six connected, pessimistic truths, flinty enough to be felt in the dark, which even I can't throw away. Bullets, not numbers.

- **You can have anything you want, but you can't have everything you want.**

It's possible I saw this on a T-shirt, or an advert for gastric reflux, but it rings true. A balanced life – full of love and health and family – will have some unfulfilled yearning in it, a wonder about what more you could have achieved. On the other hand, the application of talent, time and extreme focus can take you to extraordinary places, to heights many only dream of. But you will probably fall short in other areas. Be clear about what you want, and choose it and stop complaining. Also, it's never too late to change your mind.

- **Getting what you want won't make you happy**

Lottery winners return to their baseline mood after a few months. The relationship, job, property, sex, the faux-fur throw in cream you've been obsessed with, the high-def OLED screen that picks out individual pixels without flooding the black, these are finger plasters for The Great Wound. We're strivers, and upon getting what we think we want, we find something else. However, just as getting what you want won't make you happy, there's no reason *not* getting what you want should make you unhappy for ever. If you pride yourself on seeing through things, see through the wanting trap. Fixating is mistaking, as Buddha didn't say. There are always other possibilities.

• You will never be self-reliant

Because it's a romantic myth, at least for most of us. Winding up alone in a Canadian cabin eating forage and shitting in a trench wouldn't feel like winning. It would feel like taking your ball home because you were scared of losing. Everything that has come our way has been helped along, by luck and other people who took time and believed in us. We're only here because of someone else. Our brains and bodies were given free of charge, and it's selfish not to share. Looking after oneself is actually about learning responsibility, and knowing when to ask for help.

• It is impossible to live without hurting others

Which doesn't mean be a dick about it. Live in generosity and compassion and gentleness, and try to be better every day. But trying to keep others safe from yourself will lead to cutting yourself off. The kind of life that keeps us warm, one rich in people and places and experiences, is messy. People's damage interacts in unpredictable ways, and that's the negotiation, and that's okay. People are tougher than you think. The mess is where the growth is.

• **It is impossible to live without being hurt**

Sensitivity is good, and feeling is vital. It's a mistake to think we can protect ourself against all helplessness, rejection or uncertainty. The cost of trying is too high, and misses the point. We enter into life attached, and as we grow we learn to embrace people, philosophies and ideas of ourselves; in time we will lose many or all of them. The fact there is always more to lose shows how much you have. Pain is inevitable, and you only have a say in how you adjust. You're tougher than you think too.

• **You're going to die**

Which means you aren't dead yet. Go for a walk, you silly banana.

Better to be slapped with the truth than kissed by a lie, right? Thankfully, most of the time I don't require the slap. When I'm feeling heavy but not catatonic, touched with vapours but not the full collywobbles, there are a number of low-effort activities that always help. Going out for an amble in the park, visiting the ducks, letting fresh air hit me in the face, are all ways to mainline vitamin D and endorphins. Eating an apple – what's an apple, it's nothing, give it a go – reminds me a body can take sustenance and actually feel lighter afterwards.

Beyond these: animal company, Emily Dickinson poems and the cheese aisle rarely let me down. Video montages of Roger Federer hitting impudent drop shots.

Making popcorn. Making whoopee. Making anything. Working on my front crawl. Depressurising the boiler, so I can hang out with my plumber mates. Shining shoes, standing amid vibrant green leaves, enjoying the hang of a well-cut coat, and how it makes me feel. Putting on music and moving how I will, at any tempo that feels right. It's easy to dance like no one is watching when no one is watching. And it works instantly, showing my mind the back seat as my body and the music move us across the floor.

Everyone floats their boat in different waters, but the general principle to stick to is energy efficiency. It's not just for light bulbs. Depression takes up a lot of energy, so one must marshal what remains very carefully. I know that tiredness will batter my mood, as will alcohol and eating rubbish. I don't *not* go to the party or vacuum up the Pringles, but I understand it will take a toll if I do, and try not to complain. (And always fail.)

I also don't make plans I'd rather not. Respect for my introversion is a way to be unapologetically myself, and crucial to keeping me sane. Every day, people demand your energy for their situations, and mostly do not have the right. We're obliged to invest energy in work, relationships that matter, ideally some in a future we like the sound of. Altruistic acts, activism and volunteering are a tremendous way to feel vital and connected. This isn't about being stingy with ourselves; it's about being conscious. Energy, our most precious commodity, is more powerful when given freely, wholeheartedly. Keeping enough back for ourselves is a benign selfishness and responsible choice.

It strikes me that depression isn't as boring as I once thought it was. It's just hard to think about, so blank and inert. It has sewn itself into its own undershirt. Ideas might be more forthcoming if this was just about feeling sad. When it's bad, depression gives way to no feeling at all. It draws up the barricade. It has a meanness. Even writing this, I have felt the envious, unworthy side rising. I read in the paper about a man who'd lost his wife and sister on the same day, and think, *I never even had a sister.* I've developed this shorthand phrase, 'a good one', which refers to anyone else's catastrophe that feels more exploitable than mine. Someone discovers their daughter has been trafficked? That's a good one. Lost your legs and ability to work? A good one. Father has another family locked in a basement? That is a trauma triathlon.

What I wouldn't give for a manic episode to liven things up, I think. My friend Camilla, on the phone to a mutual friend, came up with the catchphrase *FUCK BIG GO HOME* out of nowhere, and had ordered twenty T-shirts online before James could question why she wanted his chest measurement. I don't have stories like that. But I understand that for every entertaining story I hear, there's a twin in the cupboard, a story not being told. I need to get better at seeing through to them. Not to help. Just so I feel less jealous.

Okay, maybe to help a bit. When I cast my mind over the possible benefits of depression, this ability to empathise, to connect to another being when they are most in need of it, shines out from the rest.

I also wonder about labels. Shared language is extraordinarily useful, especially with an invisible force like depression. Unless you have a name for the blizzard of bad thoughts, it's hard to ask for help. Socialising our understanding of depression allows people to discuss extremities of experience with less shame, makes it more likely they will ask for the help they need. But it's also true we don't know what depression is. Even the serotonin model is disputed. There's an absence at the centre of what we're talking about, a collection of symptoms, outcomes and remedies that varies from person to person. Trying to understand how it has shaped me has been like increasing a microscope's magnification, until I lost all sense of the room I was standing in. Wasted years, damaging behaviour – so much of what can be attributed to this illness is also the stuff of life. I'm not saying it's all in my head. I'm saying the borders of illness are porous. Grouping the experiences under a name won't redeem the time, or bring back the people lost.

Perhaps this is why I've always been resistant to medication, always bringing myself off it, trying to find a different way. I've accused my body of so much, and pathology is not empowerment for me. To talk of misfiring neurones or chemical imbalance is to throw a ball at which we can swing a chemical bat, and I'd like to avoid that if possible, to meet these feelings with understanding. Because I do understand my depression, I think. I understand it has been a filter of sorts, trying to protect me from overwhelming experiences and urges. Not to mention modernity. Given our cities' overpopulation and pollution and noise and fluorescent light, the abstracted threats of rent and mortgage, the internet and the global news, I think it would be strange to not have the heavy blues now and then. A sign of not paying attention, and not hoping for better. Maybe I just like having something to kick against.

It would be ridiculous to claim I'm cured of my depression. What I have changed is my relationship to it. Ongoing therapy has been most effective at integrating the way my mind works and the circumstances of my life. A locked box, into which I can scream the unspeakable thoughts, and realise that they cannot kill me. There is peace in affirming the paranoia, rage and sadness, realising they will have their day and move on. They are the local news. And I know how to do something with them. This will not work for everyone – people have different situations and symptoms, dependants and demanding jobs. They should try medication, different therapies . . . whatever saves, that's the most important thing. But all the talk of battling depression, fighting against myself, was leading me down an exhausting path. There is no way around debilitating sadness at times, if one is sensitive. There's no way around beauty or joy or mystery either; they're jostling for our attention. Pain arises from resisting any of their claims.

When I was self-harming, I learned to wear long sleeves at all times. Even in situations where it was absurd, such as swimming or playing football, as if I were Thierry Henry or Mr Darcy. I had to take this measure, because other boys were mocking me.

'What the shit happened to your arm?' one of them asked me in the changing room. In a fit of confused religiosity, I had carved the word "sin" next to a crucifix. 'Why does it say SINT?'

'It does not say SI—' I began, before looking down at the scabby Etch-a-Sketch on my forearm and seeing that it really did. *SINT*. Curves are hard with knives. I started laughing, as I recall. I wasn't Jesus; I was a confused child. In that moment I received, akin to a gnostic kiss, a sense of how purely, sweetly ridiculous life can be. More than anything else, this is what has saved me.

I carried on with the long sleeves for most of my twenties, however, long after I'd stopped cutting; a manifestation of my shame. If ever I forgot, or they rolled up a little way and whoever I was talking to noticed, I would clock the moment exactly. An almost imperceptible stiffening, dilation of pupils, new tightness in the voice. Usually they'd avoid the subject, look away, or make their excuses and leave. But some people asked, and that's when I started lying. It's just easier, I'd tell myself, watching relief wash over them as I explained I owned a cat that scratched. It would have had to be a snow leopard to explain the array. The scars looked a bit like canoes lining up to start a race, lozenge-shaped, strangely polite. Shiny, pale and numb, a centimetre at the widest point, they contrasted with the living brown of my arm in an obvious way. Over time, the lies grew rococo. I referred darkly to an incident with a thresher, though the closest I'd ever come to harvesting cereals was bulk-buying Coco Pops. *I was left unsupervised near a shredder on work experience*, I told people. *I train attack dogs for the police*, I'd say, looking them dead in the eye. *I entangled with a flotilla of jellyfish on holiday*. Funny how things come around.

I was angry at the people who asked, which wasn't their fault. I was angry at everything. I also knew that to talk honestly, emotionally, would cost me, and I would be laid low the next day, so I didn't. But there came a day when I wanted to stop hiding, and wear what I wanted. And people cared far less than I thought. The scars are somewhat faded now, and strangers ask about them far less frequently. Which is *almost* a shame, because I've reached a point where I don't mind talking about them. In fact, I think it's important.

Ah, yes. Another item on the list of what helps, only just below instinctive irony, is talking about feelings incredibly earnestly. Preferably face to face because, now more than ever, there's something important about people putting their bodies into the same place, giving their attention to each other. It's been one of the slower dawnings of my life, letting go the story that I don't like talking. It's what we're built to do. Our brains have an astonishing architecture, housing cognitions of monumental scale and intricacy. Not by accident did we co-evolve dextrous tongues and prodigious vocal abilities. Our thoughts reach too far to be contained in single bodies.

Cathedral-of-thought stuff aside, it's self-evidently good to connect. Most of the time it doesn't even matter what you talk about. I was on a plane a while ago, sitting next to two French women who must have been in their seventies. Most people interact glancingly in these situations, but these two obviously didn't know the drill. They requested help with seat belts, kept turning to the side to look at me. One even offered me a coconut macaron, a snack I don't care for, but to refuse at such proximity would have felt like a slap in the face. They'd never flown before, they made it known in broken English. They'd never even left Toulouse, and were now on the first leg of a journey to Dubai, via Kuwait. It struck me as an odd first trip, one you'd work up to. What about Marseilles, or even Switzerland?

These thoughts were interrupted when we hit turbulence, the kind that makes your drinks fall over, and my companions did not react well. It quickly got worse, and the cabin crew were forced to take their own seats, struggling to do up their own seat belts. The plane bucked and shook like someone was throwing Christmas trees into the propellors. As the situation deteriorated, the blood drained from the women's faces. I was scared too, though the noise was so loud I could barely hear myself think obsessive death thoughts. *Will people say this crash is my fault? Is it my fault? My S-K-I-N is my S-I-N. Who had said that? Oh, Ice Cube. Haha. Fuck, maybe I am a terrorist.* The kind of paranoid thoughts you get at altitude were spiralling around me. Maybe the women were terrorists? Always one step ahead, those terrorists. These two, with their woven hats and dithering charm, could slide through any security in the world. Where did they say they were going? What was in the macaron? I looked at them closer, and realised they were just two scared old women.

'It's okay. Turbulence is normal,' I said to the paler of the two, who was sitting next to me. She looked up wild-eyed, said something in French, and put her hand on my arm. I didn't know how to distract her. The little English she had had deserted her. '*Ça suffit*,' I said, which wasn't right. Her friend was looking at me in confusion. 'The aeroplane is *ça va*.' I repeated it with a slight accent, a technique that lets me speak any language in the world. It seemed to help. The two women were now leaning in, smiling in weak encouragement. I willed my GCSE French back to me. I had at one point memorised this stuff, so wasn't it in there? Tucked in some wrinkle of the prefrontal cortex? *How many brothers and sisters do you need?* I asked, repeating myself over the din of the engine. '*COMBIEN DE BROTHERS?*'

We continued this way for fifteen minutes, an eternity of questions about whether they prefer going to school or doing hobbies, and whether the swimming pool was nearby. They were focused on me, on my nonsensical voice, the blood returning to them; I was trying to act as if everything was fine, so that they could believe it. It was our bumbling reciprocity I can easily recall now, not the scary turbulence. Connection and vitality, interlinked. Eventually, the worst was over and the plane levelled out. '*Nous viendrons ça va,*' I said, which I'd been saving up. '*Nous sommes tout ça va.*' When we landed, they looked at me like I was Oskar Schindler, their confidence only shaken when I leaned over to pat myself on the back.

Having said that, there are occasions in life when it matters very much what you talk about, and what you can bring yourself to say. That's why I'm returning to the house near the park again, to finish what I started.

I enter the house, immediately go upstairs and remove my clothes. I change into the soft clothes that feel like this place. Polyester fleece trousers with snowflakes on, so fluffy and unnatural they would burst into flame if I stood too near the TV. It happens to be December, but I wear Christmas clothes here all year round. A brown smock top, limp to the point of transparency, over which I wear a jumper, woven with a line of dancing penguins. One of the penguins has slipped and is falling away from the others. The jumper contains sensor-activated

LEDs, that blink red and green when I move. The ensemble is completed by a hoodie that reads *Bristol Engineering: Masters of Erection*, a present from Ellie the dancing engineer.

I walk downstairs to the kitchen, where my mother is doing something unspeakable to a hen. She startles, because she never hears me come in, and then a smile opens her face. She gives me a hug, as Lily taught us. That's another piece of the answer. Touch. We shrivel without it. We never used to hug in my family, an Asian thing perhaps. There is touching of the elders' feet in respectful gesture, a hand on the shoulder. But hugs are what Lily brought into this house, an abundance of enveloping embraces, and my mother and I have learned to need them. She grasps my nose between her knuckles, which is her own twist.

'There you are,' she says. 'Do you want this? It's a nice-looking thing, innit?' She is wearing brick-red bondage trousers and her chromatic glasses that turn purple in the sun. She is holding a dustpan and brush, looking unfathomably like someone who saw the Rolling Stones at a formative point in their life and is now only allowed out at weekends. It takes a second or two to register that she is in fact talking about the dustpan and brush, which she is looking at as if it were my baby brother.

'What are you talking about?' I say. 'When is dinner?'

I get gruffer the more worried I am; I've been worried about her since the break-up ceremony, in which she learned incidentally that she might never be a grand-mother. *I am at the bottom of my spirits,* she had said in front of everyone that day, *but not all water joins the sea. Some is lost in the sand, if that is meant to be.*

We sit down to eat. Having had no notice of my visit, she ladles up a light supper: Chinese pancakes, a block of crab pâté inside a croissant, coriander veg and paneer, goujons, parsley and butter pollock, samosas, olives, pomegranate juice, coconut water, a bowl of daal and a pizza. She serves herself a small helping of rice and noth-ing else.

'That mouse has been after the chocolate eggs so I hid them, but I forgot and lost two days in looking,' she begins, apropos of nothing. She's a natural talker, I think, as good as I am bad. And then I wonder if the two may be connected, her growing used to evenings in which I can only hang my head, unable to speak. Rather than ask what is wrong, which will make me run away, she makes this a safe place, carved out of the space I need, decorated with food and stories. Eventually I start to relax, and enjoy the way her mind moves. She's currently engrossed by the Beast from the East, an Arctic air mass originating over Russia, and with which she seems to have a personal relationship, speaking as if it actually *is* Russian, and speaks Russian, and its chilly rudeness can be attributed to cultural difference.

'Did I tell you about being taken hostage in Russia?' she says suddenly. We're dipping into the family history again. This time we appear to be in John le Carré territory. I sit up, waiting for her to continue.

'Daddy had sent an Aeroflot ticket for me to come here in 1979. They were the only affordable flights. You were only allowed to bring six pounds. I had a small suitcase. Coming from a hot country, you don't think you'll need warm clothes. Ha!'

'Tell me about the hostage thing,' I say, because this is a critical juncture. There is a real risk she'll take a wrong turning inside her own anecdote.

'Oh yes, we were forced to land in Georgia and told to get out of the plane. Middle of nowhere, middle of the night. They made us surrender our passports, money, everything. They took us to a small room, no food, no water, not even for the babies. Even the stewardesses were taken. It was horrible, pandemonium. We didn't know what was going to happen.' She stops the story to pass me a plate of Parma ham, slices of which she has shrouded in a glutinous blanket of Vietnamese roll wrappers. 'I made a big, big mistake,' she says. I'm leaning forwards.

'What did you do?'

'I forgot to put raspberries inside the ham.' My eyes roll so far up into my head I can see my own bald spot.

'What. Happened. With. The. Whole. Hostage. Situation.'

'A group of journalists on board saved us. They kicked up a big fuss. Said it was an international incident, and demanded we be taken to Moscow. Very brave.'

The passengers' money and belongings were taken, she continues. 'Luckily I had very little, and no jewellery.' Was this kidnapping for robbery, or a cocktail of incompetence and corruption? She doesn't seem concerned either way. The journalists from Bangladesh succeeded, she tells me. They were all released and allowed to fly to Moscow, where they were given water and reunited with their passports, and eventually flown to Heathrow in smaller planes.

She gets up to retrieve a pouch of cooked mussels. Her eyes have been letting her down lately, and she struggles to line up scissor against plastic. While she faffs around, I go on my phone and check for supporting evidence. Not that I don't believe her, but . . . well, you know. I discover a whole Wikipedia page on Aeroflot disasters and incidents in the 1970s. According to the internet, at least every two weeks the airline was having a 'mare. I skim the highlights, unable to believe what I'm reading, or that these people were the first to get to space.

21 January 1973: Crashed into the snow near Petukhovo after being struck by a surface-to-air missile en route to Perm airport. The few survivors died in the low temperatures before a rescue team reached them.

24 April 1973: The aircraft was en route when it was hijacked by a person demanding to go to Stockholm. A device exploded in flight, killing the flight engineer and the hijacker and blowing a hole in the airframe.

18 October 1978: The aircraft took off without having been completely cleared of snow and ice. Controlling the aircraft became difficult and the crew made a forced landing in swampy terrain. The aircraft then caught fire.

16 June 1979: Stolen by a drunk pilot at Petropavlovsk-Kamchatsky airport. The plane stalled in a low-altitude manoeuvre and crashed upside down.

It goes on and on, hundreds of entries – hijackings and explosions, bullets ricocheting off cockpit doors, deaths from hypothermia while waiting for rescue teams. Flying into the side of mountains, getting tangled in electricity pylons. Cockpit-less and wingless fuselages sliding over ice. Astonishingly frequent incidents of drunk pilots performing stunts at low altitude. I read about the airline's policy of suppressing information on accidents and aeroplane write-offs, only disclosing incidents occurring beyond Soviet borders, or ones in which foreigners were killed, which meant the casualty list was likely to be higher than that publicly disclosed. I feel that shiver, the one when someone walks over your grave. My mother could very easily have been wiped out after 'a fully upward deflection of the elevator trim tab' or a pilot intentionally crashing a plane 'into the building where his former wife lived'. The odds of my being here at all are infinitesimally small. We are born into miracle, and mystery attends us at every step. I feel the cold linoleum beneath my feet, look at the old Coca-Cola bottles, my Guinness World Record, for moving jelly with a teaspoon, framed in the hallway. The half-finished cladding of the kitchen wall, the sporks and stepladders and bottles of old pills. This is enough, I think. It's more than enough.

It's no good hoping for better, you have to make better; this is the thought that comes upon me. An urge to go above my nerve, be braver than I am. Impossible. The words warp away, I'm frozen in the sight of the oilcloth, blinking, and yet I'm breathing in as if my body has a plan.

'There's something I need to tell you,' I say, opening my mouth to make a sound it never has before. 'When you were in the north, that boy—'

The drum of rain in my head grows louder, my tongue doubles in size. The control panel emits a continuous noise. Pull up, pull up. My mind goes back, to my father and how he wanted to talk and I couldn't let it happen. It goes back to lying in a bathtub, while Lily tried to talk about something I found difficult, how I grew stiff and brittle as a branch under tension, to let her know she could easily break me. *Relax your muscles, breathe*, she had to nurse me, in a softer voice, and never got her difficult conversation. It goes back to Eliza: *it's your silence that's so hard, because I fill it with the worst thoughts.* But I wouldn't break my rule for her. I think about my last therapy session, in which I'd been physically unable to talk for the whole hour, instead spending it skull-eyed and mute and hollow-chested, tears streaming down my face while

I stared at my therapist's shoes. After leaving, I'd had the distinct thought, *I can't go back*, because she had seen me, she knew what I was.

But I will be back, because I'm still learning how to talk and it's important. We don't have all the time in the world, and owe each other more than evasion and the fallout of our secrets. People are tougher than you think. I'm tougher than I think too.

'When you were in the north and I came, that boy was doing things to me . . . It was sexual abuse.'

There is a pause, but not as long as I had anticipated.

'Oh God,' she says. 'Oh God.' It feels as if I have handed her a mass of wires I do not know how to disarm. 'Why didn't you tell me?' How to say that I have been trying to tell her for thirty years? I feel dizzy. My eyes are submerged now, as if I am looking up from the bottom of a pool. She pulls me into her. 'I am so, so sorry. I didn't . . . we didn't—' I can see self-recrimination swarming over her. 'I know you didn't like going there,' she says, assembling a jigsaw in her head. 'If it wasn't for my—' She asks if anything else like that happened and I tell her about the ferry too. I don't want her to feel guilty, or that her son is broken, or lose her friendship. I forgave that boy a long time ago. All I want is to be free.

'If I knew I would have got you out of there, we would have left. It doesn't matter about anything else. And you know what Daddy would have done,' she pulls back, to look me in the eye. 'I want you to know that nothing,

nothing else matters, more than you.' I nod, feeling the warmth of tears, rather than the shame of them.

It is unbuttoning a waistcoat. Breaking the seal of paint on an old window, and flooding the room with air it had forgotten. It is also exhausting. We both go to bed before nine o'clock. On my way out of the kitchen, I take a look at the dustpan. It's teal, with orange trim and soft-touch handle, and actually is pretty nice. I slip it into my bag, and go upstairs.

The next morning, I wake earlier than usual. Instead of the feeling of having been punched in the face the night before, today there is nothing, no ticker tape of anxiety, just the smell of sunlight against the heavy curtains.

'There you are. Have some breakfast and we'll go out,' says my mother from the foot of the stairs. It reminds me of my childhood, the Saturday mornings when she would take me to the supermarket so I could carry the shopping. It's nice.

As she gets ready, I sit in a slant of light eating a block of Edam and prawns and a cup of passionfruit with an entire peeled avocado, and wonder what to do with the day, and then the rest of my days. There's cramp in my chest, right around my heart, I think unrelated to the cheese. It's a similar sensation to the hunger I used to make myself feel, the one that showed me the shape and size of my stomach in negative space. My mother appears again, wearing a normal, floral-print skirt.

'Do you want a cat?' she asks, for no reason.

'Yes.'

'I misspoke. Do you want a cap? Or hat?'

'Yes,' I say.

And then we're on the bus at the end of the road, next to each other on the threadbare tartan of the seats. Only it's not travelling towards the supermarket, it's going in the opposite direction, up the hill where the hedges grow out and the houses have bay windows top and bottom.

'Where are we going?'

'A surprising, family-friendly, free attraction in south London's Forest Hill,' she smiles, which I suspect she has read on a website. 'I want to show you something.'

It's a bright, cold Christmas morning that receives us, as we alight opposite the Horniman Museum – that is its actual name – and hobble over the road together. Middle-class couples my age are pushing prams with canvas totes slung over the handlebars, wearing enamel badges and talking to their children in a grown-up, reasonable way that I find strange. As if their toddlers are young colleagues that have to be wheeled around and bribed with tubes of yoghurt. They smile at the sight of us holding hands, not realising it's because I won't let her use her stick, as it makes her look old, and without it she'll fall over. I remember this place now, though I've not been since I was very young. A fertile Aladdin's cave of natural history set in ornamental gardens, on a hilltop overlooking the city. The sort of place you wouldn't think existed outside of books: a collection of stuffed heads and scarabs, coffins and Kalis, an aquarium full of jellyfish, sundials and ancient urns. A collection guided by its own light, and thrillingly particular obsessions.

We're not going into the main building apparently, walking past the clock tower and Christmas market selling mulled wine and organic pies towards a newer installation, near the alpaca paddock. There is an enclosure with rubber flaps over the doors. 'Go on,' my mother says. I step through a vestibule, and the world transforms around me. The chill winter air is overwhelmed by billows of tropical heat, a mass of greenery. Ferns and palms and creepers and the light falling through the leaves, cascading like coins through a change machine, sorted into colours. The floor is dappled woodchip, while the air – I don't want to blink in case the sight is wiped away – is full of butterflies, hundreds of them. I've never seen anything like it. Some of their wings are filigree, others transparent, tumbling in iridescent spirals and lazy loops all around. Some are drab brown like dead leaves – until the inside of their wings open indigo and cream and marmalade, like a secret they've been dying to tell.

'I want to tell you something too, bebe,' my mother says, choosing her words. 'I'm sorry we missed signs when you were young, and I know we don't talk much. But we are so proud of you, your daddy and me. You make us proud.' I'm something close to stricken; it means too much. Overwhelmed by the silent flapping commotion around us, strains of papaya and banana twisting through the air. It is as if the seasons have been reversed, as if I am standing on the other side of the Earth. 'Keep on writing, because these things that haunt you,' she goes on, 'they also let you see. You know that, don't you.' *One day, everything the shadow touches is yours.*

She touches my arm, then gives me space. I walk on ahead, dazed by the heat and sweetness and saturation of this world in which gravity has been undone. I pass the information board, a dictionary spelled out in leafwing and swallowtail and orange tip, tree nymphs and cattle-hearts, monarchs and malachites and postmen. Two blue morphos the size of paper planes glide past, like a summer that will last for ever. I'm lost for a time, transported, until I notice a girl of about five, standing to my side and staring at me. Another joins her, and soon another. I break out in a sweat. Why are they staring? *Cool*, one of them says. What do they see? I feel a blow to the back of my head – but gossamer light, the strike of a fairy's heel. From the corner of my eye, a little city on my shoulder, towers rising into the sky. The children whisper about the butterflies that have landed on my back. They've been drawn to the sweat, the pheromonal emanations of a brine-soaked boy. Or: sometimes the universe has a gift with your name on it.

Trying to catch a look, I disturb the hitchers and they take off, spiralling above our heads in stained glass and zebra stripe and lace. All except the one on my shoulder.

I turn away, but he remains. I can only distinguish his outline, enormous wings and frail grace.

The little girl, still standing at my side, tells me the butterfly is old.

'I can't see it,' I say awkwardly.

'Would you like me to describe him?' says the girl's mother, nearby. She's talking to me, I realise. She steps delicately closer and looks with care. 'His wings are ragged along their bottom edge, and he has a bent antennae. He's very dark violet, but above the tips of his wings at their broadest point, there's . . .' She considers. 'Shafts of muzzy white, like light through the curtains of a dark house, if you're standing inside the house.' Holy crap, I think. I wouldn't make that kind of effort if the shoe were on the other foot. Or the butterfly on the other shoulder. I guess people aren't all bad. Maybe not even mostly.

She smiles at her daughter and steps away, leaving us to it. As she does, I see my mother some way off. The only person here staring at the ground, looking for caterpillars. Typical. She looks up, excited at having found one, and we catch each other in the same moment. The first woman, still with things to show me, things I might have missed. All of a sudden I want to cry, though not from sadness. I can see the heart in her chest, a little electrical generator trying to reach mine, calling me home. It is a feeling at once particular to one person, and continental, oceanic. Stretching beyond the walls of this place and its implausible enchantments, I see a world being built of

292

love, little bricks of it every day, made of unrecorded words and thoughts and acts.

'I think he's old,' insists the little girl again. The visitor is still on my shoulder, a trembling silhouette. Although she makes a statement, there's a questioning to it. I look at her for the first time. Salmon-pink coat with a grey fur hood squiffed to one side. Bobbed hair. Wide, trusting eyes. Not too terrifying. I'm moved by the openness of her stake in our shared moment, a gentle solemnity that says, *this matters.*

'Maybe,' I say to her. 'But that's okay. He's safe now.'

Next to his mess of twigs, the duck shrugs off whatever's on his mind. Simply shakes his feathers free of it, like water off an oily, water-resistant surface. A shake of his hips – do ducks have hips? – and he plops fatly into the water once again. I've been in this unexceptional park many times since childhood. It's seen so much of me, the self-loathing and boredom and lonely walking. Serenity too, sometimes ecstasy. I remember standing in this very spot a long time ago, staring at a leaf that hung an age in the sky. It drifted leisurely from the highest tree with a turning, peaceful inevitability, to kiss my open palm. I'm going to write about the changes this place has seen in me, I decide, the mistakes and the adventures and the nothingness, and why it's all important.

An odd kind of belonging, I think that's what it comes down to. Lately I've been feeling so much tenderness and grief for everything, for the gorgeous things of this world, and the faces I pass, and the fact that we are all so much in it. Even the boys on the motorbikes, they're just chasing the feeling too. Chasing the feeling, angling towards the sun. I love being here.

Stay with a happy ending and it turns to tragedy; stay a while longer, and the story shows you something else. So keep going, is all I'd say, and make a little room for faith. That's what this story is about, at least where it is now. Still falling forwards, still seeing ghosts, but trusting my own buoyancy, and ability to endure. Trusting there will be giddy pleasures and love to come, pain too, in which we are no less vital. There's a wildness that will not be tamed in all this. Pay attention to it, I think to myself. Keep your eyes on it.

On the surface of the water, the duck alternately pushes against the river and lets it turn him, a cattle rancher in the saddle. The point of a life is not to be happy, I think, seeing him in his element. In the distance, the laughter is that of schoolkids in the other field, galloping after each other, hugging and pushing each other in the head. I walk on, passing another bird to my right, a red-and-blue bird I don't know the name of, sitting on a stump, very interested in something inside it. Jamming his bill into the mulchy top. Because the happiness comes and goes. The point of a life is just to live that life, as fully as possible, and not fall asleep on your watch. What comes after is none of my business. Having said that, I'm nosy so

I might keep an eye on it. Out of nowhere, I have the strangest intuition, a feeling that my whole soul is in that bird, and a need to know if it found what it was looking for. I turn back, and the bird has taken off.

Letter to Ma

I realised something last week. I was here for dinner and you had made halloumi and banana ratatouille with carrot and pomegranate and parsley, and it reminded me of something. All those colours, blocks and discs — it looked exactly like your canvases in the hall and front room, those bursting abstracts. I was eating your sketches, I realised.

I'm glad the Kinder Egg toys in the cabinet have been replaced by your art. I'll miss the sharky babas and glow-in-the-dark ghosts, but it's right to showcase your sculptures made of everyday things, your own talent for saving up the daylight. Millinery, rambles in brambles, learning Russian and coding and AutoCAD, you are truly the little engine that couldn't say, 'I'm not interested in that.' Now you're into street art, I worry you'll be arrested for tagging council walls. But I'm also a bit proud. Besides, you'd do well even in prison.

Oh, we are the same, aren't we? Always liking things to be sideways, and upside down. Understanding each other in ways everyone else cannot. I secretly suspected words could only put a distance between us. But it meant I hid myself, and that was a disaster.

We are also not the same. It feels strange that I was born of your body, then grew into a separate body, one capable of running away. I was so worried about you after Daddy died, which perhaps wasn't obvious from the way I left you alone to cope. I was putting out my own fire, but still it ate me up, the thought of you becoming lonely, weakened or hopeless. Perhaps that was the fire.

But you coped, and pulled me through too, which is some heavy lifting for a Yoda-sized, conga-drumming Bombay Ninja Turtle. Did I ever say how lucky I am to have you? It's a fact — you originally wanted to be a nun, and Daddy didn't want children, and you both changed your minds, so who could calculate those odds? I'm lucky to be here, and promise I will never take it lightly, or stop learning from you. You don't do things the way they're supposed to be done. It's not the kind of mothering they have in textbooks. But you go one better: you show me a way to be well. When it comes to following one's spirit, you're an illuminated manuscript.

That's why I made this for you. Sorry it's not pretty, and too heavy to stick on the fridge. But I wrote it to show you who I became, and to say thank you for my life, and that I hope I haven't let you down.

I love you.

What time is dinner?

Acknowledgements

In my fantasy of self-sufficiency this page would be entirely blank, but blank pages don't make a book any more than a man alone. Deepest thanks go to my agent Sophie Lambert, for her vision, ambition and forbearance of my bi-monthly freakzone. I also owe a life debt to Sarah Emsley, whose faith and patience and magic touch allowed me make this thing I always wanted to, and never believed I could. What a dreamboat of an editor. I have leaned on them far beyond their remit – as with my friend Suzie Worroll, who has been so generous with her time and brilliant heart, as well as supplying directions to places I've been before.

Recognition is further owed to people whose first names don't alliterate, chief among them Kira Cochrane for the commission that kicked this off, as well as Andrew Goodfellow for the early boost of belief. The family at C&W and Curtis Brown welcomed me as if I'd always belonged, whilst at Headline it was clear I'd found the perfect team. Extraordinarily touched by the hard work of everyone there, the extra miles undergone. You people. FMCM too. Cross-platform shoutout to Annabel Robinson, Emma Mitchell and Sophie Goodfellow, plus Vicky Possibly Abbott, Emma Finn and Fiona Crosby, Vanessa Fogarty, Lindsay Davies, Olivia Allen, Siobhan Hooper for the perfect cover, as well as Georginas Polhill & Moore. It's good to be the queens.

Alex Christofi gives good advice, befitting a man who has lived twenty lives in the space of thirty years. James Rowland is officially recognised for orange juice and washing up, plus years of friendship which I must point out I never asked for. Alex Dorgan you are the wisest link. Joe Lycett, your surprising investment in the daily wordcount made a difference. Charlie Gilmour, Prince of Bohemia, every day is an adventure. Love to Lily and Lilly, and everyone with a fraction of their story herein. I'd also like to thank the animals, the rocks and trees and falling rain, but I understand we've all got places to be.

Special mention goes to Eliza. This is your favourite page of any book, but you're in all the others too so here's hoping you enjoy them; I know they came at a price. Gratitude to Edna Shahaf for energy efficiency, an idea which changed everything. Hattie Berger for being a beautiful genius, tall enough to speak for heaven and earth. Aparajita Samadder for leaving trays of food outside the door while Quasimodo rung them bells within. And for quite a lot else, as should be clear by now.